The Anglo-Zulu War – Isandlwana

For my granddaughter Larissa, who died too young.

The Anglo-Zulu War – Isandlwana

The Revelation of a Disaster

Ron Lock

Pen & Sword
MILITARY

First published in Great Britain in 2017 by
Pen & Sword Military
an imprint of
Pen & Sword Books Ltd
47 Church Street
Barnsley
South Yorkshire
S70 2AS

ISBN 978 1 52670 742 0

A CIP catalogue record for this book is available from the British
Library

Typeset in Ehrhardt by
Mac Style Ltd, Bridlington, East Yorkshire
Printed and bound in the UK by TJ International Ltd
Padstow PL28 8RW

Pen & Sword Books Ltd incorporates the imprints of Pen & Sword
Archaeology, Atlas, Aviation, Battleground, Discovery, Family
History, History, Maritime, Military, Naval, Politics, Railways, Select,
Transport, True Crime, Fiction, Frontline Books, Leo Cooper,
Praetorian Press, Seaforth Publishing and Wharncliffe.

For a complete list of Pen & Sword titles please contact
PEN & SWORD BOOKS LIMITED
47 Church Street, Barnsley, South Yorkshire, S70 2AS, England
E-mail: enquiries@pen-and-sword.co.uk
Website: www.pen-and-sword.co.uk

Contents

List of Maps

Foreword

by Prince Buthelezi

The battle of Isandlwana, following the British invasion of Zululand in January 1879, not only resulted in a tragic loss of life but led to the destruction of the Zulu Kingdom. My great grandfather, Mnyamana ka Nqengelele, was King Cetshwayo's Prime Minister and Commander in Chief of the entire Zulu army. Two of his sons, Mntumengana and Mkhandumba, my grandfather, fought at the battle of Isandlwana. Mntumengana was killed while Mkhandumba lived to fight another day.

The tragic events of 1879 will be etched on my mind forever, they will, however, also recall with pride, how Ntshingwayo kaMahole, commander of the Zulu army at Isandlwana, outwitted and soundly defeated the superiorly armed invaders.

Although the Anglo Zulu war and its aftermath was a tragic disaster for the Zulu kingdom and its people, I have learned in life never to be filled with bitterness. What is important is that the truth of what happened on that fateful day in January, be told to future generations. It is equally important to know that the defeated Lord Chelmsford, the commander of British forces, deceived both his monarch, Queen Victoria and the British public, by blaming the defeat on others, in particular, Colonel Richard Glynn, his column commander and Lt Col Anthony Durnford who was unable to defend himself because he was dead.

Ron Lock's book will remove the blinkers from all those who have blindly followed those historians who have sought to portray the battle of Isandlwana as a "disaster", instead of recognizing it as a Zulu Victory against an unprovoked invasion that was responsible for the destruction of our Kingdom, the exile of our King and, under suspicious circumstances, his untimely death.

Prince Mangosuthu Buthelezi

Preface

For close on a hundred years, despite the sensation it caused at the time, the Anglo-Zulu War of 1879 was remembered as little more than just another encounter between Queen Victoria's redcoats and one of her many far-flung adversaries. Then, in 1964, the late Sir Stanley Baker released the film epic, *Zulu*, an immediate international success that is still frequently shown on British television. Within a year the film was followed by Donald Morris's tome *The Washing of the Spears*, another international success. It seemed that renewed interest in the Zulu War was not to be a brief enthusiasm. During the last half century, I would cautiously suggest that more words have been written about the Battles of Isandlwana and Rorke's Drift than have been devoted to all the other colonial wars put together.

Yet there is more to the Anglo-Zulu War – the Battle of Isandlwana in particular – than a bloody conflict that, for the Brits, evokes romantic nostalgia for Empire long gone whereas, for the Zulus, once a proud warrior nation, it engenders resentment for 150 years of subjugation. However, despite the prod, a wink and a nod, from the Colonial Secretary (to be read on page 1 hereof), it was not a conflict planned and instigated by Whitehall; it was a war, clandestinely contrived in Natal by the colonial administration, enthusiastically supported by Lieutenant General Frederick Thesiger (soon to inherit his father's title of Lord Chelmsford), the Officer Commanding HM Forces in Southern Africa. However, between the time it took Thesiger to confidently write 'I am inclined to think that the first experience of the Martini-Henry [rifle], will be such a surprise to the Zulus that they will not be formidable thereafter', and the time it took for a reprimand to follow, much had happened. Thesiger, now Lord Chelmsford, had been outwitted, his column destroyed, 1,300 men slain and 1,000 Martini-Henry rifles taken by the Zulus.

In the ensuing scurry to apportion blame, there was a similar urgency to not only be seen as disassociated with the disaster but, by finding a scapegoat, to soldier on unabashed though guilty. As an additional precaution in the safeguarding of their careers, the guilty anxiously sought the protection and patronage of the highest in the United Kingdom, and they did not seek in vain: Queen Victoria, no less, declared confidence in her defeated general.

New evidence has also challenged views of the Isandlwana battle long held sacrosanct. Perhaps the most controversial dilemma being did Lord Chelmsford fall victim to a Zulu ploy, a ploy that lured him and half his force from the defenceless camp? Was the *East London and Province Standard*, twenty-three days after the battle, justified in declaring 'The Zulus are a match for us in generalship and more than a match in cunning'? Yes, it seems it was.

I have no doubt that this book will not be favourably received in some quarters and many of its assertions refuted. Nevertheless, whether or not Isandlwana has revealed some of its long-held secrets I am sure many more are waiting to be exposed. And what better way could there be than a book penned by a Zulu author. I eagerly await its publication.

Ron Lock – Port Edward, kwaZulu-Natal

Acknowledgements

I am in debt to many people for their support and knowledge, so generously shared in the writing of this book. I am particularly indebted to Peter Robinson of Gerrard's Cross, London, for the plethora of material he unearthed a number of years ago in a variety of locations including the Public Records Office and the Royal Archives, Windsor; I would like to congratulate and thank fellow author Keith I. Smith on the publication of his *Select Documents: A Zulu War Source Book*. Now, instead of the researcher being fated to decipher cumbersome and at times almost illegible old documents, Keith's book has, in part, relieved the researcher of this onerous task; Peter Quantrill, my co-author, fifteen years ago, in the writing of *Zulu Victory*, whose interest in the history of the Zulu Nation and in particular in the action at Isandlwana has never flagged, prompting him to be the instigator of the *Missing Five Hours*, a controversial treatise on the battle; Miriam Vigar who, despite a busy life, has always found time to appraise the latest episode of my work; Major Paul Naish, for sharing both his encyclopaedic knowledge of the Anglo-Zulu War and his understanding of the terrain over which it was fought, Paul having extensively tramped the ground while lecturing his military peers from a variety of nations; a very special thank you goes to Arthur Wright who unwittingly became involved when applying his skills to our unruly family computer, then to go on to be a collaborator and friend; Arthur Kronigkramer, past chairman of AMAFA KwaZulu-Natali, and his staff for generously sharing their knowledge and tirelessly rereading the manuscript in their search for potential blunders of which they found a number; the late Chelmsford Ntanzi, once curator, like his father before him, of the Isandlwana battlefield; the staff of the Campbell Collections, formally the Killie Campbell Africana Library, who, as always were most helpful; also Lisa Hooson and Stephen Chumbley of Pen and Sword, for their advice and patience. I must once again acknowledge my debt to the members, mostly now deceased, of 'Bons', the Battlefields of Natal Society, in particular Fred Herbert and John Smallwood, both old soldiers of the 1939–45 War, who first introduced me to the world of redcoats and Zulu warriors, of the nights, during the 1960s, when we camped on the Isandlwana battlefield, then devoid of habitation, and how easy it was in those days to imagine the night cries of the jackals to be the ghostly howls of the 24th's stray dogs feeding on the bodies of their slain masters. It was a time when the battlefield was still strewn with spent cartridge cases and broken lengths of copper strapping that once bound the ammunition boxes. My final appreciation is reserved for my dear wife Brenda, for her love and extreme patience as I scattered the house with twenty-five years of research from thirty-seven box files. I am still assuring her that it will all be packed away soon.

Author's Note

In some of the contemporary quotations reproduced later in this book the words 'kaffir' or 'caffre' are used. It has been often said that 120 years ago these expressions did not carry derogatory connotations. Not so: their use was as offensive then as now. In November 1878, Lord Chelmsford issued his *Regulations, Field Forces South Africa*, which contained advice regarding the management of the Natal Native Contingent: 'Never use epitaphs of contempt such as niggers, kaffirs etc. Call them "amabuntu" (people), "amadoda" (men), or "amabuti" (soldiers).'

Abbreviations

BBG   Buffalo Border Guard
FLH   Frontier Light Horse
IMI   Imperial Mounted Infantry
NAM   National Army Museum
NNC   Natal Native Contingent
NMP   Natal Mounted Police
NMR   Newcastle Mounted Rifles
NNH   Natal Native Horse
PRO   Public Record Office
TNA   The National Archives
WO   War Office

Chapter 1

'A little war in Zululand would lead to its consolidation within the British Empire'

Lord Kimberley, Colonial Secretary

In the autumn of 1878, Lieutenant General Lord Chelmsford, Officer Commanding Her Majesty's Forces in Southern Africa, was contemplating the invasion of Zululand. Having arrived at Government House in Pietermaritzburg, the fledgling capital of Natal Colony, both he and Sir Bartle Frere, Her Majesty's High Commissioner to Southern Africa, had received alarming news from a Mr Frederick Fynney, a Border Agent in the service of the Crown. He had been tasked to relay intelligence of any Zulu military activity along the serpentine wanderings of the Thukela and Buffalo Rivers that formed the boundary between the Colony and the Zulu Kingdom. A frontiersman and Zulu linguist, Fynney had information of 'the assembly of a large number of Zulu regiments at the King's kraal …'.[1] A Zulu counter-invasion, perhaps? Lord Chelmsford thought not. Like most Imperial officers who would serve under his command, Lord Chelmsford had reservations concerning the abilities of his colonial brethren. Zulu attack or not, the rumour served as an excuse for Chelmsford to assemble additional troops for his own invasion.

Chelmsford had but a few weeks earlier inherited his father's title. Born Frederick Augustus Thesiger, Chelmsford was of German stock, his grandfather having emigrated to England where he and his family had prospered. His edlest son, also Frederick Augustus, became in turn Attorney-General and Lord High Chancellor of England. For his services to the Crown he was ennobled, becoming the first Baron Chelmsford. His son, again named Frederick, although educated at Eton, sought a military career, being first commissioned into the Rifle Brigade and sent to cold, far off Nova Scotia. On return to England he transferred to the Grenadier Guards, his father having secured him a commission by purchase. Ten years' home service followed during which, no doubt his German ancestry finding favour, he was received socially by the Royal Family. For sport he honed his skills as a boxer. Active service followed in some of the bloodiest campaigns of the nineteenth century, the Crimea and the Indian Mutiny. Then, in contrast, as deputy Adjutant-General, he accompanied Sir Robert Napier's expedition against King Theodore of Abyssinia, the most bizarre yet bloodless campaign in British military history. He was decorated with the Order of the Bath, and on return home was made ADC to Queen Victoria before returning to India as Adjutant-General. There he married and raised a family of four sons.

After sixteen years of uneventful but pleasant service, he returned to England where he found, with a grown family, the social life too demanding for his limited finances. Again he requested a posting overseas. Now, as a Lieutenant General, he accepted the first vacancy on offer, that of Officer Commanding Her Majesty's Forces in Southern Africa, where an old acquaintance from India days, and now his political boss, Sir Bartle Frere, held sway. Although Chelmsford had served in many campaigns and had exhibited tireless devotion to duty, it had so far been in an administrative capacity. Now, for the first time he would hold an independent command. He arrived at the Cape in February 1878 and although by then the outcome of the 9th and last Frontier War had become a foregone conclusion, there was still opposition to contend with. However, it was soon all over and Chelmsford had proved himself a popular general; a leader who was prepared to rough it just as rough as it came and, by and large, to eat the same plain food as his men. Perhaps the victory, the seeds having already been sown by his predecessor, came too easily and Chelmsford had found no occasion to heed the advice given to him earlier by General Sir John Michel, an old campaigner who had fought in Cape frontier wars as far back as 1851. Michel had written: 'No plan or operation of yours can in any way circumvent the Caffer. He is your master in everything … He moves three miles while you move one … they will give you a long tedious campaign … British Cavalry are utterly useless … swords are useless … always, always carry a revolver … all bivouacs at night should be half way up imminences … the tops and bottoms are too cold'. Advice Chelmsford would find to be equally applicable in Zululand.

Lieutenant General Lord Chelmsford, Commander-in-Chief HM Forces, Southern Africa.

With victory in the Cape accomplished, he was eager to conspire with those who also contemplated the conquest of Zululand. With the excuse of Mr Fynney's alarming news, he confided his punitive plans to Frere. 'The number of Zulu regiments at the King's kraal must undoubtedly be considered a menace ... I consider it only prudent to take steps to meet what may possibly be a serious attack ...'. He went on to describe his plans for the imminent deployment of various detachments of Imperial regiments along the river boundaries between the Colony and the Kingdom, the arrival of additional Imperial infantry from Mauritius, the deployment of the Natal Mounted Police (NMP), the conscription and training '... with the greatest possible despatch so that they may be available at the shortest notice ...' of 6,000 Natal natives, and the necessity to assemble, under a competent European commander, the whole available force of mounted natives along the slopes of the Biggarsberg Mountains as near as possible to Rorke's Drift. He also advised that local European regiments of mounted volunteers must hold themselves in readiness to be called out at very short notice, and that Border Police be established to patrol the border with a superintendent whose duty it would be to 'ride along the whole boundary from station to station so as to ensure and to obtain the fullest amount of intelligence'. In conclusion Chelmsford went on to say that he assumed that the Natal Government would take immediate steps to place their border natives under competent commanders so that they may be '... in a position, under their own organisation, to meet the first brunt of an enemy invasion should it be made'.[2] In referring to the conscription and training of 6,000 Natal natives (shortly to be designated the Natal Native Contingent, (NNC)), Chelmsford would find Natal was short of white men to fill the role of competent commanders and that such officers and NCOs would have to be recruited in the Eastern Cape.

A war with the Zulu Kingdom was not a new idea. In 1875 Sir Garnet Wolseley, then Governor of Natal, when contemplating Natal's neighbours, Zululand and the Transvaal Republic, mused how very useful a war between the two would be to British interests. In one stroke it would deprive the Boers of an outlet to the sea and break the Zulu Kingdom's power forever. 'I only have to give the King the slightest hint and he would pitch into the Transvaal there and then. I wish I could do so without compromising the Government at home ... I will see what can be done. If I had my way I would force on the war at once.'[3]

With the appointment of Frere as High Commissioner, the invasion was no longer a matter of conjecture. Frere had a personal mission to confederate the

Boer Republics of the Transvaal and the Orange Free State with the colonies of the Cape and Natal, together with whatever chiefdoms remained, into one Imperial territory. In this, Zululand as an independent kingdom would find no place. Like Chelmsford, Frere had seen long service in India. However, unlike Chelmsford, whose service in the subcontinent had been uneventful, his could be regarded as spectacular. From a mundane Welsh background, a family of fourteen and a modest schooling, at the age of nineteen he secured an appointment with the British East India Company. Eight years later he became Private Secretary to the Governor of Bombay and in 1847 was appointed British Resident at the State of Sattara. Following the death of the Rajah, he virtually ruled the country until it was formally annexed by Britain a year later. Frere was then appointed Commissioner of the newly-conquered territory of Sind. Returning from long leave in England, he arrived back in time to play an important role in the suppression of the Indian Mutiny and finally, to crown his service, he was appointed Governor of Bombay. On returning to England in 1867, amongst other laurels bestowed upon him, he was made a Privy Councillor and elected President of The Royal Geographical Society. With Britain recognizing the need to bring order to the turbulent state of affairs in southern Africa, Lord Carnarvon, the Colonial Secretary, offered him the post of Her Majesty's High Commissioner to Southern Africa and Governor of the Cape. The conquest of Zululand was only a matter of time.

Zululand had seen many changes since the days of King Shaka who, fifty years earlier, with military genius and utter ruthlessness had forged numerous clans of the Nguni people into the Zulu nation. And from the nation Shaka had formed an army of 40,000 men, warriors as disciplined as any regiment of Guards and held by both friend and foe to be utterly fearless. Shaka had eventually been murdered by his brother, Dingane, whose tyrannical reign followed, whilst his brother, Mpande, formed a following and an army of his own. With the aid of Boer Voortrekkers from the Cape, Mpande met in battle with Dingane on 29 January 1840.[4] Mpande was victorious but had a hefty price to pay. For the Boer's contribution to his triumph, Mpande found he was in their debt to the tune of a hefty slice of Zululand, including the potential harbour of St Lucia Bay. The Boers intended to add this new acquisition to that portion of Zululand they had already acquired by conquest, calling it, during its brief existence, the Republic of Natalia. Mpande's rule lasted for forty years and, giving due consideration to time and place, his rule can be regarded as benign. Missionaries had been allowed to promote their faith amongst his subjects (with little success, it must be said), traders did good business and white men freely hunted for both profit and sport. A sort of pally rapport existed between the Colony and the Kingdom. Mpande was also a lusty monarch with numerous wives who bore him many sons. Prince Cetshwayo kaMpande was the eldest and heir to the Zulu throne, while Prince Mbuyazi kaMpande was his father's favourite. Rivals since childhood, by the time they were young men conflict was inevitable. Each had their own adherents, Cetshwayo's, known as the *Usuthu*, considerably outnumbering the *iziGqoza*, the faction of Mbuyazi. Although only 24 years of age, Cetshwayo already had battle experience, having fought in the Royal uUThulwana *amabutho* (regiment) against the Swazis in 1852 and greatly distinguishing himself.[5] He was seen as something of a warrior prince and had a popular following throughout the Kingdom. No less admired was Mbuyazi amongst his own, but less numerous, people.

Mpande at first sought to distance his sons one from the other, providing each with a territory of his own. Cetshwayo's was located on the north bank of the Mhlathuze River, fifteen miles inland from the Indian Ocean, whilst Mbuyazi was established north of the White Mfolozi. with Mpande, acting as a buffer, taking up residence in between. Perhaps Mpande grew tired of the uncertainty and tension for he rashly gave his favourite son additional territory adjacent to Cetshwayo's domain and, as if to set one brother against the other, remarked, 'Two bulls cannot live together in the same kraal'.[6] Despite his brother's military reputation and the size of his following, Mbuyazi insolently plundered Cetshwayo's herds and fed the carcasses to his army. It was a declaration of war. On 2 December 1856, Cetshwayo, at the head of his *Usuthu* army, descended on the *iziGqoza* where, under a prominent hill called Ndondakusaka, they had assembled close to the banks of the Thukela River, recklessly encumbered not only with their cattle but also their women and children.

Although Cetshwayo was only 24 and Mbuyazi even younger, between them they had marshalled the greatest gathering of fighting men yet seen in Zululand. Cetshwayo's warriors alone numbered 20,000. Mbuyazi, at last recognizing the dire consequences of his provocation, hurried across the Thukela River to beg military assistance from retired Captain Joshua Walmsley, known to the Zulus by the name Mantshonga. He was the British Border Agent living on the Natal bank with a small staff of native Border Police. Walmsey steadfastly refused to be drawn into what was clearly to be a Zulu civil war. Not so his young assistant, 22-year-old John Dunn, a man whose knowledge and influence would, thirty years hence, be avidly sought by both future King Cetshwayo and Lord Chelmsford. His father having been killed by an elephant, Dunn, at the age of 13, '… determined to desert the haunts of civilization for the haunts of large game in Zululand'. Thus he lived amongst the Zulu as a Zulu, speaking only *isiZulu* for several years until 'caught' by Joshua Walmsley whom, it would seem, adopted him as a son and provided him with an education. In time 'there emerged a remarkable combination of a man who could pass for a Zulu or be entirely at ease in a European environment such as the Durban Club'.

As the encumbered army of Mbuyazi hurried east to find a battle position to their advantage, the *Usuthu* came into sight advancing over a nearby ridge, their massed war shields giving the impression of a moving wall. To the surprise of all, and no doubt induced by promises of a great many cattle, the common currency of southern Africa at the time, Dunn came to join Mbuyazi, leading as many of the Border Police as wished to accompany him plus a number of native trackers whom he employed as armed hunters. It was an absurd little army, if 250 men armed with spears and shields and about 40 firearms of '… every queer variety'[7] can be called an army. However, at the time, the horse was still regarded by the Zulus as something supernatural. As Dunn later wrote '… seeing a man on horseback caused a feeling of uneasiness amongst the Usuthu, a horse being at the time an object of terror …'.[8] With the sudden spectre of the horse, and a ragged volley of musketry, there was a brief moment of hesitation but then Dunn, like the *iziGqoza*, was in flight before the wrath of the *Usuthu*. Finally, with their backs to the fast-flowing Thukela, Mbuyazi's 7,000 warriors, with Dunn and his men amongst them, outnumbered three to one, stood at bay with their women and children scattered to the rear. What followed was a massacre. Women and children were killed without mercy. Only a few managed to find safety on the Natal bank. Some who did so, together with their descendants yet unborn, would, as the *iziGqoza* Company of the NNC, fight for the British against Cetshwayo in the war that lay over thirty years in the future. Dunn, still on horseback, although surrounded by a near-drowning mass of panicking humanity, also survived and, as strange as it may seem, within months had formed a steadfast friendship with Cetshwayo that would see him made a Zulu chief in his own right and Cetshwayo's brother-in-law. Despite the *Usuthu*'s heady victory it too had suffered heavily. Making their way home they passed the Mhangeni Mission Station where Mr Samuelson, a Norwegian missionary, shuddered to see the wounded '… with gaping wounds, groaning as they went along'.[9] Cetshwayo had won by conquest his heirdom to the Zulu throne but his father, Mpande, would live for many years to come.

The Thukela and Buffalo (mZimyathi) Rivers were now firmly established as the boundary between the Colony and the Kingdom but beyond, to the west where the Blood (Ncome) River rose 320 miles from the Indian Ocean, the boundary was less clearly defined. In fact an inverted triangle of land running a hundred miles north of Rorke's Drift along the Buffalo, and seventy miles east along the Pongola River and back to Rorke's Drift, was known as the Disputed Territory. It had been occupied by the Boers who had assisted Mpande in his war with Dingane. Now, due to vague agreements and ill-defined boundaries, the Boers claimed the land belonged to them. Mpande believed otherwise. Not only was the occupation of the territory in contention, so again was Cetshwayo's succession to his father's throne. Mpande, despite Cetshwayo's victory over Mbuyazi – or perhaps because of it – was favouring another son, Prince Mthonga, little more than a child at the time, to succeed him. To forestall his father's plans, Cetshwayo sought

John Dunn, the 'White Zulu', a man of many parts.

to eliminate the boy but, being forewarned, Mthonga escaped Cetshwayo's assassins, finding dubious safety amongst the Boers of the Disputed Territory. A deal was done and Cetshwayo, at least for the moment, acceded to the Boers' claims. The Boers, subject to Cetshwayo's undertaking that he would not harm Mthonga, handed the boy into his care. This transaction was concluded in 1861 at a sort of formal ceremony later called the Treaty of Waaihoek during which, to add to Cetshwayo's power and aspirations, the Boers publicly recognized him as the future king.

This did not please the British, who determined to block any Boer ambition that would give their landlocked republics a corridor to the sea. Moreover, it is possible, even at that early stage, that there were British plans to outflank the Zulu Kingdom to the west, securing access to native sources of labour to the north and expansion of Empire beyond. Enter Theophilus Shepstone, a man wholly unlike Chelmsford and Frere in birth and background, but as ardent a planner in the conquest of Zululand as both. Shepstone's parents, both English settlers, had landed at the Cape in 1820 when their son was but three years old. Apart from his English peers, Shepstone's playmates had been both Boer and

Xhosa with the result that by his early teens he was fluent in three languages. In consequence he was much in demand as an interpreter. It was in this capacity in 1838 that he accompanied Colonel Somerset's little army in its clash with Chief Matiwane and his amaNgwane when it had seemed a Zulu army was about to invade the Cape.[10] Later still, at the age of 21, recently married and again as an interpreter, he accompanied Major Samuel Charters' expedition to Port Natal which at the time was little more than a scattering of thatched huts around the makeshift Fort Victoria, inhabited by uncouth traders and Boer commandos. Critically ill with an infected throat, feeling himself to '… be at the tag end of the universe' and weary of the tedious monotony of the white sands where Major Charters bivouacked, Shepstone could not wait to accompany the Major on his overland journey back to the Cape.[11] It is likely that during this trek Charters sowed the seeds of a treaty with King Faku of the amaPondo whereby he and his people would enjoy British protection. Later a fort was built and garrisoned by British troops at a place called Umngazi on the Pondoland coast only a hundred miles south of the Mthamvuna River, Natal's border with Pondoland. The Cape and Natal coming under one Imperial administration now seemed inevitable. Shepstone, as interpreter between Charters and Faku, would of course have been privy to these negotiations. They gave him an early grounding in political intrigue and diplomacy, of which in due time he became a master. In 1845, having gained much experience in colonial administration, he returned to Natal, now formally a Crown Colony, as Diplomatic Agent to the Native Tribes.[12] Eight years later he was promoted to Secretary for Native Affairs, by which time he had built a network of diplomacy and intrigue not only in Natal but throughout the native territories beyond. In due time he learnt of Cetshwayo's liaison with the Boers and of his virtual surrender of the Disputed Territories in exchange for Prince Mthonga. All of this conflicted with British interests. Clearly, Cetshwayo had usurped his father's authority. Mpande, now in his mid-sixties, having become frail and unable to walk, decided, perhaps unwisely, to call on his colonial neighbour for moral support against his turbulent son. Shepstone, on his own authority, decided to intervene and make it clear to the unruly prince that his sickly father was Britain's friend. With a small escort Shepstone departed Pietermaritzburg and slowly made his way to kwaNodwengu, Mpande's capital, eighty miles from the Thukela border. It was, however, not a British embassy but brazenly his own.

Mpande had summoned Cetshwayo to the *indaba* (meeting) but initially he refused to attend. Then, believing it to be in his best interests, he arrived pugnaciously dressed for battle and escorted by the uThulwana Regiment, armed to the teeth. This caused Mpande's warriors to hiss and rattle their assegais in defiance. Cetshwayo, beside himself with rage, set about bawling a catalogue of accusations in Shepstone's face while the uUThulwana, screaming insults at Mpande's warriors, began to stamp and sway, moving back and forth, the prelude to a frenzy. With both factions ready to strike the first blow, Shepstone remained seated and inscrutable, knowing a wrong move or gesture could bring sudden death. As the tension rose around him he slowly rose to his feet. Curious to hear his words, miraculously the tumult lessened until, certain all could hear, Shepstone spoke: 'I know your purpose is to kill me. That is an easy thing to do as I come among you unarmed. But I tell you Zulus that for every drop of

Sir Theophilus Shepstone, Natal Secretary for Native Affairs.

blood that falls to the ground, ten thousand red-coated soldiers will come out of the sea yonder, from the country of which Natal is but one of its cattle kraals, and will bitterly avenge me.' It was more likely their admiration for his calm and manifest courage rather than his threat of retribution that brought about calm and order. Then, completely composed, Shepstone addressed Mpande and much to the surprise of both monarch and heir, he advised that the time had come for Cetshwayo to be publicly recognized by his father as the next Zulu King. Mpande dithered for a moment and then complied, declaring before the throng of notables and warriors that Cetshwayo was heir to the Zulu Kingdom.

Shepstone, the diplomat and wily intriguer, having publicly manipulated Cetshwayo's succession, could now be seen as kingmaker, and not only that, Cetshwayo was now his man and a Boer corridor to the sea had been forestalled. Shepstone, with as much pomp as his little escort could muster, returned triumphantly to Natal. He would be a future ally in Frere's conquest of the Zulu Kingdom but, having his own agenda, more a collaborator than a conspirator. Yet before the military disaster that would stun the British Empire, Shepstone would once more come face to face with Cetshwayo.

Chapter 2

'... Come and establish what is wanting amongst the Zulu People'

At the very moment Shepstone and Cetshwayo had been in confrontation at Nodwengu, 500 miles away to the west diamonds in significant quantities had been discovered. By 1870 an influx of 50,000 diggers from around the globe had reduced the hill in which the diamonds had been unearthed to a massive hole that one day, in the distant future, man would be able to discern from space. Around the hole there grew up a wild and ramshackle frontier town which the diggers called New Rush, a name that was subsequently changed to Kimberley.

The hole not only produced diamonds, it also created a demand for labour to dig them out. The warrior tribes, however, disdained both cattle and cash but when they were offered a gleaming rifle for hard work the young bucks piled their assegais at home, bid a younger brother to watch the cattle and set to with pick and shovel amongst the motley gangs of diggers. Consequently, a few months later, they were swaggering home to Natal with a gun, hidden under a newly-acquired greatcoat, and a pocket full of cartridges.

Shepstone's spy network was soon bringing alarming news that the tribes were arming, adding to his suspicion that there was a black conspiracy, manipulated by Zululand, for a general uprising throughout southern Africa. With this dreaded spectre a constant companion, and taking cognisance of the enormous disparity between the black and white populations, the possibility of an insurrection was too terrifying to contemplate. It was against this background that Shepstone received word of firearms being brought home from Kimberley by the young men of the amaHlubi, a tribe that had, at one time or another, over a period of fifty years, been plundered and pursued by Shaka, Mpande and minor chiefs from the borders of Swaziland to the Orange River. The Hlubi were a tribe that was distinctly not Zulu and made no claim to be so. In appearance they also stood apart, wearing their hair in long braids dressed with fat and red ochre. In 1848, when the Hlubi had been attempting to settle along the upper reaches of the Buffalo River, their chief, Langalibalele, received a Zulu envoy bearing a message from King Mpande:

Plait yourself a rope that will raise you from the earth to avoid the King's vengeance for so long as you remain on its surface you cannot avoid him. You may think of assistance from the frogs [the British] but this hope is also a vain one as you will find to your cost. Your destruction is inevitable. Your rocks and caves will not save you. Your cattle which you have sent away for safety shall become the inheritance of those to whose care they are entrusted when you shall be no more.[1]

Mpande's intention could not be clearer; Natal under British protection was Langalibalele's only hope. His envoy to Pietermaritzburg returned with the Hlubi request for a territory in which to settle neither granted nor rejected. So, with Mpande's wrath about to descend at any moment, the Hlubi crossed the Buffalo and settled themselves in an all-but-uninhabited territory along the foothills of the Drakensburg Mountains, where the Natal government eventually gave them grudging permission to remain. Now, a quarter of a century later, Langalibalele, no longer the warrior chief but a corpulent elder attired in white man's clothing, was well aware that his young men were harbouring an assortment of firearms.

Early in 1873, John MacFarlane, the magistrate at Estcourt, sent a court messenger to Langalibalele ordering that all firearms held by his people be brought in for registration. An impossible request.[2] The young warriors, having sweated at the diggings for six months, were not to be so easily parted from their most prized possessions. Once the guns were in the hands of officialdom, there was no guarantee that a licence would be granted. More likely the weapon would disappear into a colonial armoury. Langalibalele was unable to comply with MacFarlane's demand and the inevitable happened. The chief was ordered to present himself to Shepstone, an order designed to humiliate him and destroy his power. Langalibalele feared that, like the unlicensed firearms, once surrendered to the authorities he too would disappear into colonial custody, which in fact was what happened. Shepstone planned to charge him with rebellion, writing '… the whole tribe, it seems to me, must be removed from where it is and dispersed amongst the farmers [settlers]'.[3] Langalibalele, realizing his arrest was imminent, decided to flee with all his people into nearby Basutoland where he knew he would be welcomed. The gathering-together of all his people panicked the settler population, who believed it to be the mustering of a Hlubi army rather than a national preparation for flight. The drums beat and bugles blew: the Hlubi and its chief must be brought to heel.

Serious though the matter was, Shepstone had more momentous events on his agenda. King Mpande had died the previous year. The news of his passing, however, did not reach the Colony until four months later. In February 1873, a Zulu deputation arrived at Shepstone's office requesting '*Somtseu* [Shepstone] to come and establish what is wanting amongst the Zulu people'. The message had been initiated by Cetshwayo and his councillors, Cetshwayo's succession being as yet by no means guaranteed. Not only was Mthonga still at large in Natal, closer to home there were other and more powerful princes to contend with. Hamu kaMpande was one of whom Cetshwayo was to later remark '… Hamu is the man that has for a long time during my reign tried his best to dethrone me and get my place'. There were also those not of royal blood who would be king. What Cetshwayo wanted for all to see was that he had the backing of the British Empire. He calculated Shepstone's presence would, beyond doubt, establish such support. Eventually a formal invitation, most likely penned by John Dunn, was delivered into Shepstone's hands. Bearing in mind Shepstone's unnerving experience when confronting Cetshwayo during their stormy encounter at Nodwengu twelve years earlier, he decided to take an impressive escort, mostly drawn from colonial mounted volunteer regiments together with the Durban Volunteer Artillery, the band of the Pietermaritzburg Rifles and a contingent of armed native horsemen. Also going along amongst the many dignitaries was Lieutenant Colonel Anthony Durnford of the Royal Engineers and Henry Francis Fynn, the magistrate of Msinga District. Their presence in Lord Chelmsford's column six years hence, it would be argued, contributed much to its destruction.

Accompanying this brave, if somewhat nervous, little army, was the story that 10,000 warriors would bar their way, but even more alarming was the rumour that Mbuyazi still lived and that Shepstone was bringing him to be crowned in Cetshwayo's stead. So rife was the rumour, that once having crossed the border into Zululand at the Zinkwazi Drift on 7 August, Shepstone later said '… almost every day spies would come into the camp and follow along to see if Umbulas [*sic*, Mbuyazi] was with us'.[4] The ox-drawn wagons governed the column's speed and, apart from the rumours, its progress was pleasant, with the troops purchasing eggs and milk and fraternizing with the friendly villagers. In the evenings the band of the Pietermaritzburg Rifles, to the delight of all, played a medley of songs and marches.

John Dunn, who had now lived amongst the Zulu people for twenty years, was a chief in his own right and, it could be said, in certain circumstances Cetshwayo's right-hand man. Now, on the occasion of his coronation, Cetshwayo required

Dunn's support. Dunn not only contributed his presence but also a coronation gift, a fine carriage drawn by three grey horses. It was in this vehicle that Cetshwayo, while Shepstone fumed at the various delays that had been imposed upon him, proceeded to the first of the two ceremonies that he had carefully planned to outwit his colonial neighbour. Although he desired the nation, and in particular his enemies, to observe he had the support of *Somtseu*, he did not wish it to be assumed he was unable to claim his Kingdom without imperial backing. Thus he resolved to be crowned twice. The first ceremony would be, with the exception of Dunn, a wholly Zulu affair. Then, safely enthroned before his people, he would let *Somtseu*, with theatricals and fireworks, play the role of kingmaker.

Cetshwayo rode in his carriage, Dunn at the reins, towards Makeni, the ancient place of enthronement, close to Dingane's old capital of uMgungundlovu, with his corpulent *iziNduna* (state officials) on their underweight ponies doing their best to keep up. Nearing Makheni, the cavalcade slowed to a walk with Cetshwayo garbed in martial finery followed by thousands of warriors. But there was a faction amongst the throng who ominously showed no sign of approbation. Indeed, one powerful chief, Zibhephu kaMaphita of the Mandlakazi, perhaps more ambitious than royal, surrounded by a regiment of warriors, moved

A coach and horses: John Dunn's gift to King Cetshwayo in commemoration of his coronation.

threateningly towards Cetshwayo. Dunn later recorded ' … Usibepu's party first advanced slowly, and then came on with a rush and some of Cetywayo's [*sic*] staff … began to prepare for flight'.[5]

Cetshwayo did not immediately comprehend the danger and then wishing to avert an armed confrontation, sent several of his *iziNduna* with orders to halt the advancing Mandlakazi. Halt they did, but in Dunn's opinion due to the presence of his 200 hunters, armed as usual with guns and ammunition, ready to deploy. A coup, or perhaps a massacre, averted, the assembly moved to the sacred cattle kraal of Makheni where Cetshwayo subjected himself to the ancient rituals of coronation. Finally, with sacrifices made and with what seemed to be the whole of Zululand in attendance, Masiphula, the Prime Minister, gave into Cetshwayo's hands the Ancestral Spear of the Zulu Kings. He proclaimed him Monarch of the Nation, with the power of life and death, whereupon the great multitude in a single voice roared '*Bayete!*' the acclamation of royalty. The ceremony over, Cetshwayo gave thought to *Somtseu* and his next enthronement. But *Somtseu* was much annoyed. He had been kept waiting like a lackey on the inhospitable windswept heights of Mthonjaneni and when finally given permission to proceed, he had cause to be even more disgruntled. Having made camp, his cavalcade was soon subjected to Zulu curiosity, the warriors mingling with the soldiers in friendly rivalry. Prince Dabulamanzi kaMpande, boon companion and drinking partner of John Dunn as well as being Cetshwayo's younger brother, was a good shot with a rifle. He wanted a shooting competition, challenging anyone to hit a bottle at a hundred paces. Crafty Trooper Blamey of the Karkloof Carbineers, knowing a little drummer boy to be an exceptional shot, responded '… if you can beat this child at shooting, then talk to us men'.[6]

Dabulamanzi, who, six years hence, but for the courage and resolve of a small garrison of British redcoats, might well have left Natal in smoking ruins, was put to shame by the boy's uncanny marksmanship. Then, as Cetshwayo and Shepstone appeared, the tables were turned and hurt Zulu pride restored. Cetshwayo demanded to see the guns of the Durban Artillery in action. The troopers mounted their horses, the guns were loaded with *amalwapu* (blanks) and, down at the river, the gunners blazed away. Many years later Mshayankomo, a warrior witness, remembered '… they fired Du! Du! Du! Du! Du! … we were frightened for we were not used to guns'.[7] The troopers 'gun-trained' horses had stood firm during the racket of artillery fire but when Shepstone requested Cetshwayo to show how his warriors went into battle, 'gun-trained' though the horses were, they were not prepared for what followed. The warriors formed ranks and, raising their knobkerries, hammered their shields producing a startling thunderclap. Mtshayankomo recalled '... the horses took fright; some leaped over the kraal fence throwing off their riders, others jumped into the huts'.[8]

Shepstone was extremely irked. He turned in anger on his host, Masiphulu, accusing him of giving the Carbineers no warning of what was about to happen, Masiphulu calmly replied it was but a sport of the Zulu warriors. Shepstone refused to be pacified '... you have startled me; you have unseated my men; you have knocked over my horses; torn their saddles and broken everything'.[9] He then threatened to bring soldiers equal in number to the assembled warriors, seeming to imply he would teach the King and his warriors a lesson. Trooper Blamey had good reason to be nervous. Nevertheless, the soldiers caught and remounted their fractious horses and gave a jumping display, putting their mounts over ditches and dongas (dry watercourses) 'in grand style' and causing the astonished Zulus to again associate the horse with wizardry. One man exclaimed '... they fly over the dongas like *umtagatis* [*sic*], *amaThakathi* ...' That night, to the pleasure of all (and no doubt arousing more suspicions of wizardry), '... we had a grand display of fireworks, rockets going sky high and breaking up into star-shaped things; this was all done to show the Zulu people what wonders we had with us.'[10]

A day or so later, on 1 September, Shepstone prepared to crown the King, colonial style. A large marquee had been erected; a 'crown' of peculiar design, made of scarlet cloth adorned with a feather of the purple-crested Turaco bird, manufactured by the regimental tailor of the 75th Regiment, was ready to be placed on the monarch's head and a gilded armchair was at hand to serve as a throne. Although many of the regiments that had thronged Cetshwayo's earlier coronation had dispersed and gone to their homes, 10,000 men remained to pay homage to their king and, no doubt, to intimidate the colonials. Blamey recorded:

> ... the bugle sounded, each one saddled up and fell into line, a long speech was made to us by Major Giles, sitting on his horse in front of us. 'My men' he said 'load your rifles and revolvers now'. After this was done, he said, 'Every man of you must be on the alert whilst we are over at the coronation, and if we are attacked, fire at the Zulus for all you are worth, and die like true Britons, shoulder to shoulder.

However, they had no reason to be concerned. Cetshwayo's attitude was now entirely the reverse of the furious young prince who had confronted Shepstone at Nodwengu seventeen years earlier. Although Shepstone and Cetshwayo were roughly of the same age, Cetshwayo had taken to referring to Shepstone as his father; in fact it could be said the elders of the nation, curious though it may seem, also saw Shepstone as a Zulu patriarch.

The message requesting Shepstone's presence that had earlier been delivered to his Pietermaritzburg office had read in part:

> ... The nation had suddenly found itself wandering it knows not whither; it wanders and wanders and wanders again, for its guide [Mpande] is no more ... the nation asks that *Somtseu* may prepare himself to go to Zululand when the winter is near and establish what is wanting among the Zulu people, for he knows all about it, and occupies the position of father to the King's children ... and that he shall breathe the spirit by which the nation is to be governed ...[11]

Cetshwayo kaMpande, warrior king of the Zulu Nation.

Whilst on his way to the coronation but before crossing into Zululand, Shepstone had sent a message to Cetshwayo and his councillors:

> ... I cross the Thukela [*sic*] as the representative of the Government of Natal with an escort befitting that position and the occasion that has rendered the visit necessary to the Zulus. I carry with me the dignity of the Government that has sent me. But the head of that government has desired me to make a preliminary stipulation, namely, that his courtesy and condescension be not stained by one drop of blood. My own rank in Zululand entitles me to make another, and it is that should any Zulu be adjudged to die for any political offense while I am in the country, such sentence shall not be carried out until the charges and evidence have been submitted to me. I shall expect to meet on my way, a decided acceptance of

these conditions, or I shall refuse to proceed, as I cannot allow myself to be a witness to the spilling of blood while I am deputed by my Government only to carry out a mission of peace.[12]

Now, with the crown about to be placed on Cetshwayo's head, Shepstone had decided that if he were to play the role of father to the nation it would be a stern one. He had already discussed certain reforms which during the coronation ceremony he wished Cetshwayo to promulgate as laws. During the course of these discussions, Shepstone formed an opinion of the King's character: '... He is a man of considerable ability, much force of character and has a dignified manner; in all my conversations with him he was remarkably frank and straightforward ... I do not think that his disposition is very warlike and even if it is, his obesity will impose prudence ...'[13]

Shepstone had concocted a performance whereby having presented Cetshwayo to his people as an immature prince, he would then be taken in to the marquee, shortly to emerge, as though by Shepstone's hand, a king robed and crowned ready to rule, seated on the gilded chair. It went off well. The band played and a seventeen-gun salute was fired. Then came Shepstone's oration. He had discussed with the King and his Great Council certain conditions that

Men of the Natal Volunteer Artillery who fired a seventeen-gun salute at the coronation of King Cetshwayo. (Local History Museum, Durban).

he, as father of the nation, wished to see enforced as laws. Speaking in fluent *isiZulu* he loudly proclaimed their content:

> The indiscriminant shedding of blood to cease. That no Zulu be condemned without open trial. That no Zulu life be taken without knowledge of the King. That for minor crimes the loss of property be substituted for the punishment of death.

That Cetshwayo agreed to institute these conditions as laws was later to be vehemently denied, he asserting: 'Did he '[Shepstone]' tell the white people I made such an arrangement? Because if he did he has deceived them.'[14]

But for the moment all was goodwill and good fellowship, Cetshwayo set his people to building a new 'Great Place', a new capital at oNdini above an open plain called Ulundi. It was here that the final battle of the Anglo-Zulu War would be fought. Also, to restore both his own and the national pride, he planned to revitalize the Zulu Army which of late had become slovenly and undisciplined. Shepstone, unaware of his 'son's' plan for a revival of Zulu militarism and satisfied with his accomplishment, led his cavalcade back across the Thukela River and into Natal.

Chapter 3

'I do not think his disposition is very warlike'

In mid-September 1873, Shepstone arrived in Pietermaritzburg after eight weeks' absence to find the Colony in a state of alarm. Langalibalele had continued to defy the government and, moreover, it was claimed, gunpowder was being manufactured, his warriors were being doctored with *intelezi* to render bullets harmless,[1] and he had insulted, harassed and stripped naked two senior messengers of the Crown.[2] Even more alarming was the rumour that Langalibalele was conspiring with the Zulu Kingdom. Panic amongst the settlers was inevitable, especially amongst those in the rural areas of central Natal and along the Buffalo River close to the Zulu border. Farms were abandoned and churches barricaded. Langalibalele had to be seized and charged with treason.

A small army was assembled at Fort Nottingham, a defensive position constructed years earlier as an operational base against Bushmen raiders. Of Imperial troops there was but a scattering: two companies of the 75th Regiment, a couple of guns and a few officers. The Colonial contribution was four regiments of mounted volunteers totalling no more than 150, including 43 officers and men drawn from the Karkloof and Richmond troops of Carbineers. Many men had but recently returned from Cetshwayo's coronation.[3] The vast majority of the punitive expedition set to catch Langalibalele were hastily-conscripted Natal natives amounting to 6,000 men including a number of mounted baTlokwa tribesmen. These were led by a young chief named HlubiMolefe who, despite his forename, was not of the amaHlubi. He was so named due to his grandfather's friendship with a Hlubi chieftain.

Langalibalele and his people, rumour had it, were about to escape justice by escaping into Basutoland by the Bushman River Pass, its summit 10,000 feet above sea level. The Colonial plan was to deploy its punitive force into scattered groups in the form of a giant pincer movement. However, the area into which they were about to plunge was largely unmapped and unknown, encompassing 700 square miles of mountainous terrain, the toughest in southern Africa. To prevent Langalibalele's escape, the cavalry had to cut him off by ascending a pass south but parallel to his escape route, gain the summit, ride north along the plateau, and arrest him as he emerged at the top of Bushman's Pass.

The Carbineers, with twenty-five baTlokwas, were given the honour of leading the chase under the command of Captain Charles Barter, a man of many accomplishments – politician, big-game hunter, farmer, journalist and soldier – but, however, no longer in his prime and hard of hearing. At the last moment, perhaps because of a minor infirmity, he was relegated to second-in-command with 44-year-old Major Anthony Durnford of the Royal Engineers, more than keen to get the job, being placed over his head. Durnford had also recently returned from the coronation and although he had been soldiering in the Cape for a couple of years, he had only recently transferred to Natal as Colonial Engineer. He had been in the army for twenty-eight years

Anthony Durnford, possibly a captain at the time this photograph was taken prior to his service in Southern Africa. (By courtesy of the Killie-Campbell Africana Library)

during which time Britain had fought some of the bloodiest campaigns of the nineteenth century, the Indian Mutiny, the Crimean War and other equally epic but smaller conflicts, but it had been Durnford's bad luck, as he judged it, to have missed them all. He had yet to hear a shot fired in anger. He was eager – reckless as he would later be described – to see action and hold his own with his battle-seasoned peers.

It underlines the urgency of the situation, as seen by the Colonial Government, that on 3 November Durnford's detachment left on their mission in the pitch dark at eight o'clock at night, with the intention of reaching the escarpment, locating Giant's Castle Pass, climbing the summit and nabbing Langalibalele as he topped Bushman's Pass the following morning. Despite the darkness, for the first few miles, following a farm track, the going did not prove to be difficult. But thereafter things started to go wrong. Every man carried forty rounds of ammunition while four or five pack horses carried more in reserve. They also carried three days' provisions. The baTlokwa carried their own rations in the form of hard biscuits and dried meat. After riding for five hours in mist and rain, and having twice crossed, it was assumed, the Mooi (Mpofana) River, they were still twelve miles from the foothills of the escarpment with the best of the terrain behind them. Worse still, it was discovered that two of the pack horses carrying the reserve ammunition and all the provisions were missing, as were the men sent to find them.[4] However, instinct and the dark outline of the looming mountains against a lighter sky drew them on. By early morning, and with mist rising, Captain Barter was to write later '... we were confronted by a stupendous mountain, the sides scarred with water furrows that lay between ourselves and our destination'.

The men were now ravenous but had to make do with biscuits scrounged from the baTlokwa and a sip of rum. Durnford, however, full of energy, was eager to press on, unaware that they were completely lost. During the hours of darkness they had wandered off to the south and were now six miles short of Giant's Castle Pass, their destination, and a further ten from Bushman's Pass. Nevertheless, having found the beginning of a way up of sorts, the column dismounted and, near exhaustion, started to scramble, often on hands and knees, leading their horses, up the slippery slope to the summit that soared above. Disaster was soon to follow. Durnford, impatient to reach the top, was leading his horse, Chieftain, across a narrow ridge when Chieftain stumbled and fell, plunging down the incline and taking Durnford with him.[5] A boulder brought their fall to a halt. Chieftain rose no worse for the experience but Durnford lay motionless, concussed, with broken ribs and a dislocated shoulder. Given a little rum and rolled in a blanket, several men, at considerable risk of tumbling further, dragged him back to the ridge where they managed to reset his shoulder. After a short rest but still in great pain, Durnford declared himself ready to proceed. For the remainder of the morning they struggled upwards at times dragging Durnford on a blanket, his left arm hanging useless by his side. At noon a halt was declared, while those in the lead, still without food, waited for the stragglers. Now the terrain allowed them to mount again but it was not until after midnight, and with eleven Carbineers unaccounted for, that they faced the next frightening obstacle:

> ... the scene before us was savage in the extreme. Down the sides of the mountain hung ribbons of water showing the spot to be the very birth place and nursery of rivers. Above, huge krantzes [a wall of rocks or a ravine] frowned, whilst the masses of unburnt grass, hanging like a vast curtain, gave a sombre and malignant aspect to the scene. How we slipped and struggled, fell, struggled to get up, and struggled again.[6]

At sunset Trooper Fannin was the first man to reach the summit which would lead them eleven miles north along the plateau to the top of Bushman's Pass. A hundred yards from the top Durnford had fainted. He had been left where he fell, Trooper Erskine standing watch over him until he recovered. Captain Barter, white-bearded and older than the rest, arrived two hours later. In bitter cold weather they rested a while at a height of over 9,000 feet and at 2 am set off north, arriving at Bushman's Pass at 8 am, twenty-four hours too late.

The right-hand or northern pincer of the colonial plan that was intended to ensnare Langalibalele and his tribe, was led by Captain Albert Allison, commanding a force of 500 native levies. He had been ordered to climb the Champagne Castle Pass, travel south and together with Durnford snap the pincers closed. However, having stumbled back and forth across the base of the escarpment he discovered there was no Champagne Castle Pass and never had been. Frustrated and exhausted, Allison had, unbeknown to Durnford, returned to base where he and his men, 5,000 feet below and fifteen miles away, awaited further orders.

When on arrival at last at the top of Bushman's Pass, Durnford observed the mouth of the pass to be occupied by armed natives, he naturally assumed they were Allison's men. He was quickly disillusioned. Langalibalele had beaten him to it. With the bulk of the Hlubi he had passed into Basotholand, whilst this rearguard grazed cattle and held the pass for Hlubi stragglers. Durnford was in a predicament and it was only then that he revealed to the Carbineers that he had received orders direct from Sir Benjamin Pine, the Lieutenant Governor of Natal, that if he was confronted with opposition he was not to fire the first shot, thus leading Durnford to be later branded with the unfortunate sobriquet, 'Don't Fire Durnford'.

The Carbineers, near to exhaustion, demoralized and having eaten only a few biscuits since leaving Fort Nottingham forty-eight hours earlier, on seeing so many Hlubi cattle – beef on the hoof – harangued Barter to have one shot. They hoped that firewood could be found, a fire lit and that roast beef would be on the menu. But Durnford, obeying his orders to the letter, refused to allow a shot to be fired: instead he agreed that the amaTlokwa could slaughter a beast with a spear thrust[7] and ordered them to do just that. Not so easy. The wounded animal, bellowing in agony, careered away through the herd while enraged Hlubi warriors shouted abuse and rattled their spears. Not to be denied fresh meat, a second and then a third attempt was made to kill more of the Hlubi herd, all equally unsuccessful. Finally, with three wounded animals causing mayhem, a Tlokwa spear thrust finally found its mark. Such was the Carbineers' hunger that some ate the meat raw. Durnford was all for compensating the Hlubi but Barter insisted it would be taken as a sign of weakness. Meanwhile, more Hlubi and cattle were arriving from below, pushing aggressively through the Carbineers and Tlokwa who Durnford, brandishing a revolver, was attempting to deploy across the pass.

Durnford's threats, interpreted by Elijah Khambule, a colonial servant especially loaned to the column by Shepstone himself, were ignored. Guns were pointed, assegais were meaningfully sharpened on the rocks and Sergeant Clarke, an ex-British Army pensioner and part-time drill instructor to the Carbineers who, it would seem, had accompanied the expedition out of curiosity or perhaps for extra pay, rode back and forth among the Carbineers, lamenting in the shrill voice of panic that they would all be slaughtered.[8]

Durnford's command was now a shambles. A Hlubi elder, speaking through Khambule, agreed to take the Hlubi back down the pass but only on condition that the Carbineers led the way. An impossible stipulation. But Durnford continued with his abortive hectoring. Ominously, the Hlubi warriors, in ever-increasing numbers, began to take up positions commanding and surrounding the Carbineers, pushing, jeering and with threatening mockery demanding to know when the real soldiers would arrive? The answer to that was never.

The Carbineers and their Tlokwa allies, outnumbered ten to one, were surrounded by a throng whose excitement, at a wrong move or gesture by the colonials, could turn into a frenzy. What happened next is open to much speculation, there being several different versions all written by men who were present. Barter summed up the situation when he later wrote '... our Commanding Officer, as gallant and determined a man as ever breathed, would have cheerfully sacrificed not only us, but himself, in the execution of his orders...'. Having now watched Durnford's fruitless arguments and empty threats, the Carbineers had lost all confidence in their commander. Correctly anticipating that the Hlubi were about to go out of control at any moment, the Carbineers begged Barter to order a retreat. Barter informed Durnford that unless the order to retire was given, the Carbineers were in any event likely to depart. Durnford exploded in disbelief 'Do you mean to report to me officially that you cannot depend upon your men?' Barter confirmed that was so.

Bitter in the realization that his first independent command in confrontation with an enemy had ended in woeful disaster, Durnford shouted in desperation 'Will no man stand with me?' Only five Carbineers, Troopers Erskine, Bond, Potterrille, Speirs and Charlie Raw, rode forward a pace or two while the remainder of the Carbineers and the baTlokwa, Barter presumably having

The Karkloof Troop, Natal Carbineers, 1867. Centre, Captain Charles Barter who, under Major Durnford, commanded the Natal Carbineers at Bushman's Pass. (Stalker, *The Natal Carbineers*).

given the order to retire, formed fours and in reasonable order, turned south, leaving Durnford and his five volunteers to follow.

It was all the Hlubi needed. A shot was fired, only just missing Durnford, followed by an eruption of shouting and racing warriors. 'Ride for your life!' shouted Khambule as he was dragged from his horse and speared to death. In the mayhem that followed, Barter and the Carbineers burst through the Hlubi gauntlet and galloped south for the Hlatima Pass. Not so Durnford and his five volunteers. Ringed in, Erskine, Bond and Potterrille were also dragged from their horses and speared to death. Speirs and Raw broke free and followed the stampede south. Firm warrior hands held Chieftain's bridle while another warrior put a spear into Durnford's already injured arm. With the reins loose on Chieftain's neck, Durnford fired left and right, dropping two Hlubi, then broke clear, put spurs to his horse and galloped after his 'cowards' as he was, unwisely, to call the Carbineers. Years later when writing his memoirs, Barter remembering Durnford, penned these lines:

Cool and contemptuous in tone,
no council pleased him but his own:
proud of his flag, a soldier born,
he held the volunteers in scorn.[9]

However, it was not quite over; the survivors fought a running retreat with the Tlokwa giving invaluable support. Retiring the same way as they had come, by the Hlatima Pass, they eventually reached Fort Nottingham, having been in the saddle for fifty-two hours.

Such was the ignominious rout that it almost split the Colony, the settlers blaming the government and the government condemning the conduct of the settler-raised Carbineers. Sergeant Clarke became a scapegoat and was dismissed from the service while a Court of Enquiry found the Carbineers guilty of a disorganized and precipitated retreat with mitigating circumstances. But most of all, Langalibalele was held to be the instigator of the whole tragic affair. He and his tribe must pay and pay dearly. It was feared that Langalibalele's bold defiance and subsequent victory, as it would be seen, must lead to insurrection not only in Natal but throughout southern Africa. Retribution must be immediate and unsparing.

Hundreds of troops, mainly native mercenaries recruited from Natal natives and led by white officers, set off in pursuit, while remnants of the Hlubi who, for whatever reason, had remained in their territory, were hunted down, killed or taken prisoner. The amaPutini, a neighbouring tribe who had merely undertaken to care for Hlubi cattle when their owners fled, were held to be Hlubi accomplices and were treated with equal severity. The Colony set about the task with relish, none more so than Governor Pine. Homes were burnt, cattle confiscated, crops destroyed and Hlubi and Putini males shot out of hand while their women and children were doled out to the settlers as farm labourers. Where one newspaper expressed the opinion that the actions of the young colonials were the mere expression of youthful enthusiasm, another, *The Natal Colonist*, commented on the irony of the situation in which the authority that had issued the order not to fire the first shot, now sanctioned the 'pursuance of the horrid butchery which seems to be going on'.[10]

Whatever rapport that may have existed between the white settlers and the black tribesmen of south-east Africa dissolved as quickly as had the gunsmoke at the top of Bushman's Pass. Langalibalele was finally captured on 13 December by Captain Allison, the officer who six weeks earlier had fruitlessly sought for the non-existent Champagne Castle Pass. Langalibalele was incarcerated in Pietermaritzburg jail. He was charged with treason, rebellion and, amongst other things, to have conspired with his people to obtain firearms for the purpose of resisting authority and to having entered into treasonable communication with others unknown.[11] His guilt was already decided. He was sentenced to banishment for life, his destination Robben Island, that barren outcrop of doom situated in the Atlantic Ocean off the Cape coast.

Nine months after the skirmish at Bushman's Pass, the trial over and sentence passed, Langalibalele was made ready for his voyage into exile. However, before departing Pietermaritzburg jail, an important delegation of Zulu *iziNduna*, sent by Cetshwayo, arrived in the city.[12] Although King Mpande, it will be remembered, had, thirty years earlier, sent a message to Langalibalele advising him '… to plait yourself a rope that will rise you from the earth to avoid the King's vengeance …', Cetshwayo felt no such animosity. In fact Langalibalele was revered as Rainmaker of the Zulu Nation. In sending a deputation to the colony, Cetshwayo was making both a gesture of Zulu solidarity with Langalibalele and a silent rebuke to colonial justice. Indeed,

Chief Langalibalele, at the time of his trial in 1873.

Cetshwayo sent no less than six embassies to Pietermaritzburg requesting, most diplomatically, for the old chief's release into his custody.[13] The final deputation, after being kept waiting for several days, was at last told that they were wasting their time, the prisoner was already aboard ship on his way to Robben Island.

When the full story of Langalibalele's fate and the atrocities committed on the Hlubi and Putini people became public, there was outrage in Britain. Governor Pine was dismissed but Shepstone, with hardly a blemish to his career or a lessening of his power, survived. However, if nothing else, Cetshwayo's gesture of sympathy must have confirmed Shepstone's thinking that there had indeed been a conspiracy and that an uprising had only just been averted – at least for the moment. But if a minor tribe, with a male population of no more than a couple of thousand, could bring about the defeat of a punitive expedition, under an Imperial officer, causing panic and mayhem, what could Cetshwayo's army of 40,000 disciplined warriors do? As long as the Zulu Kingdom existed Natal could never sleep at ease.

Shepstone had recently written of Cetshwayo '… I do not think his disposition is very warlike …'. Shepstone now decided otherwise. But for the present he had to bide his time. Those equally determined to expand the boundaries of the Empire and secure the future of Natal would ultimately appear and support his vision. Three years later, as we have read, Sir Bartle Frere arrived at the Cape, soon to be joined by Lord Chelmsford. Shepstone would shortly discover that they shared with him a common objective for the future of the Zulu Kingdom.

Chapter 4

'... The Zulus have been very kind to us'

In January 1877, as though Shepstone did not have enough to fill his working day, with an escort of a mere twenty-five NMP, he set off north and without a shot being fired acquired for the Empire a territory three times the size of Natal. The Boer state of the South African Republic, commonly known as the Transvaal, had got itself into deep financial trouble, had lost several skirmishes against the neighbouring baPedi and was about to collapse into anarchy. Convincing the dubious Boer leaders that their country would prosper, as they would themselves, under the protection of the British Crown, the Union Jack was set fluttering above Pretoria. By now knighted, Sir Theophilus returned to Pietermaritzburg where he was gratified to receive a letter from the Lieutenant General Commanding HM Forces in Southern Africa. Lord Chelmsford had written:

> ... the Zulus have been very kind to us in abstaining from any hostile movements during the time we were so bitterly engaged [with the 9th Frontier War] in this colony. If they will only wait until next month I hope to have the troops somewhat better prepared than they are at present... If we are to have a fight with the Zulus, I am anxious that arrangements should be as complete as possible to make them – half measures do not answer with natives – they must be thoroughly crushed to make them believe in our superiority.

Even so, to justify an invasion, a suitable excuse would have to be found. Within days, as though made to order, unruly young warriors caused two incidents that the colonial conspirators were able to construe as a threat to Natal. The first concerned the sons of *Nkosi* (Chief) Sihaya kaXonga, a favourite *iziNduna* of Cetshwayo, who, on behalf of his monarch, held sway over a large portion of Zululand bordering on the Buffalo River, including the Zulu approach to Rorke's Drift. His eldest son, Mehlokazulu kaSihayo, believed his father's honour had been sullied by the adulterous behaviour of his father's wives, two of whom had fled across the Buffalo and were now brazenly living with their lovers on the Natal bank. Mehlokazulu, his brother and a number of their followers decided to bring the errant women back to Zulu soil where the penalty for adultery, death, would be administered. Perhaps the brothers and a few accomplices would have been more than sufficient to abduct the women. But the young men rashly got together what amounted to a war party of some thirty mounted warriors supported by an equal number or more on foot, all heavily armed including a mixture of firearms. Against whom did they intend to use their armoury? White settlers or the Natal Border Police? It was a reckless act. There was panic along the border. Both women were tracked down and, their lovers having disappeared, were dragged across the river and executed. This was a violation of Natal's territory.

Only a few weeks later, a civilian engineer, in the now Lieutenant Colonel Durnford's Colonial Engineers Department, and a local settler, inspecting the condition of Middle Drift, were apprehended on the wrong side of the Thukela by a Zulu patrol. The Drift, and the road leading to it from the heights on the Natal side of the river, had been constructed as a military road several years earlier, during the governorship of Sir Garnet Wolseley. There is little doubt that Messrs Deighton and Smith's interest in the condition of the crossing was prompted by whether or not its condition was suitable as an invasion route. And there is equally little doubt that the Zulu patrol quickly tumbled to their motive. Consequently Deighton and Smith were manhandled and some reports say humiliated by having their clothes removed. They were not, however, harmed. On both counts Sir Bartle Frere was outraged. Mehlokazulu and his followers must be handed over and stand trial in Natal. Furthermore, a fine of 500 cattle must be paid and in addition another hundred in respect of the manhandling of Deighton and Smith.

Although Frere's response to these events had been one of outrage there had been an earlier incident which should have equally given rise to Frere's wrath but which slipped by almost unnoticed. At the time Cetshwayo was endeavouring to revitalize the men of the Zulu nation into an army of warriors as they had been in Shaka's day, rather than the skiving army of husbands and herders they had become under Mpande's relaxed rule. There were far too many men providing reasons why they should be exempt from military service. For instance, it was a tradition that the *iziNyanga*, the healer/doctors of the nation, were exempt from duty and Cetshwayo saw it as no coincidence that of late there had been a flood of youths all claiming dispensation on the grounds of their therapeutic gift. The wily monarch, in setting an example, did not question their ability to heal. Instead he formed a new regiment, naming it the Nqweke, into which all the young *iziNyanga* were quick-marched. It was a regiment no different from any other, except that it was subject to harsher discipline. Cetshwayo also saw the numerous mission stations, that Mpande had permitted to prosper, as a haven for reluctant warriors. In 1876, Cetshwayo made the following observation to the Rev. J.L. Kyllingstaid of the Norwegian Mission Society.

> We cannot permit that our soldiers run to the school and become believers; because then they are running away from the King's service, and we lose our army. The believers are of no use to us and never serve us, they are lost to us when they attend school. We must refuse permission for you to take them away from us and do not permit that a soldier should become a believer.[1]

It is well known that Cetshwayo held that a Christian Zulu was a good Zulu spoilt. In fact, after his coronation he let it be known that any warrior who became a Christian would be executed.[2] However, in the case of Maqhamusela, aged around 70 at the time of his death, he could hardly have been regarded as a warrior. His crime was his persistent desire to become a Christian and his repeated declaration that he was indifferent to death so long as he was first baptised. Finally he was denounced by a local chief and his death quickly followed. An execution squad of four arrived at Maqhamusela's home and he was led away and according to the report of the Rev. Ommund C. Oftebro, written a month after the killing, the death squad had been reluctant to carry out their task, being in terror of some supernatural retribution. However, being more fearful of the King's wrath should they fail in their duty, Maqhamusela was put to death with a single musket shot through the head. His execution caused consternation and fear throughout the mission stations in southern Zululand. Shepstone, through his network of spies, was quick to hear of Maqhamusela's death. On his advice many mission stations chose to evacuate Zululand, only to return within a few weeks. The missions' opportunity to promote Maqhamusela as the first Zulu Christian martyr, and the opportunity for Frere to promote Cetshwayo as a tyrant who must be dethroned, were opportunities lost.

In the meantime the Disputed Territory was a pot of contention that continually threatened to boil over. At the recent coronation Shepstone had revelled in the role of 'Father to the Zulu Kingdom' and Cetshwayo, taking him at face value, expected some parental support in his vying with the Boers. No doubt he would most likely have got it had not Shepstone taken the Transvaal under his parental wing. Indeed, the Transvaal was now a British colony and

Shepstone its administrator. However, having lost Shepstone's support without knowing it, Cetshwayo, equally without knowing it, was about to receive a mild gesture of patronage from an unexpected quarter.

After the sacking of Sir Benjamin Pine, Natal received a new Lieutenant Governor, Sir Henry Bulwer, who, whilst Shepstone had been occupied elsewhere, had offered his services, which had been gratefully received by both sides, as mediator between the Zulus and the Boers. Bulwer, aged 43, an experienced colonial administrator who had served the Empire in many locations from Barbados to Borneo, was not only Governor of Natal but the designated Supreme Chief of the Natal African population and was firmly opposed to war with Zululand. He appointed a Boundary Commission consisting of the Hon. Michael Galway, Attorney-General of Natal, the Hon. John Wesley Shepstone (Theophilus's younger brother), Acting Secretary for Native Affairs, and Colonel Anthony Durnford. The decision of these three would settle the dispute for once and for all. They reached a conclusion finding largely in favour of the Zulus, awarding the Kingdom 1,800 square miles of the disputed land. The news was received by Frere in Cape Town on 20 June 1878. It was an unexpected setback for the war that he, Chelmsford and Shepstone had set in motion. The Boundary Commission's award had to be be put under wraps for a while.

The reader will recall how, at this stage, Mr. Frederick Fynney's news, as mentioned earlier, of the Zulu regiments assembling at oNdini, had not only sent Lord Chelmsford hastening to marshal his own forces, but had also encouraged Frere's decision to act while he was still able to do so without interference from London. It was time for Frere to put in an appearance. On 7 August Chelmsford wrote to Frere:'Sir Henry quite agrees with me that the time has arrived when it would be advisable that the High Commissioner should appear on the scene and he has told me that he intends to write to Your Excellency to come up.'[3] Sir Bartle arrived in Pietermaritzburg three weeks later on 28 September, prompting the elite of the Natal settler community to throw a Grand Ball at the hefty price of 50 shillings a ticket.

Perhaps, having thought about it, the conspirators decided that the Boundary Commission award could be turned to their advantage. It was, after all, the intention to incorporate the Kingdom into the Empire once the Zulu army had been thrashed. If farms in Zululand were to be offered as an inducement, as indeed they would be to Natal's volunteer soldiers, to cross the border and fight the Zulus, the more land the Kingdom had the better. Consequently Frere decided that the award would be proclaimed without alteration but would be immediately followed by an ultimatum which would be nothing less than a declaration of war. The King was invited to attend an *indaba* on 11 December 1878 when details of the award would be revealed. The chosen spot was the Lower Drift on the Thukela River, approximately half way between oNdini and Durban. With the river close at hand, with the green hills rising on either bank it was both a tranquil and historical location. Here, forty years earlier, the Port Natal Volunteers, as the handful of white traders had called themselves, together with 3,000 Zulu refugee followers, were virtually annihilated by a Zulu army.[4] It was also the spot where, twenty-two years later in 1856, John Dunn and the fleeing remnants of Prince Mbuyazi's *iziGqoza*, rather than face the assegais of Cetshwayo's pursuing *Usuthu*, plunged into the tempestuous Thukela roaring on its way to the sea.

Sir Bartle Frere, HM High Commissioner in Southern Africa, instigator of the Anglo-Zulu War of 1879.

An immense Natal fig tree gave shade from the midsummer sun while additional shelter was provided by a great sheet of canvas slung between its branches. The colonial delegation, having arrived the previous day, had set up camp, laid out tables and chairs which they would occupy in the deep shade, with their backs to the sun,while they relaxed and waited. The next day the Zulu delegation arrived well on time and by mid-morning all had been ferried across the river and were patiently waiting for the white men to speak. The colonials were led by John Shepstone, supported by Colonel Forestier Walker of the Scots Guards, Sir Bartle's Military Secretary, Fynney the Border Agent, and other minor officials. To impress the Zulus, they were backed up by a detachment of the Naval Brigade, complete with a Gatling gun, and twenty colonial horsemen of the Stanger Mounted Rifles, while out to sea, a British warship rode at anchor.

The Zulus were less impressive. They had left all vestiges of regalia at home and were merely clad, fore and aft, in brief skin kilts of various kinds. Other than that and an armlet or two of brass or beadwork, they were naked. Their delegation was not composed of the great *iziNduna* of the nation but more of messengers, trusted elders, one or two regimental commanders and a particularly astute and white-man-wise delegate, Gebule, of whom a Natal newspaper wrote the next day: '… very remarkable was the keen and ceaseless attention paid by this wily little Zulu to every word that was uttered.'

A Zulu escort of a company of warriors had also been ferried across but had been compelled to leave their spears and shields on the opposite bank. At 11 am the proceedings got under way and John Shepstone began to read, to the satisfaction of the Zulu delegation, the statement of their award. It was all over in a couple of hours with Zulu esteem for British justice abounding as never before. It was not all that had been hoped for but a good deal more than had been expected. It was time to return across the river and hasten the good news to the King. But wait, they were told, there is yet more news for your Monarch. After a brief pause, Shepstone began to read the terms of Frere's ultimatum and Zulu esteem for British justice rapidly changed to astonishment at British duplicity. Amongst other demands the ultimatum required the surrender of the offending hotheads for trial by a colonial court, the payment of fines amounting to hundreds of cattle and that the 'advice' Theophilus Shepstone had given to Cetshwayo at his coronation be adhered to. The current military system was to be abolished, all missionaries were to be free to return to Zululand and preach as they pleased and, the most impossible condition of all, the Zulu army of 40,000 or more warriors was to be disbanded within thirty days. Furthermore, a British Diplomatic Resident was to reside in Zululand in order to oversee the execution of the British terms and colonial interests. Should the King fail to acquiesce, Britain, he was informed would invade and enforce compliance. Copies of the ultimatum, written in both English and Zulu, were given to the confused and apprehensive delegates who were then hastily ferried back across the river.

Who was to undertake the onerous mission of giving these frightening white man's papers into the hands of the King? Clearly a task to be shunned by all. Later that day, John Dunn, who by now had been living happily for over twenty years on his Zululand farm, close to Middeldrift, received a visitor who thrust the documents into his hands and disappeared.[5] Nor was Dunn inclined to be courier to the King; instead he versed some of his staff as to the terms of the ultimatum and sent them in haste to oNdini. Dunn later wrote '… my men arrived some days before the King's own messenger reached him …'. Most likely Cetshwayo never fully understood exactly what was required of him nor what the fuss was all about. Neither he nor his *iziNduna* believed that the British would go to war over, in Zulu eyes, such petty misdemeanours as the young warriors had committed. Nevertheless, Cetshwayo decided to go along with the payment of the fines and see what would happen. Seven days after the ultimatum had been proclaimed, on behalf of the King, Dunn wrote to the Natal Government requesting more time to collect the cattle. Within a week he received an explicit reply: '... The word of the government as already given, cannot be altered. Unless the prisoners [the offending warriors] and the cattle are given up within the time specified Her Majesty's troops will advance.' Months later after Dunn had thrown in his lot with the British, in an interview with the *Cape Argus* he confessed that '... He [Cetshwayo] does not, even now, know fully the contents of the ultimatum ... the document was read over once [to the Zulu delegates at the Thukela] and its length was such that the messengers could not possibly fix the whole in their memories'. Cetshwayo and the great men of the Kingdom had not only been confounded by the demands of the ultimatum but likewise the chicanery by which they had been enticed to the meeting on the Natal bank of the Thukela River. With little option, the King summoned his generals and from every village in Zululand his warriors, young and excited at the prospect of war, hurried to join their regiments. Yet, even before the ultimatum was due to expire on 11 January 1879, Lord Chelmsford had deployed his army at four different river crossings along the Buffalo and Thukela Rivers. It was an army of consequence, equipped as it was with the latest military weaponry, namely the .45 Martini-Henry breech-loading rifle which, in the hands of a trained soldier was capable of firing twelve rounds a minute. The artillery had a variety of armaments: twelve 7-pounder horse-drawn guns, firing either shrapnel, common shell or canister shot, and four 9-pounder rocket tubes carried on mules that could deliver salvos of screaming missiles spewing smoke and flames. Finally there were Gatling guns, primitive machine guns firing between 300 and 600 rounds a minute, depending on the speed with which the crank handle was turned. There were six different regiments of Imperial infantry; elements of the Naval Brigade from HMS *Active*, comprising Royal Marines and sailors; two companies of Royal Engineers; the Army Service Corps; medical staff and finally, as far as Imperial troops were concerned, a squadron of mounted infantry. The rest of the horsemen, or cavalry, were all locally recruited from either units of the Colony's army of weekend soldiers, referred to as Volunteers, or hastily formed 'regiments' of mounted mercenaries, some white, some black, who, more often than not, were referred to as 'Irregulars', each unit varying in size from 20 to 200 horsemen. All were armed with either a carbine version of the Martini-Henry or a Swinburn-Henry, both breech-loaders and both designed to carry a short bayonet or bowie knife. Finally there were over 9,000 conscripted 'Natal Zulus', the NNC, in seven battalions, under white officers and NCOs. Of these, less than 10 per cent were armed with firearms. The rest had been obliged to supply their own arms such as spears, shields and knobkerries.

It is immediately apparent that a major segment of this hastily cobbled-together army consisted of native troops who had been pressed into service only a few weeks earlier after a peevish tug-of-war between Chelmsford on one side and Sir Henry Bulwer on the other. Bulwer by this time was firmly opposed to a war with Zululand and as Supreme Chief was equally opposed to the conscription of his native population. However, simmering with indignation, he was overruled by Frere.

Lord Chelmsford's original plan had been to launch a five-pronged attack but had later reconsidered, reducing the invasion columns to only four. No 1 Column, commanded by Colonel Charles Pearson, 3rd Regiment of Foot, was to cross the Thukela close to its estuary. No 2 Column, divided between Middle Drift and the 'Gates of Natal' on the Thukela, was commanded by Lieutenant Colonel Anthony Durnford (Durnford, since his unfortunate experience at Bushman's River pass six years earlier, had left Natal to take up a posting in Ireland. He had returned, promoted, in March 1877). Much to Durnford's disappointment, No 2 Column was to be held in reserve; No 3 Column, commanded by Colonel Richard Glyn 1/24th Regiment of Foot, was to go to Rorke's Drift on the Buffalo River. Finally, No 4 Column, commanded by Colonel Evelyn Wood, 90th Light Infantry, was to cross the Ncome (Blood) River close to the village of Utrecht.

Each column was the equivalent of a regimental depot but housed under canvas – rather than the red brick of Aldershot or the grey stone buildings of Brecon. The troops carried all the essentials for an army set to march for months and to do battle at a moment's notice. Each column staggered under almost two tons of ammunition, close on a hundred tents weighing three and a half tons dry and almost twice the weight when wet, spades, picks, buckets, camp kitchens, camp bakeries, blacksmith's forges, medical supplies, pet dogs; officers' kits (each officer was allowed 40lbs of personal baggage). cricket bats and polo sticks, spare uniforms, boots and socks, the instruments of the Regimental Band, and the Regimental and Queen's Colours (flags), which at this time were still carried into battle. But, most likely, the mess silver was not included, a lesson perhaps having been learnt at the expense of the 7th Dragoon Guards who, thirty years earlier, had lost all their silver when they were attacked by the Xhosa during the 7th Frontier War. Everything, down to the little brown clay ink bottles used by the regimental clerks, was stowed away each day aboard one or another of the hundred or more wagons attached to each column. For instance, No 3 Column, with whom we are most concerned, had 220 wagons to carry its gear,

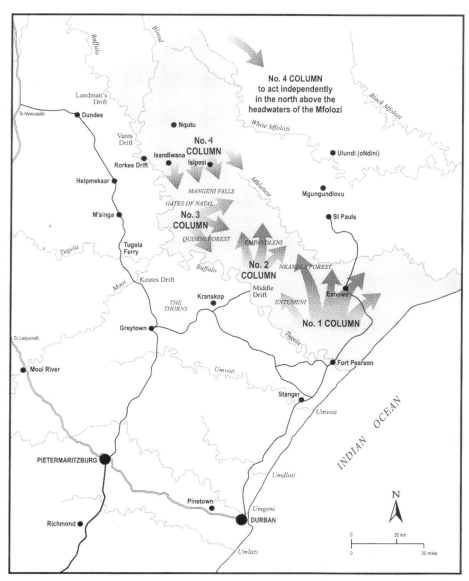

Map 1: Lord Chelmsford's original plan was to launch a five-pronged attack. He later reconsidered, reducing his invasion columns to only four.

1,507 oxen to pull them and over 300 civilians to conduct and drive them. In addition there were eighty-two mule-drawn carts ('Distribution of troops in the field, January 16, 1879.' W. Bellairs, Col., D.A.G). It is hard to imagine! The maximum speed of a column, under the most favourable conditions, was twelve miles a day. However, frequently during foul weather, they were unable to move at all. As far as the common soldier was concerned, he humped his own kit and seventy rounds of ammunition weighing in total over 50lbs. In addition, his rifle weighed 9lbs unloaded.

Opposing Lord Chelmsford, the warrior army of King Cetshwayo. The following are excerpts from 'The Zulu Army' compiled by H.D. Finney, at the request of Lord Chelmsford, in November 1878 (Durban Municipal Library, reference 968.303).[6]

Zulu warrior with unusual hairstyle and unique plaited-leather body decoration. The small shield and finery would indicate a social occasion.

FORMATION OF THE ZULU ARMY

The Zulu Army, which may be estimated at from 40,000 to 50,000 men, is composed of the entire nation capable of bearing arms. The method employed in recruiting its ranks is as follows: At short intervals varying from two to five years, all the young men who have, during that time, attained the age of fourteen or fifteen years are formed into a regiment, after a year's probation, during which they are supposed to pass from boyhood to manhood, they are placed at a military kraal or headquarters. In some cases they are sent to an already existing kraal, which is the headquarters of a corps or regiment, of which they then become part; in others, especially when the young regiment is numerous, they build a new kraal …

HOW OFFICERED

Each corps or regiment possessing its own military kraal, has the following officers: One commanding officer, one second in command who directly commands the left wing, and two wing officers … Besides the above there are company officers, consisting of a captain, and from one to three junior officers, all of whom are the same age as the men they command, while in the case of a corps the C.O. of each regiment composing it, takes rank next to its four great officers when he himself is not of them …

UNIFORM
The chief distinction is between married and unmarried men. No one in Zululand, male or female, is permitted to marry without the direct permission of the king, and when he allows a regiment to do so, which is not before the men are about 40 years of age, they have to shave the crown of the head, and put a ring around it, and then they become one of the 'white' regiments, carrying white shields, and etc., in contradistinction to the 'black' or unmarried regiments, who wear their hair naturally and have coloured shields …

STATISTICS OF THE ZULU ARMY
… for practical purposes there are not more than 26 Zulu Regiments able to take the field, numbering altogether 40,400. Of these 22,500 are between 20 and 30 years of age, 10,000 between 30 and 40, 3,500 between 40 and 50 and 4,500 between 50 and 60 years of age. From which it will be seen the mortality in Zululand is unusually rapid …

COMMISSARIAT AND TRANSPORT
As might be expected a savage army like that of Zululand neither has nor requires much Commissariat or Transport. The former consists of three or four days provisions in the shape of maize or millet, and a herd of cattle, proportioned to the distance to be traversed, accompanies each regiment. The latter consists of a number of lads [*uDibi*] who follow each regiment, carrying the sleeping mats, blankets, and provisions, and assisting to drive the cattle …

HOW REGIMENTS ARE ASSEMBLED AT THEIR HEAD-QUARTERS
In the event of hostilities arising between the Zulu nation and any other (unless some very sudden attack was made on their country), messengers would be sent travelling night and day if necessary, by the king to order the men to assemble in regiments at their respective military kraals, where they would find the commanding officer ready to receive them.

RESERVE
A large body of troops, as a reserve, remain seated with their backs to the
enemy: the commanders and staff retire to some eminence with one or
two of the older regiments, (as extra reserves). All orders are delivered
by runners. It is to be noted that although the above were the ordinary
customs of the Zulu Army when at war, it is more than probable that great
changes, both in movement and dress, will be made consequent on the
introduction of firearms amongst them.

It is strange, though true, that there were similarities between the British
and Zulu soldiery: they were both formed into regiments bound by tradition
and pride; each regiment was divided into companies; and both armies were
distinguished by their uniforms, whether they were British red coat or Zulu
otter skin headbands. Both armies were strictly disciplined and both thought
their regiments to be second to none. There were, however, marked differences:
weaponry for one.

For over half a century the Zulu army had coveted whatever firearms had
happened to come its way. King Shaka himself had acquired a number, testing
their power and range by shooting cattle
at various distances. His dream was to
equip every warrior with a musket and
he planned to this end '… to send a
regiment of men to England who there
would scatter in all directions in order to
ascertain how guns were made, and the
return to construct some in Zululand.'
Shaka's plan failed to materialize.
Thus Dingane, his successor, set about
purchasing firearms and gunpowder
from any available source, mostly from
white traders as far away as the Cape
and Mozambique. Much later, only a
year or two prior to the Anglo-Zulu War,
Cetshwayo managed to acquire, most
unexpectedly, a number of weapons with
the blessing of the Natal Government.
John Dunn, acting on Cetshwayo's behalf
had advised the Government of Natal that

An unmarried warrior with friend. Note
the broad-bladed stabbing spear, the *iklwa*.

Cetshwayo was under threat from various rival members of the Royal Family who would see themselves king in Cetshwayo's place. Furthermore, Dunn advised, Cetshwayo was too weak to avert a rebellion and unless his faction was reinforced with firearms, a Zulu civil war was inevitable. To Dunn's surprise the governor granted Dunn a permit to purchase 250 guns and ammunition on Cetshwayo's behalf.[7] On receipt of the weapons, at Cetshwayo's request, Dunn taught a number of warriors how to shoot. He combined this exercise with a hunting expedition for some of his wealthy white clients, during which a fine male lion was shot. Having skinned the beast it was decided to cook the carcass over a fire and warriors and clients alike decided roast lion was 'not too bad'.[8] By 1879 it is likely that every one in three of Cetshwayo's warriors was armed with a firearm, mostly obsolete flintlocks or inferior guns supplied by traders who would have deliberately made many dysfunctional.

The Zulu army also differed, to its great advantage, in its mobility. Whereas Lord Chelmsford's columns when on the march were fortunate to cover ten miles a day, a Zulu army, living off the land and further supplied by the local population, could comfortably cover three times that distance. For speed, its only rival was the horse which, with its rider armed and self-contained with hard biscuit and biltong (dried meat) could, if the going was good, outpace the fastest warrior. But in comparison to the heavy-booted Imperial infantryman, dressed in a uniform more suited to the Arctic than to Africa, the Zulu warrior was a nimble athlete. In the same way as the British soldier no longer polished his buttons or whitened his belt, the Zulu warrior left behind his expensive regalia of cowskin-tailed kilts and feathered headdress, for in battle with his shield, knobkerrie and *iklwa* (stabbing spear), he fought all but naked.

Although Chelmsford and his retinue had attached themselves to No 3, or the Centre Column as it was also called, the actual column commander was, as mentioned earlier, Colonel Richard Glyn, a soldier of considerable experience. During the Indian Mutiny he had fought at the relief of Lucknow and later, during the Crimean War, at the Battle of Sebastopol. More recently he had played a major role in bringing the 9th Frontier War to a close and had in fact considerably more combat experience than his commanding officer. Three years younger and at least twelve inches shorter than Chelmsford, Glyn in more ways than one would be overshadowed by his senior officer. Although, with his thickset, short stature and bristling whiskers Glyn gave the impression of a disgruntled gnome, he was both a fearless rider to hounds and a kindly, easy-going, unsuspecting person, and an obvious scapegoat for the disaster that lay ahead.

Chelmsford effectively usurped Glyn's position as Column Commander, reducing his duties and those of his staff to merely overseeing the transport, the placing of sentries and the cleanliness of the camp. Thus a prickly relationship was soon to be perceived between the staff officers of Lord Chelmsford and those of Colonel Glyn. As we will hear more of these officers, in order to avoid confusion they were:

LORD CHELMSFORD'S STAFF	
Assistant Military Secretary	Lieutenant Colonel John North Crealock, 95th Regiment. Self-opinionated and described as a waspish military man and not pleasant to deal with.
Aides-de-Camp	Major Matthew Gosset, 54th Regiment. Described as self-opinionated and haughty.
	Captain Ernest Henry Buller, Rifle Brigade. (Not to be confused with Major Redvers Buller.)
	Lieutenant Berkeley Milne, RN. Attached to Chelmsford's staff as a courtesy to the Naval Brigade.
Civilian aides	William Drummond, Intelligence Dept. and Interpreter.
	Henry William Longcast, Intelligence Dept., interpreter and guide.
COLONEL GLYN'S STAFF	
Principal Staff Officer	Major Cornelius Francis Clery, 32nd Regiment. Formerly an instructor in tactics at Camberley Military Staff College. Described as vindictive and a gossip.
Aides-de-Camp	Captain Alan Gardner, 14th Hussars. A varied career as a cavalry and artillery officer. Also served in the War Office Intelligence Department and had successfully passed Staff College.
	Captain Henry Hallam Parr, 13th Light Infantry. Had been ADC to Sir Bartle Frere who had recently released Parr from duty in order that he might take part in the campaign.
Orderly Officer	Lieutenant Nevill Josiah Coghill, 1/24th Regiment.
Civilian	J.A. Brickhill, civilian interpreter.

The main strength of No 3 Column was its Imperial infantry, consisting of the 1st and 2nd Battalions of the 24th Regiment of Foot. The 1st Battalion had been serving oversees for a decade or more, seven years in various stations in the Mediterranean and for the last three years in the Cape. There, using the new Martini-Henry rifle at the Battle of Centane a few months earlier, it had effectively brought an end to the last of the Frontier Wars. The battalion had received much local praise, the Colonial Secretary being informed that the men were 'old steady shots whose every bullet told'. On the other hand the 2nd Battalion had but recently arrived in Africa, straight from the Regimental Depot at Brecon. There seemed to be little desire between the two battalions to fraternize one with the other. The column's total strength was Staff all ranks, 20. Artillery, all ranks, N Battery 5 Brigade, 132. Imperial infantry, all ranks, 1st and 2nd Battalions 24th Regiment, 1,275. Cavalry, 346. Natal Native Contingent; 2,566. Civilian wagon drivers and assistants; 346.

The mounted troops were not cavalry in the sense that they were intended to charge or pursue the enemy with the traditional horseman's weapons of sabre and lance. Armed with a carbine, a revolver and either a hunting knife or bayonet, their task in the main would be reconnaissance, vedette duty, escort duty, acting as couriers and, when the need arose, to skirmish at close quarters with the enemy. As mentioned earlier, the only Imperial horsemen consisted of a squadron of Imperial Mounted Infantry (IMI) who undoubtedly had seen rougher, tougher service than any other body of men in Chelmsford's army. Raised in the Northern Cape four years previously, mounted infantry was at the time a new concept. Word had been put around the regiments calling for men who could ride. But those who thought their lot astride a horse would be an easier life than marching made a serious mistake. The unit had operated under several different names including 'Carrington's Horse', it having been raised and trained by Lieutenant Frederick Carrington of the 1/24th. Only forty-two strong, the men had later taken over from the NMP as escort to Sir Theophilus Shepstone at the time of his annexation of the Transvaal. Shepstone, piqued that his escort was named after a mere lieutenant, insisted the name be changed to the more imposing title of The Transvaal Mounted Infantry.[9] During the next two years the unit campaigned and rode over much of South Africa, often in the harshest of conditions until, they looked more like scarecrows than soldiers. They were described by one officer as follows: '... a more ragged crew was never got together, except for professional beggars on the stage'. Another critic went further: '... their uniform was a red coat, more or less tattered, trousers and leggings ditto, with a battered helmet. They looked like a cross between a groom out of place and a soldier after a night in the cells and a big drink.'[10]

The rest of the mounted men were either of white colonial stock or units made up of black volunteers with a grudge to settle with the Zulu King. The most senior of the white regiments, the Natal Carbineers, now commanded by Captain Theophilus ('Offi') Shepstone, Sir Theophilus' eldest son, had been raised in 1855. Now, twenty-four years later, the Natal Colony could boast of eleven such regiments with a volunteer staff commanded by Major John Dartnell, who had held the appointment since it was first promulgated three years earlier. Dartnell, aged 42, was a highly respected and experienced soldier. Born in Canada of a military family, he was commissioned into the 86th Regiment of Foot and within two years, at the age of 20, he and his regiment were attempting to scale the walls of Jhansi, a stronghold of the Indian Mutineers. Time and again the storming parties were thrown from the battlements until Dartnell, sword in hand, was over the top and fighting for his life. He received no less than four serious sword cuts and a musket ball which was providently deflected by a buckle. He was recommended for the Victoria Cross but, no doubt due to the turmoil in India at the time, the award was not pursued. After further distinguished service he retired to try his luck at farming in Natal but was soon back to soldiering again.

In the Natal Carbineers, Chelmsford was fortunate in having the most senior of the volunteer regiments assigned to his column. They could trace their origins back to 1851 when a farmer, Piet Otto, of the Karkloof area, formed his own private army, the Umgeni Rangers, to protect his cattle and his Zulu tenants from Bushmen raiders. This unit, forty strong, was the true forerunner of the Natal Carbineers, two of whom, George Shepstone (another of Theophilus's sons) and Charlie Raw, had accompanied Durnford to Bushman's River Pass. They had survived, and would serve with him again in the great battle that lay ahead in Zululand not, however, as Carbineers but as officers in the Natal Native Horse (NNH) or 'Durnford's Horse' as it was variously called.

In addition to the Carbineers two other units would march with No 3 Column: the Newcastle Mounted Rifles under Captain C.B. Bradstreet and the Buffalo Border Guard under Quartermaster D. Macphail. The latter unit, as its title implies, prior to the invasion patrolled the border between the Colony and the Kingdom. It had been the first on the scene to confront Mehlokazulu after he had crossed the Buffalo to abduct his father's adulterous wives.

The terms of enlistment applicable to the Colonial Volunteers stipulated that they would not be required to serve outside the borders of the Colony. Now that they appeared to be obliged to cross into Zululand, it was necessary for each man to give his consent, hence the term and title of 'Volunteer'. There were those who preferred to stay at home and guard their farms and families against a Zulu counter-attack and none were stigmatized for doing so. Last but not least amongst the colonial horsemen was the NMP, recruited from a good class of young men in England. The NMP was, in fact, the only full-time force of a military nature employed within the Colony. Now, as the war approached, it was placed under military command. It is interesting to note that the Zulu word for colonial mounted soldiers, *amaLenja*, was a corruption of the word 'ranger' taken from the Durban Rangers, a mounted regiment disbanded prior to 1879. While all armed and mounted soldiers were known as *amaLenja*, it was a term quite distinct from the Xhosa word *nongqai*, meaning armed mounted watchman. Somehow or other, the NMP acquired this native name, hence Fort Nongqai, later to be the headquarters of the NMP at Eshowe. Excluding the NMP, the Volunteers had material benefits to consider. A trooper was paid five shillings a day, compared to one shilling a day for a British soldier, plus an allowance for his horse. The horse he rode was most likely his favourite means of transport that not only carried him around the farm, into town, out hunting and, on occasion, to regimental camps and manoeuvres.

However, now that the Volunteers were actually going to war and were about to invade Zululand, there was, apart from their pay, the prospect of loot in the form of Zulu cattle. Some of the invading columns would be more proficient at plundering than others, provoking jealousy and criticism by those who saw themselves as getting less than their fair share. There was in addition the prospect of a farm in Zululand for every Volunteer, once the Zulus were conquered and the war was over. Carl Muller, an officer of the Stutterheim Mounted Police, had met Lord Chelmsford in the Eastern Cape, at which time Chelmsford had requested Muller to recruit horsemen for service in Natal. Muller recorded that he was instructed to '... recruit young men who were strong and could ride and shoot well'. They were promised five shillings a day and a uniform if they were successful in quelling the 'rebellion'. They would also receive a farm of 3,000 morgen (approximately 6,550 acres). '... I was to recruit a hundred men immediately and they were to be equipped in Natal.' Wally Stafford, who was destined to be one of the few survivors of what would become known as the Battle of Isandlwana, when reminiscing many years later on his terms of recruitment as an officer of the NNC, recalled that he was offered fifteen shillings a day and after the war a farm in Zululand. Similarly, Trooper Fred Symons remembered that after parading in Pietermaritzburg before marching off to war, '... Lord Chelmsford promised each of the Carbineers a farm in Zululand when the war was over'.[11] Later, however, a brief paragraph in the

Natal Mercury of 11 July 1879 put an end to all hope of free farms across the Buffalo River. It read: 'In providing for the future of Zululand, no grants will be made to volunteers.' But before the 'Volunteer' could hope for loot and farms, he had to put money up front by providing his own horse; and what did a good horse cost? When in 1874 Durnford had landed at the Cape, he had commented '… Kafir ponies could be had for a hundred shillings each. These were not much to look at but they gave fifty miles a week and never required to be fed'. In the autumn of 1878, when it was suddenly appreciated that a Zulu warrior was just about as fleet as cavalry, the cry went out for good horses. It was found that the 'Plate' (River Plate) horses from South America, of mixed Arabian blood and of great hardiness, could be had – unbroken of course – for 300 shillings. Cheap unbroken horses were doled out to inexperienced riders. An officer of Irregulars wrote: '… the mode of selection was primitive in the extreme. The horses were driven into a stone enclosure called a kraal, every man then went with a halter and from a plunging mass selected what suited him.' That, however, was later in the campaign. Now, in the autumn of 1878, a trustworthy horse cost around 360 shillings, a figure that would double within months. An officer arriving in March of 1879 paid six hundred shillings for a Basutho pony and 1,200 shillings for a 'good mover'.[12] When the conflict to come entered into months of arduous campaigning, the Basutho pony would emerge as the ideal warhorse.

There was one quality sought before all others, however, that the horse be 'salted', a term used to describe a horse that had contracted 'horse sickness', and had survived, and was now immune. As early as July 1878, six months prior to the invasion of Zululand, Chelmsford had written to the Duke of Cambridge, the Commander-in-Chief in faraway London, '… I am afraid there will be great difficulty, however, in keeping the mounted branches effective owing to the climate of Natal and the Transvaal being so unhealthy for horses. I understand there are only four months in which horse sickness, as it is called, does not prevail.' He did not, however, mention which months these were. It was a disease that could kill a troop of horses as efficiently as a volley of musketry. A disease that though common was more prevalent in some areas and at certain times of the year than others. It was inflicted by the midge, a small blood-feeding fly. The symptoms were the onslaught of a high fever, difficulty in breathing and frothy discharge from the nose, followed by sudden death. An officer of the NNC, by the name of Fenn, marching up to Natal from the Eastern Cape in 1878, recalled, '… the season for horse sickness was fast approaching when we should, in all probability, lose as many as sixty percent of our horses. This was not a pleasant outlook for a cavalry regiment with only twelve percent reserve horses.'[13] It was indeed a threat but although the sickness stalked the columns it never killed at anything like the rate predicted until much later in the campaign, when the search was on for Cetshwayo, now defeated and a fugitive, amongst the swamps and low lying flats of the Black Mfolozi River valley. A British officer recorded, 'the horses, poor brutes, were covered in them [ticks], indeed as many probably had more ticks on than their own hair, but this does not say much for as many of our horses were completely bald! What we were most afraid of, however, was "horse sickness", a deadly disease for which we had no remedy. It was quick, horses apparently well in the morning being dead by night.'[14]

On 6 January 1879, just four days before the British ultimatum expired and the juggernaut that No 3 Column was fast becoming was poised around the hamlet of Helpmakaar in the hills of the Biggarsberg ready to descend to the Buffalo River, the correspondent of the *Natal Mercury* reported activity on the enemy bank opposite to Rorke's Drift. '... It was considered probable that the Zulu force seen on the banks of the river intended to attack the camp, and the Volunteers all eagerly waited for the opportunity of having the glory of having the first brush with the enemy and giving them a taste of their quality.'The reporter also mentioned another matter the Volunteers were eager to have settled. In addition to having the right to decide whether or not they served beyond the borders of the Colony, they had the right to elect their commanding officer. They had already exercised this prerogative, having chosen Major Dartnell as their leader. Perhaps Lord Chelmsford and his staff were unaware of this colonial privilege. It would certainly seem to be so, as, on arriving at Helpmakaar, Major Crealock, on Chelmsford's orders, usurped Dartnell's position, giving command of the Volunteers to an Imperial Special Service officer, Major John Cecil Russell of the 12th Lancers.

Russell, aged 40, was not only an experienced cavalryman, having served in three different cavalry regiments, he had fought in the Ashanti War. He was also extremely well connected having been ADC to Major-General Sir Archibald Alison, Chief of Intelligence at the War Office; moreover, he had held the appointment of ADC to, and was the friend of, the Prince of Wales. Furthermore, Russell was a friend of Lord Chelmsford. Russell had already ruffled feathers amongst the mounted men – again on Chelmsford's orders – by superseding Lieutenant Edward Browne, the officer commanding the IMI, a position Browne had held most competently almost from the inception of the unit. Resentful though the IMI may have been, there was nothing they could do about it. However, ruffling the Volunteers was a different matter. The correspondent went on to describe the scene after Captain 'Offi' Shepstone

had read the General Order containing Russell's additional appointment '...
can your readers wonder that the Volunteers stood amazed after hearing such an
order? It was so unexpected that the men could not realize it nor decide upon a
line of conduct; for a short time there was complete silence'. 'Offi' Shepstone
spelt it out for them. '... Men, you know under what conditions you signed
your names and agreed to go into Zululand ... by this order Major Dartnell is
superseded and Captain Russell, raised to the rank of Brevet Major, is placed
in command over you. Now is your time to speak I ask you now, therefore, do
you accept Captain Russell as your commander or no?'[15] The men of one accord
shouted 'No!' and with that 'Offi' Shepstone mounted his horse and was off
at the gallop. The NMP, Dartnell being their commandant, were particularly
angered. Trooper Symons of the Carbineers recalled that on hearing the news
the NMP started packing and were determined to leave for Pietermaritzburg.
What could have escalated into a sort of permissible mutiny was, with Dartnell's
cooperation, settled amicably enough. Chelmsford, with a little loss of face,
solved the problem by promoting Dartnell to his staff as 'Cavalry Adviser'
which in effect put Dartnell in a position where he could politely dictate to
Russell. Honour was satisfied, and the Volunteers, having saddled up with the
rest of the column, made their way down to Rorke's Drift.

Chapter 5

'A big fuss over a small matter'

Everyone was delighted to leave the dismal windswept heights of Helpmakaar where they had endured almost constant mist and rain for days on end, turning the roads and horse lines into a morass of knee deep mud. The horses themselves made their aversion to the Helmakaar plain to see by escaping at every opportunity: the NMP, putting their horses out to graze, lost sixteen in one night, the wiliest being eventually recaptured over a hundred miles away in the Orange Free State.

Speculation was rife as to how the Zulu army was going to react to the build-up of British forces on its doorstep. The correspondent of the *Natal Mercury* wrote '… it was rumoured an *impi* of eight thousand warriors was assembling on the Zulu bank'. However, the correspondent went on to reassure his readers what the fate of the Zulu army would be should it oppose the British crossing:

> … it will be a day long to be remembered by the Zulu nation, and all African races. Across the river is a fine open battlefield: imagine one thousand five hundred men firing, say, a shot a minute, a battery of six guns cannonading sharply, a Native contingent, two thousand strong attacking, and a charge of four hundred cavalry armed with revolvers: imagine such a thing, and no refuge or shelter of any kind within three miles and you can realize what the remnant of the Zulu army would be in a couple of hours.

The correspondent went on to speculate that there would be a large concourse of spectators to witness the crossing of the river and the anticipated battle. He did not, however, specify whether they would be colonial or Zulu.[1]

At 2 am on 11 January a trumpeter of the 24th Regiment sounded Reveille and No 3 Column advanced towards the river, only to be foiled by an all-enveloping mist of such thickness all sense of direction was lost. It was not until two hours later that two companies of the 24th, one in each of the recently arrived pontoons, were safely hauled across to the opposite bank. There they quickly deployed into a skirmish line that would shortly, as more troops crossed, expand to three miles in length along the Zulu bank. By 6 am only six guns of the Royal Artillery remained, with a company of infantry deployed on rising ground to cover the crossing. Before the day was out they too would be put aboard the pontoons and, like the wagons, hauled across the river. It was a successful operation without a casualty, despite a man of the IMI, Private Price, being swept from his horse midway to the Zulu bank. He was saved by the heroic conduct of an NNC officer, Captain Hayes, who '… had been sitting on his horse close to the bank. He rode in and held out the butt of his rifle to the struggling man. In doing so, however, his horse also got swept away and he separated from it; but he nevertheless managed to rescue Price at the imminent risk of his own life and bring him into shallow water. His gallantry and coolness called forth the encomiums of all who were present and was thought worthy of notice in Column Orders and afterwards in General Orders.'[2]

During the course of the day, seven riders were seen approaching from upstream along the Zulu bank, causing a stir of excitement. Much to the surprise of all they turned out to be from Colonel Evelyn Wood's No 4 Column, situated thirty-two miles to the north, led by Captain Robert Barton, a Special Service officer seconded from the Coldstream Guards. As a Natal Carbineer later recorded they had been 'out exploring the road, and meeting with no resistance had penetrated right through to our camp … the kaffirs all along the road had been friendly and given them information and milk.'[3] How unlike the anticipated *impi* of 8,000 warriors!

The crossing of the Buffalo, despite the rumours and speculation, had been unopposed. The Zulu army, 40,000 strong, being still at oNdini, fifty-five miles away to the east, was undergoing its ritual preparations for war. The warriors had marched fifteen miles to the emaKhosini valley, the sacred burial place of Zulu monarchy where, in the presence of King Cetshwayo, the war doctors had communed with the ancestral spirits of the Zulu Nation beseeching them to accompany the army into battle and to grant the *amabutho* (warriors) victory over the red soldiers of the White Queen. The great host of warriors, war doctors, the King and his counsellors, had spent the night in prayer and at first light all had returned to oNdini where the individual regiments were required to *hlanza* (vomit) into deep pits specially prepared for the purpose, an ancient ritual of cleansing the body before battle.[4] To ensure each man was not slack in performing this function, all were compelled to take a deep swallow of a concoction containing amongst other things herbs, the flesh of brave animals such as the lion and buffalo, and the body dirt of the Nation that might, for instance, be scraped from a gateway or a seat that was in constant contact with human skin, thus acquiring a patina of grease and grime. The brew might also contain the body parts of an enemy or a man who in life had been courageous: the bone of the right forearm, the cartilage of the breast bone, even the rectum was also included, in the belief that its inclusion would subject the enemy to diarrhoea and confusion.[5] Should a warrior attempt to evade a gulp of this repugnant brew the war doctors were close at hand to have at him with sticks and cudgels. The ceremony of *hlanza* completed, the pits were quickly covered lest an enemy procure a portion of its contents and with due alchemy turn the brew to his advantage.

Next the fiercest bull of the royal herds, essentially black in colour, was driven into an enclosure where it was tormented, driven to and fro, round and round, not only to tire it but to madden it into a frenzy. Then a favoured regiment of the king, unarmed and barehanded, would rush the beast and by sheer weight of numbers, incurring casualties in the process, bring it down. As the bull fought and squirmed, many endeavoured to hold its kicking legs while a dozen warriors or more, laying hold of its horns, twisted its head until, with a crack that could be heard above the clamour of the throng, the neck broke. Fires having already been prepared, the war doctors and their assistants fell upon the carcass, quickly skinning and demolishing it into thin strips of meat ready for the fire. Barely cooked, the meat was tossed into the air to be caught by eager hands; one bite and the strips were tossed again to be snatched by those yet to grab and gnaw a morsel. So the ceremony continued until the war doctors were satisfied that every precaution against ill fortune had been taken and that, with the goodwill of the ancestors, the enemy would be scattered.

Now that No 3 Column had successfully crossed into Zululand, there was a feeling of euphoria throughout. It was going to be a walkover. The mounted troops were particularly active. While Major Dartnell led a reconnaissance to ensure there was no hidden army ready to pounce, Chelmsford with an escort of colonials set off north at a leisurely pace seemingly with no more anxiety than had he been out for a ride down Long Valley at Aldershot. He had a previously arranged rendezvous with Colonel Wood; they were to meet at Mkonjane Hill, nine miles north of Rorke's Drift. For some there was a dreamlike, surreal quality about the ride; instead of a pitched battle all was peace and quiet. Like the Zulus Captain Barton had met the previous day, the people were unperturbed, going about their business and tending their cattle with no more concern for

Chelmsford and his escort than had they been a party of traders up from Port Natal. They were met along the way by Major Redvers Buller, Wood's second-in-command, escorted by a troop of the Frontier Light Horse (FLH). This was also a colonial regiment but not of weekend soldier volunteers such as the Natal colonials: the FLH were mercenaries, mostly from the Eastern Cape. Not only were they mercenaries, they were also the most proficient cattle rustlers in southern Africa.

Whilst the commanders and their staffs discussed tactics, Chelmsford's escort took the opportunity to off-saddle and stretch out in the grass; not so the FLH. They set about looting with the efficiency that comes from long practice. During the three-hour interlude, during which the officers conferred, the FLH scoured the countryside lifting hundreds of cattle, the first of the estimated 7,000 head they would loot within days of crossing into Zululand.[6] This form of plunder was designed to both demoralize and starve the enemy into submission. It was also a profitable business. Every man, white and black, of the column shared in the proceeds derived from selling the cattle to contractors and butchers as far away as the Orange Free State. Chelmsford's escort was not slow in taking a cue from the FLH. On the way back to Rorke's drift the Natal Carbineers pillaged a number of beasts, goats and sheep promoting the villagers to '… shout defiance but not fire in retaliation'. Some Imperial officers began to appreciate that a posting to No 3 Column could be a financially rewarding one. On 18 January 1879, Lieutenant Curling referring to the column's crossing of the Buffalo River, seven days earlier, wrote home that 'fortunately the Zulus had all retreated and gave no trouble. They had left behind them nearly 3,000 head of cattle which we captured which means five pounds [sterling] each at last … I am extremely well off here for the very simple reason that there is nothing to spend money on.' Although Chelmsford in his *Regulations for Field Forces South Africa 1878* had laid down '… Natives will be treated with kindness. Commanding officers will exert their influence with all ranks to prevent their being in any way molested or oppressed', these fine principles had already fallen by the wayside.

On arrival at Rorke's Drift and having attended to their horses, the colonials of Chelmsford's escort were dismissed. They immediately headed for the river which had subsided somewhat, stripped off, plunged in and frolicked about. It was only after they were back on the bank drying off that they realized someone was missing. Trooper Dickson had drowned without anyone having noticed. He became the second casualty of the Anglo-Zulu War.[7]

That night the column put up their tents and camped along the three-mile skirmishing line that had been taken up on crossing the river. Despite the pre-dawn reveille of the previous day the column was again woken early at 3:30 am. Five miles away to the north-east, amongst cliffs and caves, stood the hilltop homestead of *Nkosi* Sihayo kaXongo Ngobese. The first serious blow of the war was about to be struck. It was from Sihayo's homestead that his fiery son Mehlokazula, with a posse of young warriors, had crossed into Natal and subsequently executed his father's adulterous wives. What better place to be the target of Britain's first act of retribution.

Although the previous day's contact with the local Zulu people had been somewhat uneventful, Lord Chelmsford was taking no chances. Apart from a reserve, the whole force would march on Sihayo's 'Stronghold', as the homestead would be called after it had been conquered. They set off at sunrise, the column under the command of Colonel Glyn with Lieutenant Colonel Russell taking charge of the cavalry, 200 in number. It was not long, however, before Lord Chelmsford himself took over.

As the column drew close to Sihayo's homestead eerie chanting could be heard, the defiant 'war song' of the few who remained. Most of the warriors, including Mehlokazula himself, had already left to join their regiments at oNdini. The 1/3rd NNC was under the command of Major Wilsone Black of the 2/24th, with Commandant George Hamilton Browne at its head leading the way. Browne was a mercenary by profession, having served around the globe in many military outfits including the Royal Horse Artillery, the Papal Zouaves and as a volunteer during the on-going New Zealand wars between the indigenous Maori and the European settlers. He had thus acquired the nickname 'Maori' Browne, a title he put much store by. Browne was eager to get to grips with the enemy but a jumble of rocks and boulders of immense size, mostly covered in a tangle of thorn bush, barred the way. Suddenly a voice called in English demanding to know their business and on whose authority they had entered the Zulu Kingdom? An officer, so legend has it, shouted that they were there by 'Orders of the Great White Queen'.

Despite Glyn being nominally in charge, Chelmsford and his staff pressed well to the fore with Chelmsford calling Browne aside, instructing him to secure the Zulu cattle but on no account to harm women and children. Turning to his men, Browne repeated the General's instructions and further cautioned that anyone harming a woman or child would be shot. Soon the advance was faced by the heights of the stronghold through which a 'V'-shaped defile cut its way, sheltering the remaining inhabitants and their cattle. The Zulu defenders, though greatly outnumbered, fought hand-to-hand with the NNC before retreating onto the broken ground above. Taking cover amongst the rocks they commenced firing upon their pursuers. Before Browne and his NNC could reach them, the soldiers of the 2/24th, bringing up the rear, opened fire, driving the Zulu sharpshooters back into the open mouth of a deep cave. Browne was highly critical of his troops except for 'three hundred real Zulus' who formed part of his 1,200-strong B Company NNC; it transpired they had been warriors of the Ndluyengwe Regiment that had defected from the Zulu army in December 1877.[8] Finally Browne and his men reached the heights and the cave itself. The fight for Sihayo's homestead was all over, bar some risky moments spent in forcing the surrender of the last Zulu diehards. Lieutenant Henry Harford of the 99th Regiment, a Special Service officer now with the NNC, who had grown up in Natal and could speak Zulu, exhibited particular bravery in calling the most defiant of the defenders to surrender.[9]

To complete the victory the Volunteers, displaying the value of mounted troops, had galloped around the east side of the fortress, cutting off all means of retreat. They could clearly see the enemy on top of the krantzes keeping parallel to them until, having come within range, the warriors opened fire with all manner of firearms, including an old elephant gun. The horsemen were ordered to 'Number Off' and those of even number to dismount with the men on the right taking hold of the reins of his horse. Those afoot quickly formed a skirmish line, firing as they moved forward. Trooper Symons of the Natal Carbineers described what happened next. '... Our sergeant took the three of us onto the right and advanced towards a pile of rocks behind which we had seen some mounted Zulus disappear.' (By this time the Zulus had lost their fear of horses and no longer regarded a horse to be an *amaThakathi*. In fact it was now a matter of prestige to be a mounted warrior. Many members of the Zulu Royal Family also rode and the horse was fast becoming a factor in Zulu reconnaissance and travel). Symons continued, '... What's going to happen now thought I but I wasn't long in doubt for V-O-O-rrr went a pot leg or some cumbersome missile over our heads. At this we too opened fire along the whole line ... a frightful waste of ammunition ... we saw no sign of the enemy and a number of horses were grazing quietly about half a mile to the right ... we went after them and when we had covered about half the distance we saw some Zulus charging down on us'. Symons and his comrades, outnumbered and on foot, were suddenly in a tight spot. The order was given to fix bayonets and just as Symons with a Zulu in his sights was about to press the trigger, the 'enemy' threw up their hands. They were men of the NNC who, in fear of the Zulus, had pulled off their distinguishing red bandanas and fled.

Trooper Clarke of the NMP, who had also formed part of the skirmish line, reported that everything combustible was burnt to the ground and a large herd of cattle taken. The cattle were later sold to the butchers at thirty shillings a head and the contractors resold them to the military at £18 each.[10] Nevertheless, all in all, Lord Chelmsford considered it a British victory and released the prisoners. Trooper Symons summed up the day's operations as 'a big fuss over a small matter'. The correspondent of the *Natal Witness* had a different opinion. He bellowed in triumph at his readers, '… I have seen the bare green hills of Zululand enlivened by the white tents, and the red or blue uniforms of men who have been gathered there to vindicate the just cause of an offended civilization, and to assert the outraged authority of the British Crown. I have seen the climax of a policy which must end in the undisputed supremacy of British rule over all the native tribes that live south of the Limpopo.'[11] Charles Norris-Newman, the Special Correspondent for the *London Standard*, in a more practical vein, commented on Lord Chelmsford's release of the prisoners: '… His policy in doing so was not approved by the officers who best understood the Native character and could not see the benefit of allowing men and women to come into the camp either as prisoners or to surrender themselves, and to be fed well, treated kindly and allowed to go when and where they liked. Considering the experience we've had in the last Cape War, surely this should not have been permitted.' The skirmish at Sihayo's homestead had indeed been 'a big fuss over a small matter' and the casualties, British twelve, Zulus twenty-eight, insignificant compared to the carnage that would occur ten days later.[12]

There is little doubt that within an hour or so of the last shot having been fired, King Cetshwayo, sixty miles away at oNdini, would have been fully informed of the taking of Sihayo's homestead. Whilst the British with a heliograph (soon to arrive in South Africa), provided the sun shone and there was a clear line of sight, could flash messages over considerable distances, the Zulus communicated by shouting from hill to hill, astounding strangers by the speed at which information could be conveyed over vast distances. Eustace Fannin, a magistrate and a Zulu linguist, would claim to be the first white man other than those who were actually present to hear of what would shortly be the great Zulu victory of Isandlwana. He was in the Kranskop area, above the Thukela River, some fifty miles south of Chelmsford's camp and had heard the news from Zulus shouting from hill to hill. The young H. Rider Haggard, then 23 years old and earning a living as Shepstone's secretary, was in Pretoria 200 miles away on the day of the Zulu victory. The following morning his native washerwoman told him many redcoats had been slaughtered by the Zulus. It was not until twenty-four hours later that an exhausted horseman arrived with the news. Similarly, Cannon Mullins of the Church of England, 450 miles away in Grahamstown, also heard of the battle from a servant the morning after it had happened; and L.H. Samuelson noted: '… particular arrangements for forwarding news were made by them [Zulus] in times of war and lines of communication were established from hill to hill.'

With the news of the destruction of Sihayo's 'stronghold', King Cetshwayo despaired of negotiating with the British. He was still unable to comprehend why the Colony should go to war over what even a white man must regard as but trifles. He bitterly reflected that there was no option other than war with faint hope of victory. Not so, however, the warriors of the Zulu army, who Sir Bartle Frere would describe as '… celibate man-slaying gladiators', whilst his spinster daughter, Mary, would nervously write '… the Zulus travel nearly as fast as men on horseback. They are reckless of death.'[13]

Chapter 6

'Deceit is your most valuable asset in war'

Xenophon, 360 BC

Having safely crossed the Buffalo and having won a skirmish with but few casualties, No 3 Column was full of confidence and Lord Chelmsford was eager to push on into Zululand. In the evening after the skirmish, Chelmsford had written to Sir Bartle Frere: ' I am in great hopes that the news of the storming of Sirayo's stronghold and the capture of so many of his cattle may have a salutary effect in Zululand and either bring down a large force to attack us or else produce a revolution in the country.'

A month earlier Chelmsford had written to Colonel Wood telling him that he had recently read Chase's *The History of Natal*, and had found; '… that in 1838 Andreas Pretorius, with a command of over four hundred men, took only six days to march from Rorke's Drift to the hill where Retief and his party were massacred [twelve miles from oNdini]. They entered Zululand on 13 December during the rainy season '… the road Pretorius took is the same as Glyn's Column will move along'. Chelmsford went on to say that he had spoken to an ancient Boer who had actually accompanied Pretorius' commando and confirmed the route was hard and open all the way to the White Mfolozi River, approximately twenty-eight miles from oNdini. However, Chelmsford was mistaken. Pretorius' commando had not crossed into Zululand via Rorke's Drift but forty miles upstream and closer to present-day Dundee.[1] In any event in 1838, there was no crossing known as 'Rorke's Drift' as Rorke only acquired, by Deed of Grant, Colony of Natal, number 2254, the land of which the Drift formed part, in 1860.

The route that No 3 Column was mistakenly about to take through the Batshe Valley, passing a huge isolated landmark turret of rock called Isandlwana, was anything but 'hard and open all the way'. Chelmsford justifiably complained of the lack of maps. (After the Coronation, Colonel Durnford had spent some time wandering around Zululand ostensibly, no doubt, as a tourist/hunter, but in reality he was compiling a map of the country he traversed which Chelmsford later regarded as 'not very helpful'. The same applied to this map drawn up by Captain James Alleyne RA, which Fannin, the Border Agent, considered '… more or less misleading'.[2])

Shortly Chelmsford would attempt to explain his difficulties to the Duke of Cambridge ' … I have already pointed out to your Royal Highness how impossible it has been to obtain really reliable information regarding the country even from those who ought to know it well. They have never been accustomed to look at any of the roads from any but a trading point of view, and are therefore unable to give the detailed information which is so important when movements of troops are concerned.'[3]

The 'roads' that he was referring to were little more than imprints in the soil left by the passing of occasional traders' wagons. The difficulty in getting his 220 laden wagons through would be immense and very time-consuming. But the 'roads' turned out to be far worse than the tracks he had mentioned to the Duke. Having reconnoitred the route for a short distance on 16 January, Chelmsford protested to Frere that a rapid advance into Zululand during the

The problem of non-existent roads was immense. Here Natal Mounted Police struggle their way into Zululand.

rainy season was '... absolutely impossible ... No 3 Column ... cannot possibly move forward even eight miles until two swamps into which our wagons sink up to the body have been made passable'. So while the infantry and the NNC either stood guard over the all but stationary convoy or, up to their knees in mud, digging, pushing or pulling, the Volunteers in small detachments rode ahead reconnoitring as far as the Ityotyosi River, twenty-eight miles to the north-east. They encountered no opposition but their vigilance gave the column confidence that it was immune to surprise attack.

Meanwhile, Chelmsford turned his attention to Colonel Durnford and his No 2 Column deployed at Middle Drift, hundreds of dizzy feet below the Greytown Helpmekaar road. No 2 Column had, on Chelmsford's orders, begun to move closer to Rorke's Drift, its destination Sandspruit, a few miles short of Msinga. By 13 January the column was spread out over several miles and was still on the move when Durnford received intelligence from Bishop Schreuder, the Norwegian Missionary, once a crony of old King Mpande and a long-term resident of Zululand. He was unkindly described by Sir Garnet Wolsley as being '... more or less half kaffir and very like a gorilla'. Despite such derogatory remarks the Bishop had a very efficient spy network and any information of his could not be ignored. Schreuder passed word that in retaliation for the destruction of Sihayo's homestead a large *impi* was about to cross at Middle Drift and cause havoc in Natal. Durnford, holding an independent command, felt compelled to take the initiative and about-turned for Middle Drift. He sent a galloper with a brief note to Chelmsford advising of his intent and prepared to counter-attack the anticipated enemy. Long before the column was half way back to Middle Drift, a courier on a sweat-drenched horse drew rein and handed Durnford what was a reprimand rather than an order:

Dear Durnford unless you carry out the instructions I give you, it will be my unpleasant duty to remove you from your command and to substitute another officer for the command of No 2 Column. When a column is acting separately in an enemy country I am quite right to give its commander every latitude, and would certainly expect him to disobey any orders he might receive from me if information which he obtained, showed that it would be injurious to the column under his command – your neglecting to obey my instructions in this present instance has no excuse, you have simply received information in a letter from Bishop Schreuder, which may or may not be true and which you have no way of verifying. If movements ordered are to be delayed because of reports that hint at an invasion of

Natal, it will be impossible for me to carry out my plan of campaign. I trust you will understand this plain speaking and not give me any further occasion to write in a style which is distasteful to me.[4]

Durnford's aide-de-camp, Captain Haye of the NNC, who was riding close to him at the time, remembered the look of disgust on Durnford's face as he read the order and, guessing at its content, went on to say that despite what appeared to be a reprimand, every man of the column was ready to follow Durnford and march straight on to Ulundi.

———————◦○◦———————

Four days after the skirmish at Sihayo's homestead and whilst the wagons still floundered, Chelmsford with his staff and an escort of fifty mounted infantry, left Rorke's Drift camp at daylight. Riding at a leisurely pace they shortly came upon the bogged down transport where relays of men were scouring the countryside for any sort of material that the marsh barring the way would gobble up and give purchase to bogged-down wheels. The wooden poles of nearby native dwellings offered a solution and soon all the huts within sight were systematically dismantled and pushed into the mire.

Campaigning in Zululand entailed rough living. This column was lucky enough to have a field kitchen and bakery.

A further three hours at walking pace brought Chelmsford's reconnaissance ten miles into Zululand as far as the rocky pinnacle of Isandlwana. A halt was called, everyone dismounted and tucked into a picnic breakfast. The rain had stopped and the day was clear, allowing the patrol a distant view of a whale-shaped eminence, Isipezi, twelve miles to the east. In between Isandlwana and Isipezi lay a rock-strewn plain dotted here and there with strange-shaped hills and outcrops. But strangest of all was Isandlwana itself, towering behind them. An interpreter mentioned that the Zulus compared its shape either to that of a small hut or a particular part of a cow's intestines. To those men of the 24th Regiment who partly formed the mounted escort, the likeness was more obvious: Isandlwana Hill clearly resembled a sphinx, their regimental crest, an honour awarded for gallantry in Egypt many years before and now the revered emblem of their regiment. A weird and oddly disturbing coincidence. Chelmsford decided that this spot, with Isandlwana at its back and with an open field of fire stretching away over five miles to the fore, would be No 3 Column's first base camp in Zululand.

At about this time, Chelmsford received two unexpected visitors, the first being Mr J.J. Uys who, forty years earlier, had fought the Zulus at the battle of Blood River. He gave Chelmsford some unsolicited advice, warning him to beware of Zulu spies and to laager his wagons, a wearisome task that in Chelmsford's opinion would be overcautious. More to Chelmsford's liking was the arrival of Sir Theophilus Shepstone who had, on his way with his entourage from Transvaal to Durban, made a detour of seventy miles to witness the near fulfilment of his long-planned strategy, the conquest of Zululand.

Soon all the wagons would be through the swamp unloading their conglomeration of kit and supplies, and with a camp laid out 'Aldershot fashion', the column would be poised for its advance on oNdini. Breakfast concluded, a large herd of cattle was seen heading in their direction. An enticement to an ambush? The IMI rode off to investigate. Chelmsford was pleased to learn it was a sub-chief, Makumdana, who wished to give up his weapons and surrender that portion of his herd belonging to the King, the King's cattle being of such immense number that they were farmed out to the care of various chiefs throughout the Kingdom. A large number of assegais and a few guns of assorted origin and in dubious working order were handed over but the scrawny cattle offered as those belonging to Cetshwayo were rejected. The IMI were not to be deceived and so rounded up another herd more worthy of royal ownership.[5]

The reconnaissance was about to return to Rorke's Drift when more cattle were seen approaching, herded it seemed by the whole local community, men, women and children. They were led by none other than Gamdana kaXonso, a younger brother of Sihayo, who appeared submissive and prepared to cooperate. Chelmsford was elated, until Gamdana ingratiatingly announced that he had already surrendered to Mr Fynn, the resident magistrate across the Buffalo River at Msinga. Gamdana's surrender had, in fact, been a fait accompli for several days. Chelmsford was astounded. Here was a civil servant, Fynn, finalizing peace terms with the enemy, an enemy that he, Chelmsford, might have attacked not knowing that the man enjoyed safe conduct. The political implications could have been considerable. It then occurred to Chelmsford he could use this incident to his advantage. He had known of Henry Francis Fynn for some time, the man's father of the same name being the first of the Port Natal traders to have made contact with King Shaka back in 1824. Furthermore, during Mpande's long reign, Fynn Snr. had become the Monarch's friend and confidant to the extent that Mpande gave Fynn's Zulu name, Mbuyazi, to his favourite son. Although Fynn had led a polygamous life, taking many Zulu girls to wife, he had also taken an English wife, Christianna Brown. Henry Junior was their first child. The boy grew up on the Cape frontier and in the outposts of Natal, his childhood friends being not only those of his own people but also Boers and Zulus. Consequently by his early teens he was fluent in three languages and was much in demand as an interpreter. In the capacity of both clerk and linguist, he secured employment with the colonial government and accompanied Shepstone's expedition to the coronation of King Cetshwayo. A year later he was appointed Resident Magistrate of the Msinga District, an area as remote as any and taking in much of the territory along the Buffalo border. A month before No 3 Column was due to cross into Zululand at Rorke's Drift, Lord Chelmsford had advised Colonel Glyn, the Column Commander: '… You should at once put yourself in communication with Mr. Fynn the magistrate of Msinga, and ask him to let it be known on the opposite side of the Buffalo River, what the orders are which you have received. He should also explain that you do not cross with any hostile intentions, but simply to show that the demands of the High Commissioner must be complied with.' Fynn was also employed as an interpreter in translating the ultimatum to the Zulu delegation.

There were few white men who could excel Fynn's knowledge of the Zulu people or surpass his expertise as a Zulu linguist. Moreover, he was known throughout the Kingdom by his Zulu sobriquet of *Gwalagwala*, a name derived from his habit of wearing the tail feather of the purple-crested turaco in his hat. That he could do this was a rare compliment to a white man since the feather had associations with Zulu nobility. Chelmsford concluded that if anyone had the ability to source the intentions of the Zulu army it was Fynn. In later life

A group of colonials. Henry Francis Fynn Jnr., second from the left, back row, Major Dartnell on Fynn's left.

a Zulu girl, Baleka kaMpitikazi, recalled her father visiting Fynn and greeting him with the salutation: 'You, son of Mbuyazi of the Bay [Port Natal]; you son of the finch that came from Pondoland; Chieftainship does not start with you, for we lived with your father, a chief.'[6]

Chelmsford's existing political staff included the Hon. William Drummond, second son of the Viscount Strathallan, aged 34, who had spent years knocking around Natal and Zululand shooting game. He was also a Zulu linguist. One of his exploits was to have shot twenty-three hippopotamus in one morning. The other officer, Henry Longcast, also a civilian, was, like Fynn, a product of the African frontier. Aged 29, he was the son of a Natal innkeeper but having been orphaned at an early age, had been adopted by the Rev. Robert Robertson and his wife and taken to live at kwaMagwaza, thirty miles south of oNdini. Longcast's playmates and friends had been predominantly Zulu and, like Fynn, he was fluent in *isiZulu*. Whilst still in his teens he had married a Zulu girl, one of Robertson's Christian converts. Longcast, a man of both worlds, was a valued member of Chelmsford's staff but both he and Drummond lacked the contacts and spy network that Fynn controlled on both sides of the Buffalo River.

Soon the idea of drafting Fynn into No 3 Column began to take root: 'Mr. Fynn would be most useful with Colonel Glyn and I hope the Lieutenant–Governor may be able to spare him', Chelmsford wrote.[7] Having crossed the

Buffalo River and successfully dealt with Sihayo's Stronghold, Chelmsford determined to have Fynn as a personal aide. But Bulwer's refusal to concur caused Chelmsford to write peevishly to Frere ' I wish Sir H. Bulwer would allow Mr. Fynn to be with me. I have no one to consult with as regards my duties as Resident in Zululand. [It would appear that Chelmsford had already been offered and had accepted – once Zululand had been conquered – the post of British Resident.] I am afraid unless I am allowed his services I shall not be able to deal satisfactorily with any chiefs who are anxious to tender their submission …'. Clearly Chelmsford had formed a high opinion of Fynn's unique association with Zululand and was not to be thwarted by Bulwer. With the excuse of reprimanding Fynn for authorizing Gamdana's surrender, Chelmsford summoned Fynn to report forthwith to Column HQ. Within a day or two Chelmsford looked to Frere to pacify the ruffled Governor. 'I hope you will be able to pacify Sir H. Bulwer with regard to my annexing Mr. Fynn. It was only after seeing how essential it was in the public interest that he should be with me, that I decided to summons him to headquarters.'[8]

Two days later, on 19 January, Fynn, who was about to unwittingly precipitate the impending British disaster, reported to No 3 Column bringing with him intelligence Chelmsford was eager to hear. Fynn later recorded:

> It was planned for this Column to proceed northwards, jacht pad [jag pad, hunting road], or nCome [Blood] River line of road for central Zululand [Chelmsford still mistakenly believed No 3 Column was on the same track as taken by Pretorius in 1838, hard and open all the way to the Mfolozi.] In such case I pointed out the Zulu plan [author's emphasis] to descend the Mange [*sic*] Valley of the Mhlazakazi mountain there to shelter in the Qhuedeni forests until the column had moved forward sufficiently to enable the Zulu army to creep round from the Mange Valley up the Buffalo River, and to cut off the column from the rear and close upon them.[9]

Fynn went on to inform Chelmsford that a certain Zulu *iziNduna*, Matshana kaMondisa, a man who with his clan had spent many years in Natal until, having had a confrontation with colonial officialdom, including John Shepstone, had fled into Zululand. Matshana had not only been welcomed by Cetshwayo but had been given the beautiful but almost inaccessible wilderness of the Mangeni Valley to occupy. Furthermore, Fynn continued, it had originally been the Zulu King's intention that Matshana, knowing the territory so well, was to command the attack on the British column but '… other great leaders mistrusted him'. Consequently Matshana was now merely tasked with guarding the area incorporating the Qhudeni Forest, Mangeni Falls and the Malakatha Hills. All in all it was a stunning example of Fynn's inside information. No doubt everyone, including Drummond, was convinced Fynn had revealed the whereabouts of the Zulu army. Drummond wrote '… of course, knowing as we did that this spot [looking down into the Mangeni Valley] contained the enemy it was searched carefully with jealous glasses [binoculars].'[10]

On riding back to Isandlwana Chelmsford and his weary reconnaissance were gratified to see the column base camp had been laid out in the most orderly fashion. The white bell tents of both battalions and those of the white officers and NCO' of the NNC straddled the entire eastern base of Isandlwana pinnacle. The horse lines and tents of the artillery and mounted troops were situated in between. The natives of the NNC, with no tents provided, had been left to make do with whatever protection they could scrounge from either the camp or the countryside.

On the 20th, Fynn led Chelmsford, Colonel Glyn, Major Dartnell and members of both staffs on a reconnaissance to show them where the Zulus were concealed in the Mangeni Valley: '… an immense valley of precipitous depth, the cattle on the broad circular plain below looked like ants. Glasses were put to use but only a few cattle were discernable. That the Zulus were there there were no doubts expressed however.'[11]

The following day, the 21st, Fynn again led the General and his staff in search of Gamdana, finding him '… hiding on the Buffalo River in fear of Zulus as well as European forces'. Fynn gives no reason why Chelmsford found it necessary to see Gamdana again at such a critical time, Chelmsford having, as a result of Fynn's intelligence already initiated the first move in what would be known to history as the Battle of Isandlwana. Fynn, in a matter of hours of arriving at headquarters on the evening of the 19th, had convinced Chelmsford that his, Fynn's, intelligence, was of so compelling a nature that Chelmsford changed the strategy that he had planned over the previous weeks. There is no question that Fynn himself was not utterly convinced of his facts and the part he was playing. Fynn never mentioned the source of his information or the name of his informant but there can be no doubt that it was none other than Gamdana, the brother of Sihayo, the friend and confidant of the King.

Although Fynn was the resident magistrate of Msinga, twenty miles from the Buffalo River, he was remarkably familiar with the terrain on the Zulu bank: '… I proceeded with Lord Chelmsford to show him where the Zulus were concealed … I guided Lord Chelmsford, Colonel Glyn, and the two staffs to the kraal of the Zulu chief Gamdana.' It would seem, then, that the association between Fynn, the Natal magistrate and Gamdana the Zulu chief was more involved than that of being mere acquaintances. The document containing Fynn's above revelations is a transcript (lodged with the Campbell Collections, University of Natal, Durban) of an article written by Fynn and published in the *Natal Witness* not, however, until 22 January 1913, exactly thirty-four years to the day after the Battle of Isandlwana. Meanwhile, there is yet another mystery surrounding Fynn and Gamdana to consider. Fynn's article contains the following extract: '… before dawn next morning down the valley southwards of Sanhlwana [*sic*], past the kraal of chief Gamdana (Fynn's Ally) …'. What does 'Fynn's Ally' mean? Just what did Fynn believe Gamdana to be? His ally and his spy? It would seem so. But could it be that Gamdana was more than that? A double spy? A double agent and a loyal subject of the Zulu King working in collaboration with his neighbour, Matshana? In view of what was about to happen there is little doubt that Gamdana was both. As with the Boers during their punitive expedition against Dingane in 1838, the British had a phobia – and not without reason – regarding Zulu spies, the native population of Natal, mostly ex-Zulu nationals, being over 300,000',[12] to say nothing of the 2,370 NNC in the British camp. Since the days of King Shaka it had been the strategy of the Zulu Army to infiltrate its enemy with spies. One renowned Zulu agent, Nongila, over a period of forty years spied for no less than four Zulu kings.[13] He went as far as the Cape on Shaka's behalf and later, after being away for many months, reported on the activities of the white people. 'He used to precede [the army] by going to see what the country to be attacked was like. He spied out the country's forces. He was as a rule accompanied by others, that is, when the *impi* was actually campaigning. He used to go out alone when on a tour of preliminary inspection.' A Mabaso by birth, Nongila was made a hereditary Zulu by Shaka in acknowledgement of his espionage services and was created '*iziNduna* of all Spies'.[14] The Zulu Army appreciated the value of spies to the extent that each regiment had its own espionage unit: Mpatshana kaSodondo of the iNgobamakhosi regiment recalled '… spies were selected for common sense and ability to describe carefully what they had observed. I myself was a spy at Isandlwana.[15] Selected spies would also be chosen to go ahead and live with the people to be attacked. Such were our guides, men who knew well the enemy to be attacked.'[16]

Chelmsford, now aroused by Fynn's confidence that a Zulu army was concealed nearby, was determined to locate it, ordering for the morrow a reconnaissance in force to be led by Major Dartnell. The composition of this force, with the exception of several officers of Chelmsford's staff, was in all respects colonial: cavalry drawn from the NMP and Volunteers and 1,600 men of the 3rd NNC, commanded by Commandant Rupert La Tour Lonsdale, who had only been discharged from hospital the previous day, having suffered concussion following a fall from his horse eleven days earlier. Lonsdale, 30 years old and an ex-Imperial officer of the 74th Regiment of Foot, had left the army five years previously to settle in the Eastern Cape where he later became involved in the 9th Frontier War, leading with considerable ability and courage a locally-raised unit of native troops. He now held command of the 3rd NNC. The reconnaissance was about to scour some of the roughest terrain in Zululand: the horsemen to climb and sweep the precipitous jumble of the Malakatha and Hlazakazi Hills while the NNC were to head south, skirt the turret-shaped shoulder of the Malakatha and then push their way through a thorn-covered ravine leading into the Mangeni Valley where, two days earlier, Fynn had observed '… that the Zulus were there there were no doubts expressed'.

Where possible the horsemen and the infantry were to collaborate and eventually rendezvous in the vicinity of Chief Matshana's stronghold where a waterfall of the Mangeni stream tumbled to the valley below. The reconnaissance had made no attempt to depart stealthily or to take the enemy by surprise; the correspondent of the *Natal Witness* reported '… the morning of the twenty-first gave every promise of the great heat we afterwards experienced when after a considerable amount of noise, in the way of bugles, the NNC started, followed by an ambulance wagon which, however, did not get far.'

It was a six-mile hike across a scrub- and rock-strewn plain to the base of the Malakatha, a 3,000-foot climb to the top for the horsemen, and a 1,500-foot descent to the Mangeni River for the NNC, before the actual search commenced. Then, all being well, the whole force would proceed east for eight miles, combing the terrain, until it reached Matshana's stronghold. There, on Chelmsford's orders it was to about-turn and march ten miles back to camp, a minimum round trip of twenty-six miles plus the ascents and descents already mentioned. It was a tough assignment at the best of times but at the height of summer, and with the conditions underfoot, an ordeal to say the least. It is not surprising then that the NNC, with its white NCOs marching with the rank and file, expecting to be back in camp for supper, wished to carry as little as possible. Therefore they had left their rations behind. Strangely enough, the horsemen, with little excuse for doing so, had followed suit. Thus the whole force, apart from a few who had squirreled a pocketful of biscuits, was not only without food but also blankets.

Reaching the base of the Malakatha, the Carbineers and the Newcastle Mounted Rifles under Captain 'Offi' Shepstone dismounted and leading their horses started to climb, while the NMP followed the base of the mountain east towards Matshana's stronghold and the Mangeni waterfall. Eventually, after an arduous climb, the Carbineers were the first to sight Matshana's homestead nestled far below between perpendicular krantzes, '... overgrown with thorn trees under cover of which thousands of men might lay unsuspected ...'.[17] Here they numbered off, even numbers off-saddled and took a rest while the remainder stood to their horses or formed vedettes. Of the NNC there was no sign. The lucky ones spread out under whatever shade could be found. Apart from the chink of curb chains, and the champing of bits, the silence was utter until all were startled by the sound of a distant shot coming from the direction taken by Dartnell and his men. One shot and nothing more. Silence again. Those stretched out in the shade were finding the urge to doze hard to resist when, close at hand, came a clatter of hooves and more pistol shots. All at once they were on their feet, scrambling to mount, but, as Trooper Symons recorded, '... it was only Drummond, galloping after a steinbok and shooting at it with his revolver'. The leading scouts of the NNC, led by Commandant Lonsdale, appeared shortly after.

The ascent from the valley had been rocky, steep and tiring but the men had worked cheerfully and well. It was 2 pm. A junction between the units had been made as planned. There was little to report except that 'Maori' Browne, on questioning two youths under duress, believed them to be temporary absentees from a nearby Zulu army. Other than that, it was time to go if they were to be back in camp by suppertime as ordered. Thus, in a cheery mood the men fell in and prepared for the rough descent when Inspector George Mansel, now nominally in command of the NMP since Dartnell's elevation to the staff, arrived with startling news. The enemy were in sight: '... a body of Zulus on a hill to the left of the road to the number of seven to eight hundred; one of the scouts told us that upon another hill he had seen several thousands of them'.[18] It coincided well with 'Maori' Browne's interrogation. Excited, yet disappointed at turning their backs on rest and supper, the horsemen briskly made their way to the Mangeni track leaving the NNC to follow.

It transpired the first contact with the Zulus had been made earlier in the day, just as Dartnell and his troop reached the vicinity of the Mangeni falls. They found the enemy in strength and '... very anxious to fight'.[19] However, it was difficult to make out their number with any certainty as they occupied a large kloof (ravine) from which any aggressive move by the NMP brought forth, '... with the greatest readiness ...', more warriors. As the NMP were at the time well in advance of the Carbineers, Dartnell prudently awaited reinforcements. So the stand-off between the adversaries continued until the Carbineers eventually arrived. Dartnell, uncertain as to whether or not the enemy were merely Matshana's clansmen or were the vanguard of the King's army or both, was determined to find out. He ordered Mansel to take four NMP troopers, and endeavour '… to make them really show their force'. It was near sundown and the Zulus for the moment had retired into their kloof. Mansel related '… immediately they saw us come up they came out again and throwing out their flanks they made to surround us. In my anxiety to see their numbers I stayed almost too long and very nearly got caught. The Zulus must have received orders not to fire as they never fired a shot but they tried to catch us. If they had fired I think they must have shot us.'[20] Mansel later told Milne of this encounter, how he and his men found themselves right in amongst the *impi*, describing it as a wonderful sight, the way in which the warriors immediately spread out like a fan trying to surround them. Trooper Symons, had a more vivid description of Mansel's encounter:

We watched anxiously as the small party [Mansel's NMP] disappeared over the brow of the hill and when we saw them [coming back] at a much more rapid pace than when they went up, we knew something was after them … from one end of the ridge to the other, as if by magic, rose a long line of black warriors advancing at the double at short intervals of skirmishing order. It

Officers of the Natal Mounted Police. Major Dartnell centre front row, Inspector Mansel on Dartnell's left.

was a magnificent spectacle that no British regiments could excel in keeping their distances in skirmishing at the double. They uttered no sound and on reaching the brow of the hill their entire centre halted while the flanks came on forming the noted 'horns' of the Zulu *impi*. We all thought we were to be attacked but a shout came from the hilltop answered by one from the right horn. The *impi* then halted, another shout and the Zulus slowly retired till only three or four were visible on the ridge.[21]

This was no performance by Matshana's clan; these were warriors of a disciplined regiment. A Zulu army had been encountered just where Fynn had said it would be found. Dartnell took the decision, no doubt after discussion with Chelmsford's staff officers, Major Gossett and Captain Buller, to disregard his orders to return to camp before dark and instead to bivouac with his command on Maphungu, a flat-topped ridge overlooking the Zulu position. Gossett and Buller were ordered to hasten back to the camp and report to Chelmsford. The behaviour of the Zulus was baffling to say the least. It was nevertheless clear that they were under orders to both stop Dartnell's advance and at the same time to avoid provoking an attack that could possibly reveal whatever secret they were there to guard.

Dartnell's reconnaissance was not the only encounter with the Zulu army that day. At first light, Lieutenant Browne, with four men of the IMI, had set out east across the Isandlwana plain heading towards the massive Isipezi that, rising to 5,000 feet, obscured all sight of Zululand that lay beyond, territory as yet to be scanned by the British. During the course of the morning Browne and his men had seen several groups of the enemy moving away from them towards Isipezi. Clearly there was an enemy presence not far away but in which direction and in what number was yet to be revealed. More alarming for Browne, on making his return to camp he and his men were almost cut off by a Zulu detachment of eight mounted warriors and thirty on foot. There was a brief firefight in which two Zulus were killed, together with two of their horses, while the IMI managed to gallop away without incurring a casualty. Closer to the camp and the Nquthu plateau, which formed the left flank of the British camp, for ten miles or so, '… one or two mounted bodies of Zulus were seen hovering … and such as thought at all on the subject, anticipated fighting on the morrow.'[22]

Lord Chelmsford himself was also about to have a Zulu sighting. After breakfast, as we have read earlier, he with Fynn, Colonel Glyn and other officers, despite the rumour of Zulu activity, had ridden again to visit Gamdana and found '… he was in hiding on the Buffalo River'.[23] Whatever their business may have been with Gamdana is not recorded but, it would seem, it was inconclusive, for later in the day Gamdana reported to the camp where, as Crealock put it, '… he could therefore see whether it was defended or not by earthworks or wagons'.[24]

Gamdana said that he had heard Zulus were present in force to the right of Isipezi Hill (the location of Dartnell's bivouac), as indeed they were, but he made no mention of the Zulu activity as witnessed by Browne. Lord Chelmsford himself later wrote to Frederick Stanley, the Secretary of State for War, stating that the only native report of enemy activity he had received was that of Gamdana's at 4:30 pm on the 21st, advising '… that the umCijo Regiment was assembled not far from Isipezi Hill'. This confirmed the report which had just come in from Major Dartnell that a large force was in front of him.[25]

In riding back to camp from their abortive visit to Gamdana, Chelmsford and his officers encountered Captain George Shepstone (another of Sir Theophilus's sons), of the NNH, Colonel Durnford's staff officer, who had ridden over from Sandspruit requesting further orders. Chelmsford had no hesitation in instructing him to return with all haste. No 2 Column, having climbed the dizzy heights from Middle Drift was now to descend from Msinga down to Rorke's Drift. Nevertheless, No 2 Column was about to take an aggressive, rather than a defensive, role. Durnford would be delighted.

Having sent Shepstone on his way, later in the afternoon Chelmsford and his staff set out to inspect a road working party.[26] Satisfied with progress they rode on to be shortly overtaken by Gossett and Buller who, having ridden hard, brought news of Dartnell's encounter. Major Clery recorded '… they informed the General that Major Dartnell had come up with the enemy in considerable force …', furthermore, that it was Dartnell's intention to '… attack the following morning'.[27] Lieutenant Milne, Chelmsford's Naval ADC remembered '… Major Dartnell sent in for instructions as to what he should do. In the meantime, if no order were sent, he intended to bivouac on the ground he had taken up and watch the enemy. Orders were immediately sent to Major Dartnell to attack as and when he thought fit. Food was also sent for his force.'[28]

However, more than two months later, when a culprit was being sought to blame for the disaster of Isandlwana, that at the time was less than twenty hours away, Chelmsford's recollection of what he had said was entirely different, writing that his orders to Dartnell were '… that he [Dartnell] was to return to the camp after completing his reconnaissance …' and that he, Chelmsford, was much vexed that his orders had not been 'attended to'.[29]

Riding on, Milne remembered they got

> … up to the high land' [the Nquthu Plateau] ' on the left of the camp, the
> ascent was steep, but possible for horses. On reaching the summit of the

picquet hill [iThusi], I counted fourteen Zulu horsemen watching us at a distance of about four miles. They ultimately disappeared over a slight rise. Two vedettes were stationed at the spot from where I saw the horsemen: they said they had seen these men several times during the day and had reported the fact. From this point the ground was very nearly level; there were slight rises, however, every now and again, which would prevent our seeing any men who did not wish it.[30]

This assemblage of incidents – Browne's encounters, groups of enemy horsemen having been seen several times, slight rises in the ground that could conceal an enemy, groups of Zulus hovering around and the immediate sighting of fourteen enemy scouts, all relatively close to the camp (yet so far from where it was believed Dartnell held an *impi* at bay) – seemed to have aroused little concern in Chelmsford other than his determination to reconnoitre the Nquthu Plateau the following day. In fact, he did not deem one incident worthy of mention in the long report he wrote to Frere that evening.[31] Nor is there any record of Chelmsford's proposed Nquthu reconnaissance having been implemented. Did he, after all, decide it would be superfluous? Dartnell had found the Zulu army just where Fynn had said it would be found. Rather than listening to Fynn, Chelmsford should have taken heed of the journal of Nathaniel Isaacs, an early Port Natal trader, who forty years earlier had written of King Shaka's spies and scouts, '… these persons were always directed to make such observation … as might be useful in leading the troops to the scene of action with the surest chance of arriving at their position without being discovered on the one hand, or surprised on the other'.[32] Even more imprudent was Chelmsford's tacit order to Dartnell '… to attack as and when he thought fit'. Had Chelmsford both overrated Lonsdale's NNC and underrated the enemy, causing him to send Dartnell's poorly-armed and unsupported command against a Zulu army?

As the light began to fade, Chelmsford and his staff lost sight of the fourteen Zulu horsemen but had conditions been more favourable, and had they ridden on to Mabaso Hill where the enemy scouts had lingered, and had they glanced into the valley below, they would have seen, not seven miles from the camp, hundreds of warriors about to bivouac for the night. Thus it is reasonable to conclude that the intelligence fed by Gamdana to Fynn was entirely false and that the Zulu high command had never intended, or had long since changed its plans, to advance up the Mangeni Valley. Yet it had been a ploy of such conviction that it would lure Chelmsford into taking almost 70 per cent of the column's strength out on a wild goose chase.

Chapter 7

'... The Zulus are a match for us in generalship, and more than a match for us in cunning'

East London and Eastern Province Standard, 14 February 1879

T he Zulu army, after the war doctors had completed their mystic tasks and after many of the King's 50,000 warriors had slept for weeks in the valleys around oNdini, split into three divisions.[1] Despite Cetshwayo's deadly weeding out of reluctant warriors, such as his earlier dealing with the *iziNyanga*, as rumours of war with the Colony grew daily, so did sickness in many forms prevent more and more of the warrior class from reporting for duty. In Zulu husbandry a sick beast is done away with lest it infect the rest of the herd. In the same manner Cetshwayo dealt with his ailing warriors. They were '*goquoza*'d', put down.[2] *Impis* of trusted soldiery were dispatched to villages throughout the kingdom and the infection was swiftly eradicated. The first division of a now fit, eager and able army was dispersed to strategic locations, its first priority to guard the approaches to the inner kingdom. The second division, approximately 5,000 strong, under its commander Godide, moved south towards the coast, past the Rev. Ommund Oftebro's now-deserted mission station at kwaMondi, there to linger in ambush for the British. The third and largest division of 20,000, commanded by Ntshingwayo kaMahole, an elderly warrior in his sixties, having been received by the King and his prime minister, Mnyamana kaNgqengelele Buthelezi (who '... stirred up the *impi* to make it burn like a fire'),[3] had left the great military kraal at Nodwengu on the afternoon of 17 January. Once Ntshingwayo's *impi*, accompanied by a mini-army of sons and brothers, some as young as eleven years, known as *uDibi*, the carriers of their senior's shield, mat and cooking pots, had crossed the Mfolozi River, it marched as a single column. But on the fourth day it split into two, three miles apart, with mounted scouts, all men of Sihayo's clan, riding ahead while detachments of warriors, fully armed but otherwise unencumbered, scouted the flanks ready to decoy and lure away any enemy from sighting the advancing regiments.

By the 20th, the day Fynn had led Chelmsford and his staff to the Mangeni Valley to show them where he believed the Zulu army was concealed, Ntsingwayo's *impi* was actually approaching Isipezi Hill, ten miles north-east of the Mangeni Valley.[4] Here it bivouacked, except for a detachment of the uMcijo Regiment which, in collaboration with Matshana's warriors, now confronted Dartnell's apprehensive column.

The NMP and Carbineers, having skirmished with the uMcijo, had together with the NNC, retired to high ground overlooking the enemy position some three miles away. As darkness fell the enemy location was defined by sparkling campfires while Zulu scouts, much closer, harangued the colonial camp with a barrage of graphic taunts describing what the warriors intended to inflict on the sisters and mothers of their jittery foe. The prospects for Dartnell's troops, weary, famished, without blankets or food, was bleak. Furthermore, before daylight had completely faded, the number of warriors had been seen to increase alarmingly, causing Dartnell to reconsider attacking without Chelmsford's permission. Milne subsequently stated 'The force which was in front of Major Dartnell on the night of the 21st January, was the advance guard of the large '*impi*' which was halted close to Isepezi [*sic*] Hill'.[5] Consequently Dartnell conscripted Lieutenant Davey of the NNC to ride back to Isandlwana camp with a note requesting orders. With nothing but the stars, when they appeared, to light the way, and with the enemy close at hand, it was a dangerous undertaking; and most alarming for both parties when Davey bumped into a group of horsemen coming from the opposite direction. Great must have been the relief when Davey discovered they were IMI, led by Lieutenant Walsh of the 13th Light Infantry, on their way to Mangeni with rations and blankets. Walsh also carried Chelmsford's blessing for Dartnell's proposed dawn attack; Davey's journey had not been necessary but he nevertheless rode on to Isandlwana.

On arrival at Mangeni, Walsh immediately informed Dartnell that he had Chelmsford's full support for his proposed attack. Dartnell, however, had second thoughts. On top of the growing number of warriors as witnessed earlier, the rash of campfires was equally perturbing.[6] He had good reason to believe he was facing both a disciplined and numerically-superior enemy while he had only, more or less, only 160 colonial horsemen who, after all, except for the NMP, were but weekend soldiers, supported by 1,600 poorly-trained (as the night would prove) and badly-disciplined NNC who had never been expected to play the role of assault troops. Without support Dartnell decided an attack would be a reckless undertaking. He scribbled a note requesting the support of two or three companies of Imperial infantry and instructed Walsh to hasten back to Isandlwana.

In the meantime Davey had delivered Dartnell's original note, not to the headquarters tent of Colonel Glyn, the column commander, but to that of Lord Chelmsford's staff officer, thus giving a clear indication that even junior NNC officers assumed Chelmsford was in command of the operation. However, Major Gossett, who took the note, followed correct protocol and at about 9 pm sought out Colonel Glyn and informed him of Davey's message, Glyn promptly instructed that Davey, who had gone off to bed, should be found at once, ordered to return to Dartnell and inform him that the General had directed that '... he was at complete liberty to act on his own judgement as to whether he should attack or not'.[7]

It took Major Clery, Glyn's chief of staff, searching in the darkness of the tent town, some time to locate Davey who, after an exhausting eighteen hours, was rudely awakened. Having given Davey Chelmsford's instructions, Clery ordered him to repeat them until he was satisfied. Davey was then given a horse and sent, no doubt cursing his luck, post-haste back to Dartnell. There is no record of his return ride but, more than likely, he again encountered Walsh and his escort hurrying in the opposite direction. The fact that Davey survived the coming day confirms he reached Mangeni safely.

On arriving at Isandlwana it was now Walsh's turn to seek the general but being an Imperial officer he was well aware of protocol. At about 2 am he woke Clery who, after dealing with Davey, had been fast asleep, and gave him Dartnell's message. Having read it and perceiving that a Zulu army might well be at bay, Clery nevertheless correctly woke Glyn. Having scanned the note, Glyn resignedly passed it back, knowing full well that Chelmsford would take command. He urgently directed Clery to '... take the note to the General'.[8] Now it was Clery's turn to ignore protocol. Bypassing Staff Officer Crealock and shielding a lighted candle with a cupped hand, Clery passed the sentry guarding the entrance to Chelmsford's tent and shook the General awake. Kneeling beside Chelmsford's camp bed, Clery '... read out from the crumpled piece of paper written across in pencil word after word'.[9] Chelmsford was awake at once. The Zulu army had shown just as Fynn said it would. Chelmsford would often be accused of vacillation but on this occasion he did not hesitate. He immediately gave orders for six companies of the 2/24th, four of the RA's six guns, a company of engineers and the IMI to be ready to march at daybreak. An explosion of activity followed. The sleepy troops, raised by shouts and curses, stumbled grumbling into the pre-dawn chill, guns were limbered, horses saddled and the men fell-in ready to march. Durnford and No 2 Column, ten miles away at Rorke's Drift, was sent an order by Clery to move and 'take command' of the Isandlwana camp.[10] However, in the blizzard of blame for the disaster that would shortly befall the camp, the veracity of Clery's contention that he had ordered Durnford to take command, like other factors, would be held to question.

Lieutenant Horace Smith-Dorrien, a 20-year-old Special Service Officer of the 95th Regiment, was selected to ride with Clery's hastily-scribbled order. As Smith-Dorrien set out alone, Colonel Glyn, who as column commander had no intention of being sidelined, demanded of Chelmsford whether, as stipulated in *Field Force Regulations*, reserve ammunition was to accompany the column? It was a pertinent question for it would be required to be carried by ox wagon reducing the column's speed to a crawl. Chelmsford attempted to compromise. Ox wagons were out of the question; reserve ammunition would remain in camp but loaded aboard his own mule-drawn cart and ready to leave at a moment's notice. It was no more than a gesture. The reality was the column would have no reserve ammunition and if, as anticipated, it came to grips with the Zulu army twelve miles away, the mule-drawn cart would either never arrive in time or flounder amongst the dongas on the way. The column would have to manage with the seventy rounds that each man carried. Greatcoats and blankets were also to be left behind. Glyn, however, ordered an ox wagon to be loaded with rations, tinned meat and biscuits, which with a small escort could slowly follow on behind the column.[11] As for the reconnaissance of the Nquthu plateau, it was casually forgotten. For the moment there was no time to lose in confronting the enemy and having given them a taste of the Martini-Henry, '… crush them … to make them believe in our superiority'.

Meanwhile at Mangeni, after Davey and his escort had come and gone, the weary and apprehensive troops had settled down in hollow square formation atop the ridge, the NMP and Volunteers on one side, the NNC on the remaining sides with the Volunteers' horses ring-tied in the centre. A further 200 men of the NNC formed outlying picquets. The ground underfoot was rough and stony, the night was cold and sleep difficult. Nevertheless, in the flickering light of the scattered fires the NNC had somehow coaxed into life, the men fitfully dosed and slept until, as if to justify Dartnell's worst fears that the NNC lacked discipline and staunchness, there was a sudden uproar. Shots were fired, shouts were heard followed by a stampede as '… the NNC sprang to their feet with a roar like the Howick Falls in flood, striking their shields with their sticks and firing their guns; then losing all self-control they broke ranks and rushed about like so many demons'.[12] Some got in amongst the horses and had to be driven back with the butt end of a rifle. A number of the NNC officers' horses, not ring-tied like those of the Volunteers, broke loose and, terrified, galloped in and out amongst the equally terrorised NNC while the NNC picquets, as they fled in panic from the outposts back into the square, were mistaken for the enemy and were wounded or worse by their comrades '... who freely used their assegais'. It is probable at this time that two NNC officers, Lieutenants Holcroft and Avery, deserted and rode back to Isandlwana camp, there within hours to die. Another NNC officer, Captain John Maxwell, slept through most of the uproar to be suddenly awakened and to find himself alone. He had been so exhausted that the NNC had charged right over him. Finally, discipline was restored and by dawn every man was in his place again with the square reformed. Nevertheless, Maxwell contemplated '... had the Zulus attacked we must have been cut to pieces'.[13]

Chelmsford's column marched out of Isandlwana camp at dawn, heading east into the rising sun and on towards Mangeni, two and a half hours slog away. Lieutenant Charles Pope and his G Company were the only men of the 2/24th, due to their being on picquet duty that night, to remain in camp. They were still in position as the column came past causing much banter and evoking considerable envy in those left behind at the sight of their comrades marching away at a swinging pace, rifles at 'the trail', to do some 'real fighting'.

As the column disappeared into the mist which had descended as the sun rose, so did a sense of decorum prevail in the camp. For those left behind, well, they might miss a bit of fighting but in the meantime, apart from sentry-go, it could add up to a day off. There was no sense of impending danger except, perhaps, for Captain Barry's picquet of No 6 Company 3rd Regt. NNC, which had been on duty for thirty-six hours at Magaga Knoll (Makweni Hill), a lonely spot, out of sight of the camp, on top of the Nquthu plateau. In the growing light Barry's picquet had seen Zulus close enough to speak to.[14]

Lord Chelmsford and his staff, with an incautiously small escort of only twelve IMI, '... rode on quickly',[15] and had soon outdistanced the rest of the column. The Isandlwana plain, that from a distance had appeared level and without obstruction, was found to be crossed with dongas of staggering proportions into which the four guns, under the command of Lieutenant Colonel Arthur Harness RA, had to be lowered and then pulled out by drag ropes. It was not long before Captain Henry Mainwaring of the 2/24th, marching with his men, observed two horsemen watching the column's progress. Taking them to be vedettes he was surprised when, on close inspection, they proved to be Zulu scouts. Writing later in his journal Mainwaring reflected '… they were placed there to watch our force depart preparatory to the attack on the camp by the Zulu *impi*.'

Dartnell's beleaguered command were, no doubt, hoping to see 600 red coats striding down the track but Lord Chelmsford's arrival, with a handful of officers and a dozen IMI, could hardly have inspired a cheer. Chelmsford was also disappointed. Expecting to find a Zulu army he only saw '… their scouts were here and there visible'.[16] How strange. Dartnell was not a man whom one would dare to call an alarmist. The Zulu army had been here, now it had gone. Chelmsford determined to find it. Without waiting for the column to arrive he immediately ordered the weary Volunteers to saddle up and scout the broken country that the Zulus had occupied the night before and in which their camp fires had burned only hours earlier. (It is well to pause for a moment and mention that there are so many primary-source accounts that differ one from the other, in respect of time and distance, that it is not possible to vouch for the accuracy of either in the conflict of the next two days. There was no town hall clock by which to set one's watch; there were no accurate maps so distances were also guessed at. For instance the time of arrival of Chelmsford's column at Mangeni varies in different accounts by as much as two hours while the distance from Isandlwana to Mangeni, from between ten to twelve miles or more.)

Yet the Zulus were still around. But for the moment, not in substantial numbers, or so it seemed, but scattered provocatively on hilltops, mostly out of rifle range and moving slowly to the north. When the column finally arrived, after a stiff march and an hour or more after Chelmsford had cantered in, the pursuit of the elusive enemy commenced. A long line of skirmishers was thrown out; the six companies of the 2/24th in the centre, supported by the artillery, with the NNC, having recovered from the terrors of the night, on either side. The Volunteers, under Dartnell, were sent at a brisk trot away to the right in the hope of outflanking the enemy. The NMP rode straight for the ravine, where Mansel and his troopers had nearly been caught the previous afternoon, but they found it empty. The Carbineers, on the extreme right, moving at a trot towards Nkabane Hill, a known habitat of Chief Matshana, suddenly came upon a body of Zulus, about eighty in number, who took up an aggressive stance, shields to the fore with assegais at the ready. However, they quickly had a change of mind, disengaged, split up and raced towards Nkabane where its northern face would not only prove too steep for horses but also provide caves for refuge. The Carbineers also split up, groups of twos and threes pursuing individual quarry but over rough ground gained little distance on the fleeing enemy. Not to be outdone, everal troopers reined in, dismounted and opened fire. Two or three near-misses gave them the range and a following shot sent a victim tumbling over.[17] The next moment Captain 'Offi' Shepstone arrived. Although he complimented his men on their marksmanship it was followed by a severe dressing-down for having dismounted. Joining their captain, the troopers galloped off towards the sound of more firing to find some of their comrades shooting at a single warrior, a casual fellow who seemed indifferent to being shot at. He strolled nonchalantly across the line of fire to a lone boulder and prepared to shoot back but his musket, by misfiring, let him down. Unperturbed and amidst a volley of shots he '… stood up and walked quietly over the brow of the hill'.[18]

Lord Chelmsford, his staff including Fynn, the artillery and the IMI had moved far to the left with the infantry and NNC in between. The early impression that the enemy had gone with the dawn was soon dispelled. The Magogo Hills, rising a thousand feet from the valley below, were suddenly alive with warriors gesticulating and shouting insults yet moving almost

Captain 'Offi' Shepstone, inspecting men of the Natal Native Horse, most likely at Pietermaritzburg during the build-up to hostilities. Most appear to be armed with both the Martini-Henry carbine and a spear.

inperceptibly north. Crealock was later to write '… we had been advancing with Colonel Glyn's column against a Zulu force that fell back from hill to hill as we advanced, giving up without a shot the most commanding positions'.[19] They did indeed, gradually drawing the column further and further away from Mangeni and the track that led back to Isandlwana camp.

Chelmsford decided on a frontal assault. To the far right of the line the Volunteers were still in contact with the enemy. In an effort to encircle them, the IMI were to be sent to the left, up the Magogo Valley and out onto the eastern end of the Isandlwana plain shortly before it merged into the slopes of Isipezi. The infantry and NNC, supported at a distance by the artillery, were to traverse and attack the Magogo Hills. Chelmsford led off at a brisk trot accompanied by his staff and the IMI. Captain Penn Symons of the 2/24 later wrote '… we saw the enemy in scattered bodies of ten to five hundred disappearing and retreating in front of us in all directions. It was hunting a shadow, as men who well knew the Zulus and their tactics declared at the time, that the cattle that had been seen and retreating bodies of men were simply decoys to entice us away from the camp …'.[20] Drummond was to write '… although they showed themselves in very considerable form all along the hilltops, they kept retiring, according to what, as after events taught us, must have been their preconceived plan. The General, however, did not, of course, at this time, imagine that the Zulus were carrying out a concerted scheme but thought they were probably falling back on their supports.'[21] It had not occurred to Chelmsford, or his staff, that they were the victims of a Zulu ruse. However, a message from Lieutenant Colonel Harness, struggling over a nightmare terrain of rocks, gullies and boulders with his four guns, ammunition carriages and mule carts, reporting that it was impossible to keep up, caused Chelmsford to abandon whatever plan of pursuit he had in mind. At that moment he must have realized the futility of his infantry, at the height of summer, clad in thick uniforms and heavy boots, attempting to catch and engage an army of athletes clad in little more than nothing and wearing sandals. The minor success that the Volunteers were currently achieving by inflicting sixty casualties, the only dead and wounded of the whole operation, would emphasize the necessity of cavalry against a foe, '… who are as fast as men on horseback and reckless of death'.[22]

Chelmsford, now having abandoned the pursuit, decided to have breakfast and then set about establishing a new base camp at Mangeni. Under the circumstances, the spot chosen for breakfast could not have been more pleasant. Commandant 'Maori' Browne who had been summoned to report direct to Chelmsford remembered '… never shall I forget the sight of that peaceful picnic. Here were the staff quietly breakfasting and the whole column scattered over the country'.[23] Browne could not help but wonder what would happen if the Zulu army they were seeking should at that moment descend upon them. He had even more cause for concern when he was ordered to return to Isandlwana '… to assist Colonel Pulleine to strike camp and come on here'.[24] However, Browne decided his was not to reason why and with his 1/3rd NNC pushed on round the southern shoulder of Silutshana and onto the Isandlwana plain and so back to the camp twelve miles distant.

The column was, indeed, scattered; scattered over a seven-mile line, the Volunteers to the right, the IMI to the left with the rest of the column spread out in between causing Captain Henry Hallam Parr of the 13th Light Infantry, formerly Sir Bartle Frere's Military Secretary but now a member of Chelmsford's staff, to write '… the morning was spent in endeavouring to get to close quarters with an enemy who could, and did, avoid us at [his] ease'.[25]

What was particularly memorable of this moment was the arrival of an NMP trooper on a sweat-soaked horse. He had galloped from Isandlwana camp with a half-sheet of blue foolscap paper bearing a pencilled message: 'Staff Officer – Report just come in that the Zulus are advancing in force from the front of the camp (8.5am). HB Pulleine, Lt.Col.'[26] Hallam Parr took the message, noting the time as 9:30 am. It had taken the trooper an hour and twenty-five minutes to gallop twelve miles and find the general. What did the message convey? Little that was concise. It was if anything ambiguous. No estimate of enemy numbers; no appraisal of their distance from the camp or speed of advance and, above all, no cry for help. It was Pulleine's first independent command and it would seem he was determined not to be labelled an 'alarmist'. Hallam Parr handed the note to Clery who passed it directly to Chelmsford. Having read it, Chelmsford said nothing and handed it back.Clery questioned '… is there anything to be done on this?' to which Chelmsford replied 'There is nothing to be done on that'.[27] In the recriminations that would later follow the disclosure of this incident, Chelmsford would deny that he had made such a remark but Clery, backed by Glyn, would not be shaken.

Despite Pulleine's note failing to cause even a hint of trepidation, there was, indeed, cause for alarm. The messenger, after being dismissed, fell into conversation with some soldiers along the track who had witnessed his arrival. Whether or not the trooper had been prematurely dismissed by Chelmsford it is impossible to say but it would seem he carried far more dramatic tidings than did Pulleine's note. He told the inquisitive soldiers that the camp was under attack and being surrounded. An officer, overhearing the conversation dismissed the trooper's tale as 'banter', remarking that if it were true, everyone would be marching back to camp as fast as they could go.[28]

While the rest of the column was still to get within rifle shot of their elusive enemy, the colonials were occupied at close quarters. Captain Maxwell of the NNC, after endeavouring to get to grips with the enemy for over an hour, recalled that firing was heard followed by the appearance of the Volunteers '… in skirmishing order at the gallop, and gallantly riding at the enemy until they obtained shelter in the caves of a krantz'.[29] The enemy were undoubtedly the remnants of Matshana's forces: in fact Matshana himself had been recognized and, hotly pursued by 'Offi' Shepstone, had escaped at the last moment by flinging himself from his horse and disappearing from sight over the edge of a krantz. Shepstone, however, took Matshana's black horse as a trophy. Nearby, Trooper Symons who was guarding nine prisoners, puzzlingly recalled the arrival of some men of 'Durnford's Native Horse', also bearing news of fighting at the camp. This is a difficult piece of the Isandlwana jigsaw puzzle to place. Durnford and his men by all accounts were either en route to Isandlwana from Rorke's Drift or had already arrived at the camp. Yet there was no hesitation in Symons identifying the arrivals as being those of Durnford's Horse. Nor at that moment was Symons perturbed by this news or the sound of heavy firing that could be heard in the direction of the camp. He was too intent on securing one of his nine prisoners, '… a cheeky '*insizwa*'[young man] robed in a new fur coat, who refused to give up his arms and laughed at the idea at first'.[30]

At the other end of the column, to the north, Russell and the IMI had exited the Magogo Valley onto the eastern end of the Isandlwana plain while Chelmsford, at about 10 am and now concerned by Pulleine's message, ordered Lieutenant Milne RN and Captain Penn Symons, with a party of signallers, presumably to carry Milne's telescope and tripod, to the shoulder of nearby Silutshana Hill, approximately 500 feet above the valley floor.[31] Having watched the camp through their telescopes for an hour, both Milne and Penn Symons agreed that apart from the oxen having seemingly been herded in close to the tents, nothing unusual was happening. Penn Symons particularly noted that all seemed quiet in the camp '… and at that time it was certain that no firing was going on'.[32] The two officers then turned their attention to activities closer to hand. Milne noted the main body of the enemy, that had been in front of the column all morning, had now assembled at the foot of Isipezi Hill, watching the advance of the IMI, while small clusters of warriors occupied every hill top observing '… our movements'.

Milne and Penn Symons, having descended Silutshana to find breakfast finished, reported their observation of the camp. Chelmsford, satisfied that nothing appeared to be amiss at Isandlwana, decided to hurry on with the establishment of the new base camp. He ordered Captain Alan Gardner, 14th Hussars, of Colonel Glyn's staff, together with Major Stuart Smith, RA, Lieutenant MacDowel, RE, and Lieutenants Dyer and Griffiths of the 2/24th, to return to Isandlwana and speed things along. It was hoped to have the column's tents and kit established at Mangeni before nightfall. The troops remaining at Isandlwana, together with Durnford's column, could move up the following day or the day after. Of the five officers returning to the camp, only Gardner would survive the day.

During the course of the morning,

Lieutenant Archibald Berkeley Milne, RN, the only naval officer on Lord Chelmsford's staff. (By courtesy of John Young)

Inspector Mansel, in pursuit of the elusive enemy, had been drawn far to the north '… into some very broken country where it would have been madness to follow'.[33] On calling a halt, Mansel had been surprised to see Chelmsford and his staff at breakfast in the valley below. Perhaps in the hope of being offered a bite, Mansel decided to take his men down and make a report. He did not record whether or not he was offered something to eat but, as he was ordered to escort the artillery back to Mangeni, rather than to harass the enemy, it was indicative that Chelmsford had abandoned the operation.

Having sent Gardner and the other officers on their way back to Isandlwana, Chelmsford and his staff prepared to ride in the direction of the gunfire caused by the Volunteers' encounter with Matshana. Milne recalled saddling up at about 12:30 pm and riding with the General in a roundabout way over the Magogo Hills to the Mangeni Valley. Thus for a while, Chelmsford ceased to be in contact with his scattered troops. As Milne later wrote 'the messengers sent by Commandant Brom [sic, Browne] failed to find the general. The latter is so rapid in his movements, that with the exception of his personal escort, it is sometimes hard to tell where he has gone.'

The whole operation, starting twenty-eight hours earlier, with many of the men not having eaten since, had been one wild goose chase. Only the IMI were, with little enthusiasm, still actively chasing the enemy. Russell had moved up the Magogo Valley as directed to '… see where the masses of the enemy were and if possible to make our way round by the right to meet the Mounted Police',[34] but Mansel and his men were already on their way back to Mangeni. As they marched they were joined by Dartnell, the rest of the NMP, Volunteers and the NNC led by Commandant Lonsdale. The artillery and infantry stopped at a large open space, where it was intended to set up the next base camp. The mounted troops took the opportunity to off-saddle, strip off their clothing and bathe in the Mangeni stream. Russell and the IMI, however, were still facing the enemy five miles away with Chelmsford, Glyn and their staffs somewhere in between. It was at about this stage that Commandant Lonsdale, still suffering from the after-effects of concussion, aggravated by the hardships of the last two days, decided he would best serve the operation and himself by getting out of the way and hastening to his bed back at Isandlwana camp. Meanwhile, the IMI, isolated now, had nevertheless given chase to a number of the enemy who appeared to be heading for the Isandlwana plain. Russell later reported 'I therefore pursued them for some distance but finding that there were few of them and going very fast I ceased doing [so] and rode up the valley at the foot of Isipezi Hill. This hill was covered with the enemy in very large numbers and we saw the spoor in the valley where their masses had come down from the hills where they had been in front of the General in the morning.'[35] The spoor Russell referred to was, in fact, that left by the passing of the Zulu army as it had made its way the previous day – with its remnants continuing to do so – on to the Nquthu plateau above the Isandlwana camp.

It is difficult to assess the strength of Russell's patrol. The total of the IMI has been given as 111 all ranks. Some had remained in camp and perhaps twenty had stayed as escort to Chelmsford. It is therefore likely that Russell's strength was no more than, say, sixty or seventy all ranks. In any event Russell did not intend entering into unknown country and allowing '… my retreat to be cut off'. So he decided to retire and later stated rather vaguely '… to try and re-join the General'. However, as the enemy Russell had been following suddenly opened fire, the IMI moved out of range and, having decided to give their horses a rest, withdrew and off-saddled for half an hour. It could be said that the whole operation had by now become a shambles lacking both purpose and enthusiasm as illustrated by the lethargy of the hungry and weary troops. Mansel, for instance, had abandoned the pursuit by making the excuse of reporting to Chelmsford, the artillery had found, with good reason, the going too difficult to overcome and so retired, Dartnell allowed his men to strip off and bathe while Russell, seemingly at a loss as to what to do next, became equally slothful. When at about 1:15 pm, a mounted European of the NNC galloped up saying that he had been sent to tell the General that the camp was under attack, Russell's own reaction as he recalled, was 'we could not tell him where the General was, but he was told whereabouts he had been that morning'. There was no indication of alarm or urgency. Russell rambled on to say that he had instructed the IMI to '… move quietly along the outskirts of the hills', while he went in search of Lord Chelmsford, but not finding him. However, on rejoining his men Russell was told that they had seen the guns in the camp firing. Soon a second mounted European arrived from the direction of Isandlwana confirming what must have been abundantly apparent by this time, that the camp was under attack. This prompted Russell into despatching two separate parties of scouts, one officered by Captain Davey and the other by Captain Walsh (who it will be remembered had spent most of the night riding to Mangeni and back to Isandlwana), to 'find and inform the General' while Russell led the remainder of the IMI back to Mangeni. On the way they overtook Harness and the artillery from whom they learned Chelmsford had been informed twenty minutes earlier (2:10 pm) that the camp was under attack. Russell's report continued '… I pushed on to report to HE [Lord Chelmsford] whom I met about half a mile further on'. Lord Chelmsford, according to Crealock, had been aware of the firing near the camp, '… not that the camp had been in any danger'.[36] However, Colonel Harness, a bachelor devoted to his profession and to the artillery in particular, was to think differently. He was proceeding with his guns, still escorted by two companies of the 2/24th commanded respectively by Captains Church and Harvey, when two horsemen were seen galloping across the plain coming from the direction of Isandlwana camp. Captain Church immediately borrowed a trumpeter's horse from the artillery and galloped to intercept them. The message they carried from Commandant 'Maori' Browne was staggering to the point of disbelief. 'For God's sake come back, the camp is surrounded and must be taken unless helped at once.'[37]

Chapter 8

'Startled by a calamity so sudden. So great and so close ...'

Sir Bartle Frere to Queen Victoria, 10 February 1879

Harness paused to take counsel with Major Wilsone Black, also of the 2/24th, who was marching with the column, and, with Black's concurrence, about-turned the guns only to encounter Staff Officer Gossett who, guessing Harness's intent, strongly advised Harness that he would be disobeying orders and not to do so. Disregarding Gossett, Harness and Black set out at once for Isandlwana with the infantry and guns while Gossett hurried back to Mangeni where, unlike other riders who had sought the General in vain, Gossett was immediately successful.

We have earlier seen, as with Colonel Durnford, that Chelmsford did not countenance his officers disobeying orders except, as Chelmsford had put it, when '... it would be injurious to the Column not to do so'. It could be argued that any delay in hastening to the beleaguered camp with four guns and two companies of infantry would be injurious and such was Harness's fearless evaluation of the situation. Nevertheless, for all that, Chelmsford ordered Gossett to gallop back and give Harness a direct order to return to Mangeni. The exact wording of his reprimand has never been revealed. However, at about 12:30 pm, when Chelmsford and his staff were nearing Mangeni, it struck Drummond that something untoward was happening at Isandlwana. Some of the NNC were insisting that fighting was taking place and that big guns could be distinctly heard. In addition, Longcast, Chelmsford's interpreter, on questioning a prisoner was told the King's army of 25,000 men was expected hourly. Almost within minutes, as if to confirm the growing doubts and rumours, a black horseman, most likely another of Durnford's men, arrived at the gallop gesticulating and shouting wildly. Fynn, rushed forward to interpret the man's hysterical tirade: 'The Zulus have taken and demolished the camp at Isandlwana completely!' he was screaming.[1] This messenger was shortly followed by yet another courier, Trooper Hayhoe of the Carbineers who, on encountering the column, delivered a message to Major Dartnell. Trooper Jones of the NMR later recalled that Hayhoe '... Had escaped from Isandlwana and had brought news of the disaster with him. We started back immediately, meeting the oncoming reinforcements, [commanded by Harness and Black] who were given orders to go straight back, [to Mangeni].'[2] Chelmsford and his staff rode to the top where Milne, training his telescope on the distant camp reported, as he had earlier in the day, all appeared quiet. The sun was shining brightly on the white tents, there was no sign of gunsmoke and although bodies of men could be seen moving about they were naturally put down to be Imperial troops or NNC. 'This was at 1:45pm and not the faintest suspicion of any disaster had then crossed our minds. We believed an attack had been made on the camp and had been repulsed, as those who knew Lord Chelmsford's disposition for defending it had every right and reason to believe.'[3] Strange words to have been written by Drummond who must have been fully aware that virtually no dispositions had been made for the camp's defence. (The sun still shining on the tents at 1.45 pm, is questionable as the sun was partly eclipsed at that time.)

Chelmsford and his staff spent an hour on the top of Mdutshana, presumably pondering the recent rumours and watching the distant camp whilst the troops hung around wondering if they were ever going to eat again. It was at about this time, 2 pm, that further down the track, Harness and his infantry escort, as ordered by Gossett, turned their backs on whatever dreadful fate the camp was about to endure. Crealock later wrote that Chelmsford, not thinking that there was anything wrong in the camp, decided to take forty Volunteers, plus Russell and his IMI who had just arrived, and see for himself what was happening at Isandlwana. Drummond commented '... it is likely that anxiety to hear what the attack on the camp had really been, induced the general to return to it in person ... no vestige of the suspicion of the real truth had, as yet, entered our minds.'

Trooper Symons had noticed the dull, oppressive nature of the day but did not realize it was due to an eclipse until later. He and his mates, after their encounter with Matshana's clan, were off-saddled near the Mangeni stream trying to brew some tea, that they had scrounged when the distant boom of artllery was heard disrupting the band that was playing at that moment and causing an uneasy presentment. It was an incongruous scene: the Carbineers sprawled by a sparkling stream eating tinned fish while the regimental band of the 2nd Battalion, 24th Regiment, played soldiers' favourites, perhaps, 'Let me kiss him for his mother' or 'The girl I left behind me', while distant guns boomed loud enough to strike a chord of apprehension in all those that heard them. But the trooper's idle was soon interrupted by Chelmsford and his escort trotting past in the direction of Isandlwana. At once a trumpet sounded and soon the Carbineers were hastening after Chelmsford only to shortly encounter Colonel Harness, the artillery and their infantry escort, having about-turned as ordered, back to Mangeni. Meanwhile Chelmsford had pressed on, soon coming in sight of 'Maori' Browne and his 1/3rd NNC.

After leaving Mangeni at 10 am, the NNC had not gone far when they encountered two Zulu scouts. Having killed one, Browne learnt from the other that a Zulu army was close by on its way to attack. Even so, Browne and his men continued on their way until, three miles further on, large formations of the enemy were seen advancing between them and Isandlwana. A halt was called and a second man, a white NCO, was sent galloping back to Mangeni with orders to 'find the General' but neither he or the earlier messenger were successful. These were undoubtedly the men who had encountered Russell and the IMI earlier in the day. Nevertheless, Browne continued to advance, hoping to get in front of the enemy and into the camp, at the same time despatching a third messenger in search of Lord Chelmsford. By 1:30 pm Browne was close enough to Isandlwana to see the movements of the artillery in the camp and to witness the smoke from the heavy firing that was taking place in front of the tents. Shortly, the cannons ceased firing altogether and fighting could be seen amongst the tents which were still standing. Browne then sent his fourth and famous message 'For God's sake come back ...'. Nevertheless, Browne and the NNC continued to move forward until Browne saw three large bodies of warriors crossing his front, intent on attack so he thought. As those of his men fortunate enough to carry a firearm, rather than a spear, had only fifteen rounds of ammunition each, he decided to retire and take up a defensive position on a nearby rocky outcrop. But he need not have concerned himself, the enemy were intent on looting the camp and were not to be deterred by the prospect of killing a battalion of 'Natal Kaffirs', as they would have contemptuously called the NNC.

At 2:30 pm, as estimated by Browne, all resistance ceased, the battle of Isandlwana was over. The Zulu army had accomplished an overwhelming victory and Browne got himself and his battalion as far away from Zulu notice as possible, back along the track to Mangeni. It was at this point that Russell and the IMI, leading Chelmsford and his staff, were seen crossing the plain in the direction of Isandlwana. Browne sent yet another rider, Captain Hayes (who it will be remembered had saved the life of a drowning infantryman eleven days earlier when crossing the Thukela), to intercept Chelmsford with the grim tidings that the camp had been overrun. Chelmsford, not daring to believe Browne, spurred on towards Isandlwana. Then perhaps the most extraordinary incident of an extraordinary day occurred. A figure, slumped in the saddle, riding a pony at a slow walk came into view. It was Commandant Rupert Lonsdale who, still suffering from concussion, had earlier left Mangeni riding his pony Dot to seek the comfort of his bed back at Isandlwana. Riding in a complete daze, he had not been aware, as he meandered into the camp, of the racing Zulu regiments, the artillery fire, the rattle of musketry and the clamour of battle but had ridden slowly into the camp itself. The crack of a bullet passing close to his head made Lonsdale suddenly aware of his surroundings; a red-coated black man holding a rifle brought him instantly alert. Reason falsely told him that the black man was one of the NNC who had carelessly discharged his gun. A moment later, as he passed close to a tent, he was appalled by the emerging apparition of another red-coated black man with a blood-covered assegai in his hand intent, by his look, on making Lonsdale his next victim. With the realization of his cataclysmic position, Lonsdale dragged Dot's head around and applied spurs; but Dot, tired, hungry and longing to be off-saddled, was intent on heading for the picquet lines. For a moment pony and man stood locked in desperate confrontation while warriors, firing and throwing spears, surged forward intent on dragging Lonsdale from the saddle. Slowly Dot got going into a reluctant trot and, with animal instinct sensing danger, plunged into a gallop, miraculously taking her rider clear of the camp. Now even more exhausted after their close encounter with certain death, both man and horse ambled back towards Mangeni. '… We were met by a solitary horseman coming at a foot-pace from the direction of the camp who, as it came nearer, was recognized as Commandant Lonsdale whom we knew to have ridden on. It is little exaggeration to say that those who heard him tell the General "the camp is in possession of the enemy, Sir!" will not soon forget it.'[4] (it is interesting to note that the discrepancies in time in the various accounts of Chelmsford's

Commandant Rupert Lonsdale, Natal Native Contingent, who unwittingly rode amongst the looting warriors and lived to tell the tale. (By courtesy of John Young)

encounter with Lonsdale are considerable: Penn Symons, 1:15 pm; Maxwell, 2 pm; Hallam Parr, 3:30 pm; Crealock, 4 pm).

Chelmsford, showing no trace of the anxiety he must have felt, immediately ordered Gossett to make haste back to Mangeni and not only recall Harness, his guns and his escort but also Colonel Glyn and all the troops remaining there. Meanwhile, still unable either to comprehend or accept that such a catastrophe could be possible, Chelmsford ordered Russell and the IMI forward to make a closer reconnaissance of the camp. Russell found it to be 'in complete possession of the enemy'. Legend has it that Chelmsford, utterly dumbfounded exclaimed 'but I left a thousand men to guard the camp!'. Was it at that moment that the first ghastly inkling occurred to him that somehow he had been decoyed and out-generalled? It was probably too much, there and then, for him to deduce that the trail of this monstrous catastrophe led directly back to Fynn, Fynn the oracle of Zulu intent and strategy whose services he had gone out of his way to acquire. Had Fynn, who had believed emphatically in the credibility of his intelligence sources, been himself outwitted? It is unlikely that anyone, except perhaps Frere, would ever be told of the deception, a deception that would remain an unmentionable secret between the General and the Msinga magistrate for the rest of their lives. Yet it would be only hours before the military, the press and colonial population would stridently declare that Chelmsford had been outwitted. In the meantime, now at a distance of about five miles from Isandlwana camp, Chelmsford and those about him waited with 'unspeakable impatience and anxiety' for the Mangeni troops to come up while, at the same time, watching '… the Zulus swarming like bees in the camp'.

When Gossett, after a gallop of eight miles, arrived at Mangeni, his horse completely blown, he found the troops scattered in all directions. Assuming, quite rightly, that they were to bivouac where they stood, most, except for the picquets, had set out in search of anything edible. Therefore, despite the urgent call of the bugle to 'Fall in', it was some time before the furthest-flung forager appeared. It is ironic that the ration wagon, ordered by Colonel Glyn to follow the column, arrived simultaneously with Gossett. Consequently the food it contained was not distributed until after dark when the column had reached Isandlwana. It was after 4pm when Colonel Glyn, well to the fore, was ready to march. Penn Symons recalled, '… a whisper ran through the column that the camp had been taken and sacked. It was barely credible. The majority refused to believe it.' Hallam Parr, in his letter to Bartle Frere, wrote 'I myself felt quite cheerful on the way home [to Isandlwana] feeling convinced that we should take the Zulus in the rear still attacking. Near the camp we came up with the General and Crealock.' Hallam Parr found Chelmsford, Crealock and the staff, like the IMI and Volunteers dismounted. The time was 6 pm. They had been waiting at a distance of about two miles from the camp, watching the final agonizing moments of its destruction. The tents which had stood all day, doing much to deceive Milne and Hallam Parr that all was well at Isandlwana, were no longer to be seen. The victorious Zulus had cut out the tent tops leaving the skirts, with guy ropes, still hammered into the ground.

Chelmsford, never a great orator, addressed the troops, his words intended in particular to inspire the infantry: 'Twenty-fourth, whilst we have been out yonder the enemy have outflanked us and taken our camp, they are probably holding it now; at any cost we must take it back tonight and cut our way back to Rorke's Drift tomorrow. This means fighting but I know I can count on you.'[5] Hardly a blood-stirring rally and the plight of their situation was not lost on the men. Everything the column possessed, except for the four guns and the ration wagon, had been left in the camp. They were now behind enemy lines without food, low on ammunition and with only the clothes they stood up in. Nevertheless, the infantry gave three cheers which in turn were taken up by the NNC. The weary troops were then ordered into battle formation: the IMI leading, followed by the NNC, the artillery in the centre supported by the infantry on either side and with the flanks protected by the Volunteers.[6] Major Dartnell, however, was far from happy. He begged Chelmsford not to put the NNC in front of the infantry, stating that if attacked they would most likely bolt '… throwing the rest of the column into confusion'.[7]

As the troops advanced, stumbling in the gathering darkness, it was, nevertheless, still light enough to see masses of the enemy moving out of the camp with cattle and other spoils which, not realized at the time, would include the two 7-pounders of the Royal Artillery. Scattered fires still gave hope that there was resistance within the camp. It was a hope short lived. The horses, shying and ill at ease, were the first to sense the horror of what lay about them. In the gloom, the artillerymen were forced to feel on their hands and knees for the cause of their horses' terror and then pull away the corpses before the animals would pass. The NMP marched in half-sections with even numbers dismounted. Trooper William Clarke, unlucky enough to be one of those afoot and more than nervous, constantly called to his half-section, who was leading Clarke's horse, telling him that on no account, in the event of a scare, was he to clear off with his horse. 'The dead were lying in such numbers that we constantly fell over corpses, whether Europeans or Zulus it was too dark to see.'[8] January 22nd 1879 was the day of the 'Dead Moon', as it was later to be called, the last day of the Lunar cycle before

New Moon. The Zulus called it *Olumnymana*, or the black day.[9] A century later, historians would argue, inconclusively, whether or not this phase of the moon influenced Zulu strategy and the outcome of the battle itself.

A mile and a half closer to the tent lines, the sort of scare that Trooper Clarke had feared might deprive him of his horse, suddenly occurred. Out of the gloom, figures were seen slowly advancing on the column. A halt was called. Mounted scouts were sent forward and shortly opened fire, dropping one man and sending the rest scuttling for cover behind some rocks. The column held its breath. Then a tirade of indignant Zulu verbiage as three figures emerged, asserting they were NNC, as indeed they were, who had miraculously survived the battle. A fourth man, he who had been shot, also emerged wounded but not badly. The column heaved a sigh of relief and again moved forward.

Although there was no moon, the outline of Isandlwana rock, the 'Sphinx' to some, or, perhaps to the more anxious and imaginative soldiery, the outline of a crouching beast, was clearly visible as were the wagons on the nek between the Sphinx and Mhlambamkhosi, a small hill ever after to be known as 'Black's Koppie'. It was decided that if the enemy were present their most likely place of concealment would be amongst the wagons. Chelmsford ordered the guns forward and a salvo was fired, '… to the most beautiful effect from an artistic point of view but none whatsoever as far as discovering the position of the enemy was concerned'.[10] Next the infantry were ordered to fix bayonets and, under the command of Major Black, to attack and hold Mahlabamkhosi. The bayonets of the 2/24th rattled briefly as they connected with their rifle sockets and then the infantry were gone into the gloom.

Out of sight, Black and his men were storming Mhlambankosi, a steep and rocky climb in daylight but in darkness a task best suited to the tough and bloody-minded soldiery who were, at that moment, scrambling up its slopes. Then, hours later it seemed, they were at the top. What better way to proclaim their achievement than by British cheers. Drummond recalled, '… suddenly through the darkness we heard the 24th cheering away to our left and knew they had taken the hill which was the key of the position. These cheers were taken up all along the line'; and here Drummond paid a compliment, a rare occurrence, to the British infantry whom the Zulus had mocked and jeered all day: 'Had the Zulu nation only heard them [cheering] and known as we did, that they were the cheers of a handful of English troops, having lost half their number, besides everything they possessed, and who believed themselves to be advancing against an enemy ten times numerically stronger, and under cover, and in the dark, I fancy they would have understood that they had considerably undervalued our "footmen" as they contemptuously called them.'[11]

The camp, for what it was worth, had to be retaken. It contained little except the mutilated bodies of dead comrades, the corpses of Zulu foes and the debris of what until a few hours earlier had been a British column with the capability, it was believed, of defeating the Zulu army. Now its supplies, equipment, the dozens of wagons and the hundreds of oxen that had carried all the paraphernalia of this military juggernaut had been either taken or destroyed. A thousand breech-loading rifles and 200,000 rounds of ammunition were in the hands of the enemy and what of the 1,500 men who had been left to guard the camp ... ?

The General gave the order to 'Form square!'. The infantry, two deep, facing the Rorke's Drift road, the guns and cavalry facing back towards Mangeni and the NNC on both flanks. Chelmsford, despite it being the most calamitous day of his life, personally saw to the placing of the sentries and was courteous enough to apologize to an NNC officer whom he had wrongly accused of some indiscretion. Major Dartnell, ever concerned and never afraid to speak his mind, saw to it that the NMP and Volunteers had correctly ring-linked their horses and had then further protected them with a circle of troopers two yards apart. Trooper Clark remembered '... the ring [of horses] of which I had charge, was a constant source of worry because it was almost impossible for the horses to move without stepping on a dead man which caused them to shy and keep on the move all night'. Continuing to delve, Dartnell inspected the guns and warned Harness to have them unlimbered and '... brought into action'. Then, in company with Harness, he went in search of Chelmsford but was told by a staff officer that the General was lying down and could not be disturbed. Finally Dartnell returned to the Volunteers and NMP and told them that in the event of an attack '... we were to leave the horses and fight it out back to back with the 2/24th'.[12]

Apart from those on picquet, most, utterly exhausted, lay down where they stood, more often than not to find themselves in company with a corpse caked in blood. The NNC were particularly distraught and restless. Their great chief, Gabangaye kaPhakade of the amaChunu clan, had been left in camp. It was feared that he together with 400 of their clansmen were dead. It was not surprising then that, during the terrible night that followed, the NNC caused several false alarms by firing off their rifles at enemies imagined and by drumming their shields. 'One of the weirdest sounds that I have ever heard in all my life', wrote Captain Mainwaring. It was not this incident, however, that would cause the Column to hold its breath, finger on the trigger and nerves a-jangle: '... at 1pm a shot was fired and a sort of half whistle, half shiver, ran thro' the ranks and a confused volley was fired. It was impossible to get hold of Colonel Clery's or my horse, some mules broke loose, and there was confusion in the centre of the square – luckily it was a false alarm.'[13] Fynn, with a thousand doubts and questions of his own racing through his head, was asked by Lonsdale to '… keep the natives quiet and in their places'. Fynn added '… for they were excited about the absence of Gabangaye their presumptive chief, son of the hereditary chief Pakade Chunu. Their restlessness was seriously dangerous for in the event of a sound from the Zulus, these natives would have rushed precipitously southwards over the whole column.' Apart from weird sounds, there were also unexplained lights or fires illuminating the skyline in the direction of Rorke's Drift. Some, aware that there was a contingent of Royal Engineers at the drift, suggested that the illuminations were the result of some electrical device. More realistically, others contended the Zulus were across the Buffalo and rampaging their way through Natal.

Chapter 9

'What excitement this will cause in England and what indignation'

Lieutenant H.T. Curling RA, in a letter to his mother, 2 February 1879

I n Zululand at midsummer it is light at 4:30 am and Chelmsford intended to get his men on the move before they could see the horrors that darkness had concealed. They formed up into a ragged column;the IMI and Carbineers led, closely followed by Lord Chelmsford and his staff, then the infantry with the NNC on either wings and the NMP covering the rear; but they were not alone. Large bodies of warriors still moved around the periphery of the camp and more could be seen on the Nquthu plateau, while closer, villagers, men and women, came to stare. Milne believed them to be people with blood on their hands, robbers of the dead, and regretted there was no time to kill them. The NMP, forming the rearguard, had time to witness the chaos of the camp: the dead, men and animals, were strewn everywhere, tents destroyed, wagons run into dongas, and everything that was once of value torn, broken or burnt. Yet there were exceptions. An ox was found alive and still yoked to its upturned wagon. He was cut loose, struggled to his feet and, with his tail up, trotted off with the column towards Rorke's Drift. Trooper Clarke, taking a chance and disobeying orders, slipped off in an attempt to find his tent and to see, if by chance, his spurs were still where he had forgotten them two days before. In the confusion of what remained of the tent lines he was unsuccessful and, on making his way back to his troop, he came upon the body of a comrade, Trooper Stimson, still booted and spurred. Rather than leave Stimson's spurs to be looted by the Zulus, Clarke dismounted only to be pounced upon by Inspector Mansel who, much to Clarke's indignation, severely reprimanded him for 'robbing the dead'.

The regimental band of the 2/24th, despite the rigours of the retreat, still humped their unwieldy instruments and as the despondent column shuffled forward, ludicrously it must have seemed to some, gallantly struck up a marching air. It was not to last for long. Masses of Zulus, numbering in their thousands, unexpectedly appeared on both flanks. One *impi* marched parallel to the column at a distance of three miles while another was close enough to converse with. The martial music was judged to be of too challenging a nature and the band was immediately ordered to cease playing. But both were beaten armies, both anxious to avoid further confrontation and Chelmsford '… deemed it wiser not to bring on an engagement as the crucial point, the Thatshe [*sic*] valley, lay before us in which were unknown dangers and we short of ammunition'.[1] The British, were unaware, at the time, that they were passing the downcast warriors of several combined Zulu regiments, over 3,000 strong. Having been given a bloody nose by the garrison at Rorke's Drift, the regiments were retreating back into Zululand. Prince Dabulamanzi kaMpande, he who at Cetshwayo's coronation, it will be remembered, lost out in a shooting competition with a colonial drummer boy, would have as much explaining to do to his King as would Chelmsford to his Queen. Yet, for all that, just one careless act of provocation could erupt into a bloody set-to. There were several close calls. One warrior, perhaps drunk on looted grog, took potshots at the passing troops. He was finally dispatched, it taking '… a great want of ammunition to polish him off'.[2] The NMP rearguard were especially intimidated. A vast crowd of warriors came to within 300 yards, cutting off some NNC stragglers who had been looting on their own account.[3] Dartnell gave orders to fire if necessary and then galloped off for reinforcements. He soon returned declaring angrily 'These are all the supports [a troop of NMP] I can get. "They" [author's apostrophes] have refused to give me any so I brought back the only troop of our men that were near.'[4]

On the left flank, to the front of the column, there was an even more dangerous act of incitement. As the weary soldiers passed a mass of squatting and evidently exhausted warriors, one sprang to his feet and frenziedly implored his comrades to attack. No one moved. Undeterred and alone the warrior rushed madly downhill to be shot dead only thirty yards from the British line. His comrades, unmoved, continued to squat and stare. Apart from shouted insults as they passed the Zulus, there were no further provocations and after a march of four hours the column came in sight of Rorke's Drift where the homestead could be seen still smouldering. Figures appeared here and there busy amongst the buildings. Friend or foe? One emerged on top of a roof waving a flag. Another Zulu ruse, perhaps? The IMI and Volunteers were ordered forward to find out. While the IMI forded the river, the Volunteers dismounted and lined the bank to cover their retreat if required. Tense moments. Then a British cheer followed by a man of the IMI shouting 'All right! They're our men!'

The river was still running high, but the cavalry, at the expense of several duckings and the loss of one carbine, crossed at the drift. The NNC waded further up, while the staff, infantry and artillery, keeping their feet dry, were carried across on the pontoons which, to the astonishment of all, were still in working order. The column then discovered the miracle. A cosmopolitan mix of British soldiery but mainly of the 2/24th, totalling 129 men all ranks, and two civilians, in the ramshackled buildings of a mission station unprepared for defence, had fought and defeated a Zulu army of several thousand in a battle lasting from late afternoon on the 22nd until early morning the following day. British losses were fifteen killed and nine wounded. The estimate of Zulu killed varied considerably. For instance Hallam Parr wrote that there were 170; Mainwaring: 300; and Clarke: 375. Little was said of Zulu wounded. Clarke coldly stated '... altogether we buried three hundred and seventy five dead Zulus and some wounded were thrown into the grave. Seeing the manner in which our wounded had been mutilated after having been dragged from the hospital [men who were wounded in the skirmish on 12 January] we were very bitter and did not spare wounded Zulus'.[5] Fynn was awestruck by the multitudes of Zulu dead, chiefly of the uThulwana Regiment, 'heaped and strewn all around'.

The Battle of Rorke's Drift has been fought many times in every form of media and it is not the purpose of this book to fight it once again. However, Rorke's Drift cannot be dismissed without mentioning that no less than eleven Victoria Crosses were awarded for its defence. Despite the unquestionable courage of its defenders, this was an unprecedented number for a single action. It created the suspicion that such a volume was a ruse on the part of Lord Chelmsford to divert worldwide attention from the disaster of Isandlwana to the glorious defence of Rorke's Drift. Not only that, envy drove others to protest. In order to present the two officers in charge of the defence as the stuff that 'Boy's Own' heroes are made of, the Victorian press somewhat implied that they were mere boys. Indeed, it was true that neither ranked higher than a lieutenant, yet John Rouse Chard, the senior of the two, a Royal Engineer officer, was 32 years of age and Gonville Bromhead, of the 2/24th, 34. The major gripe of the dissenters was that Chard and Bromhead, who were both awarded the Victoria Cross, were merely doing their duty; there was nowhere to retreat, they had no option but to stand and fight. Lieutenant General Sir Garnet Wolseley, who would eventually relieve Chelmsford of his command and perform the duty of decorating Chard and Bromhead with their VCs, was himself brave to the point of insanity but, unlike a number of his peers, had somehow repeatedly missed out as a recipient of Britain's most coveted decoration. Wolseley's ire is clear when on 16 July 1879, he confided to his diary 'I presented Major Chard, RE [both Chard and Bromhead had recently received rapid promotion] with his V.C. and a more stupid looking fellow I never saw … Bromhead of the 24th Regt. who was 2nd in command of the post is a very stupid fellow also.'[6] These unseemly reflections were also echoed by others. A young officer who had miraculously escaped from Isandlwana and who, no doubt, had experienced as terrifying an ordeal as both Chard and Bromhead, wrote home to his mother: 'It is very amusing to read the accounts of Chard and Bromhead. They are about the most commonplace men in the British Army. Chard is a most insignificant man in appearance and is only about five foot 2 or 3 inches in height. Bromhead is a stupid old fellow, as deaf as a post. Is it not curious how some men are forced into notoriety.'[7] Nevertheless, soon copies of Lady Butler's famous painting depicting Chard and Bromhead directing the battle would adorn the walls of boys' bedrooms throughout the Empire.

Following the euphoria of having survived the last two days, the defenders of Rorke's Drift, '… after their desperate exertions were hysterical and could not speak. Others, overjoyed at their escape and our arrival threw their arms about, waved their caps and cheered. All were begrimed with powder and blood and smoke and smuts from the burning hospital.'[8] The immediate desire of both the defenders and the column was for food and sleep. Food there was in plenty (the NNC had not eaten since the night of the 20th), but for most sleep would have to wait. The mass of dead warriors had to be buried before their decaying corpses could cause more deaths. As the NNC had an aversion to physical contact with the dead, they dug a mass grave while the white men, officers and other ranks alike, worked shoulder-to-shoulder carrying the Zulu corpses to their final resting-place.

Apart from burying the dead, there was much to be done. Only the Buffalo River separated Rorke's Drift from Zululand and the victorious Zulu army. The mission station was now Natal's first line of defence and the remains of No 3 Column would be its unfortunate garrison for many weeks to come. What was left of the mission buildings had be fortified, defences extended, the guns brought inside and mounted either pointing towards the river or in the direction from which the enemy had come the previous day. Patrols were sent out and Russell was dispatched with Chelmsford's written report to Helpmekaar, six miles away, not knowing whether or not the small British garrison had been attacked and overwhelmed. However, all was well.

Chelmsford, whatever his faults, did not lack the grit to sit down and scribble to Sir Bartle Frere what must have been the most difficult epistle he would ever write. The revelation of its contents would spread panic throughout southern Africa and rock the British Empire. It began 'I regret to inform you that No. 3 Column has maintained a terrible disaster …'. He went on to describe the events of the 21st and 22nd while evading any mention of Fynn, Gamdana or the instructions that he had given Dartnell. Nor did he mention Hamilton-Browne's imperative messages and his own delayed responses. He merely stated: 'On learning that the camp was attacked I commenced to move towards Isandlwana and the Native Contingent, the Mounted Infantry and the Natal Volunteers, having the artillery and the 2/24th and Natal Police form an encampment under Col. Glyn. At the time I had no doubt but that the reported attack was of small significance and that the force in camp would be sufficient to beat it off.'[9]

Presumably one of Russell's infantrymen acted as despatch rider with Chemsford's report. If so, he was already a day late with the news. Two officers of the NNC, having escaped from Isandlwana, had paused neither at Rorke's Drift nor Helpmekaar but had ridden on with the news to Pietermaritzburg. Russell returned in the evening to announce that Helpmekaar was secure, and he brought with him a few survivors of Isandlwana.

When at last the weary troops were permitted to rest – except for those on picquet – it was found that not only were there no blankets or greatcoats, but that the men were to be packed within the mission station defences 'like herrings in a tub'.[10] The General, Colonel Glyn and their staffs took occupation of the roofless house while the white troops were allocated space within the temporary defences. The NNC, except for their white officers and NCOs, were left to get on with it as best they could outside the dubious barricades. With only one man in ten possessing a rifle and a few rounds of ammunition, without officers or NCOs and with gross prejudice, they were to be, in the event of a Zulu attack, both assegai-fodder and Natal's first line of defence. It is not surprising then that by the following morning the NNC had turned into a sullen mob, refusing to muster, searching for food and killing any Zulu wounded they happened to come across.[11] They unanimously requested that they be discharged; they wanted to get home to their villages where their women, children and cattle were vulnerable to Zulu attack. There were a dozen or more drifts along the Buffalo and Thukela Rivers where raiders could cross unopposed. In their absence no one else would protect their interests. They wanted out.

Men of the Natal Native Contingent. Like their Zulu kin across the Buffalo River, the NNC fought all but naked – unlike their European NCOs. As can be seen, one man in ten is armed with a Martini-Henry rifle. Those taking up the rear are armed with spear and shield.

On being informed of their request, Chelmsford, fearing that his force was about to diminish by half, angrily ordered the NNC on parade. He called on Drummond to interpret his reprimand – Drummond, not Fynn, it will be noted. Fynn, who at Lonsdale's request had calmed the obstreperous NNC only hours earlier, had departed. Fynn, whose services Chelmsford had gone to so much trouble to acquire, is never referred to again. Had there been an unmentionable dialogue of recrimination between the General and the Msinga magistrate, eventuating in Fynn's banishment? We will never know. Fynn, however, did resume contact with Chelmsford. Coming down from Msinga the following May, he again accompanied an expedition led by Black – now Brevett Lieutenant Colonel Black – to the Isandlwana battlefield, writing: 'Months later [15th May] I found Lord Chemsford's written orders of the night of Tuesday 21st January, 1879, amongst the rocks close to Col. Glyn's headquarters tent and sent them to Lord Chelmsford.'[12] Fynn did not lack good reason for leaving Rorke's Drift; his wife and children were at the Msinga Magistracy a few miles away. Nevertheless, he would have best served his family and his comrades by remaining at his post. Whatever the circumstance of his leaving, Fynn arrived at Msinga at twelve noon on the 24th, and 'silently and grimly embraced his distraught wife and three children'.[13]

The NNC, having been ordered to parade, with Drummond interpreting, were addressed by Chelmsford: 'He informed them of the penalty for desertion and on no account, unless leave was granted, were they to leave.'[14] Thus having issued his last order to No 3 Column, the column he had taken upon himself to command with such disastrous consequences, Chelmsford and his staff, departed for Pietermaritzburg at 9 am on the 25th, leaving Colonel Glyn amongst the desolation of defeat but in command of his column once again. During the two days that Chelmsford was at Rorke's Drift he would have spent many of his waking hours contemplating his awesome responsibilities: the loss of No 3 Column and the safety of Natal being the foremost. But perhaps what caused him to fret the most, was making the decision of whether he should concede that he had been decoyed and outgeneralled? Whether by deliberate Zulu ploy or a stroke of Zulu good fortune would make little difference, and his masters at Horse Guards (headquarters of the British Army) would be hungry for answers. Crealock (described by Wolseley as 'that offensive snob who is Chelmsford's ruin'),[15] as Chelmsford's chief of staff was also implicated. Together, they schemed to evade responsibility. They decided to convene a Court of Enquiry, the members of which, it would seem, were to be directed to reach neither a conclusion or offer an opinion as to the cause of the disaster. This duty (under the circumstances) appearing to have been done for the moment, the conspirators would have time and opportunity to compile their own version of events and to allocate blame. And so, during the brief moments Chelmsford would spend at Helpmekaar later that day, he and Crealock would find time to set their deception in motion. Amongst the military flotsam and jetsam – either fortunate survivors of Isandlwana or personel caught on the road to Rorke's Drift – that had washed up at Helpmekaar during the last couple of days, Chelmsford would find Colonel F.C. Hassard RE, a recent arrival in Natal and the senior ranking officer at the outpost. Hassard, however, had no wish to take command and had smartly handed the responsibility to Colonel Bray of the 4th Regiment of Foot, who had also been stranded at Helpmekaar. Hassard then seemed to be the right sort of unassuming and unambitious officer to head up a Court of Enquiry along the lines the General required. He would head the court supported by Colonel Harness and Lieutenant Colonel Law RA. Harness, being a member of the court, would be prohibited from giving evidence and neither Dartnell, Lonsdale nor Black were called. On 3 February, less than a month after the Court of Enquiry, Chelmsford wrote to Colonel Wood, the commander of No 4 Column, saying, 'Poor old Hassard and his adjutant Baxter, went off in an ambulance today for Durban, en route for Capetown. The former is very weak and I shall be glad to hear he is alive and on board ship'.[16] However, six months later, Hassard was still in Capetown, Wolseley remarking at that time '… Colonel Hassard RE, who is the Comd. Officer here, whom I had known in the Crimea, has no interest in his profession …'.[17]

A Court of Enquiry, by definition one would assume, would be tasked with determining the cause of a particular happening – usually an unfortunate one, as was the case with the disastrous defeat of No 3 Column. Whether by lack of understanding of its duty or because it was directed to do so, Hassard's court would merely take a brief statement from Major Clery outlining the events of Chelmsford's reconnaissance in force on the morning of the 22nd. It contained a paragraph from Colonel Glyn stating, more or less, that as far as he was concerned he just took orders from Lord Chelmsford; a statement from Crealock, similar to that of Chelmsford's, outlining events of the 22nd, and accounts from five surviving officers relating their own personal experiences. Other statements were taken but not recorded, and in due course the court would be severely censured for this. The court would offer no opinion nor would it point an accusing finger, thus all were exempt from accountability, including the commanding general.

Amongst the entourage accompanying Chelmsford to Pietermaritzburg that day were several NNC officers destined for the Eastern Cape with orders to recruit replacements for the fifteen officers and thirty-six NCOs of the 3rd NNC who had been killed at Isandlwana. It would be a more difficult task to find replacements for the 467 black soldiers of the NNC who had perished in the battle. When the NMP heard that the General and his staff were about to depart for Pietermaritzburg, it was not surprising that there was a great keenness amongst the troopers to be part of Chelmsford's escort. Trooper Clarke was particularly disappointed. He lost out because he was late bringing his horse up from the river and so was not selected. He was later told by his mates who had formed the escort, that it had been no holiday. Chelmsford, anxious to reach civilization and know the worst, had pushed men and horses to the limit. On reaching Helpmekaar, there had been more disturbing news. The men of the 2nd Battalion NNC, under the command of Major Bengough, who had as yet to enter Zululand, had all but mutinied, and refused to march. Bengough, concerned that they were about to desert, taking their rifles with them, had decided to disband them on the spot.[18] They were in the act of departing when Chelmsford arrived. Furious with Bengough for acting without orders, Chelmsford immediately commanded that they fall in, forming three sides of a square. Three companies of British infantry, from the Helpmekaar garrison, formed the fourth side. Chelmsford, astride his horse, harangued the despondent NNC, informing them that they were to march to Msinga (where Fynn would have recently arrived), and there protect the Magistracy and prevent the enemy from crossing the border. There was much shuffling of feet and no indication of compliance until Chelmsford put it plainly 'any man who deserted would be shot',[19] whereupon the battalion reluctantly obeyed orders and marched away to Msinga.

But the problems with the NNC were far from over. For the men at Rorke's Drift, observing the General and his staff, Commandant Lonsdale, other NNC officers and the Volunteers departing, it was too much. The universal reaction was 'If they're going, so are we!' W.J. Moody, the Resident Magistrate of Ladysmith, in his report of 3 February 1879, put it plainly: 'Very many of the natives, [the NNC] on their return from the front reported themselves to this office … to use their own words, said to me, "we saw that the Government was driven out of Zululand and the wind blew us back also". In their extreme ignorance many thought that the Commander-in-Chief's visit to Maritzburg was a flight from the enemy.'[20] Captain Maxwell also had something to say: 'The General and staff left for Maritzburg … and shortly after they had gone our natives of the Contingent began to leave in small bodies. We warned and threatened, but it was no use – go they would, and, to tell the truth, I don't think one officer or non-com of the Contingent was sorry to see them disappear. Provisions we had in plenty but no clothing or blankets for them. They, like ourselves, having lost all they had – with the exception of what they stood in – and that was little.' Commandant Hamilton-Browne went even further. In defiance of Chelmsford's determination to retain the NNC, he addressed, with bitter recrimination, the 3rd Regiment and dismissed the lot. Despite Hamilton-Browne's scathing remarks, the joy of departure and that they were permitted to retain their issue blanket, saw them gaily bounding off '… laughing and joking and performing all sorts of antics, making beelines for their homes'.[21] When Chelmsford eventually heard the news of the NNC's departure, to add to his morass of troubles, he tactlessly inferred that Sir Henry Bulwer – with whom it will be remembered he had earlier squabbled on the subject of the NNC – was in some manner responsible for their going.

Chelmsford and his retinue covered sixty miles on the first day, killing two horses in the process, and spent the night in the postcart stables at Modderspruit, twelve miles short of Ladysmith. Early the next morning they pushed on another sixty miles to Estcourt where Chelmsford dispensed with his escort and travelled the remaining distance of ninety miles to Pietermaritzburg by carriage. 'By carriage' it will be noted, not postcart, which was the fastest way of covering distance by wheeled transport. Was it in the privacy of the carriage that Chelmsford and Crealock discussed the defeat of Isandlwana (for which they were largely responsible) and decided to pass the blame onto the shoulders of others? After all, Glyn was the column commander – and what of Durnford?

Chelmsford reached Pietermaritzburg on the evening of the 26th to discover the city and the whole of Natal in a state of panic. The victorious Zulu army was expected to invade at any moment. No's 2 and 3 Columns had ceased to exist. Colonel Charles Pearson's No 1 Column had crossed into Zululand by the Lower Thukela Drift and on the 22nd had fought and won a battle at the Nyazane River. Then, having pushed on into Zululand, the Column found itself besieged in the Lutheran Mission Station of kwaMondi, soon to be known as Fort Eshowe, the place where the first Zulu Christian martyr had met his death two years previously. Only Colonel Evelyn Wood's No 4 Column, now laagered 200 miles away at Thinta's Kop in the Disputed Territory, remained intact. However, at Utrecht, the nearest town to Thintas Kop, 'complete panic prevailed'.

Along the border road between Rorke's Drift and Greytown, the invasion route traversed only six weeks earlier by No 3 Column with bands playing, was now a dangerous territory littered with supply wagons abandoned by their drivers fleeing to the dubious safety of Greytown where, within its laager, thirty-two criminals were imprisoned in three small cells guarded by one white official and four native policemen. The jail also served as an arsenal for a quantity of rifles and ammunition. The nearest troops were sixty miles away, the Zulu border only forty. An army convoy close to Helpmekaar, carrying ammunition destined for Rorke's Drift, had halted immediately on encountering the first of the fugitives. Fearing its precious load of ammunition might fall into enemy hands, the ammunition had been off-loaded and buried, never to be found again, torrential rains obliterating all traces of its location. Norris-Newman, the war correspondent, also along the border road, encountered various troops and convoys, all stunned, anxious and incredulous at the rumours of the disaster that fleeing fugitives, both black and white, spread as they fled onward into Natal and beyond.[22]

At Pietermaritzburg and Durban the citizens, and what remained of the military, organized defence committees. Entrenchments had been dug, buildings had been sandbagged and loopholed and barricades erected. Town guards had been formed and in Durban fifty-nine different buildings, including the Masonic Hall, the Durban Club, a convent, the Town Hall, warehouses, homes and banks had all been turned into mini-fortifications.[23] These buildings sheltered a total of 2,700 women and children who were protected by 500 town guards, 100 Royal Durban Rifles and 171 men, all ranks, of the 88th Regiment,recently arrived from the Cape. The disparity in numbers between local and imperial soldiery gives an indication of how few British troops remained to defend the Colony. One lady commented 'I rubbed my eyes when I awoke this morning, scarcely realizing the fact that I was safe in my bed and no Zulus outside in possession of Durban.' However, for many colonists feeling safe in bed in Durban was not safe enough. They would feel more secure in the Cape. Suddenly, there was an exodus. Within days the ships *Nyanza*, *Dunkeld*, *Roman*, *Venice* and the Royal Mail steamer *Africa* were busy evacuating the population of Natal. The passengers were mainly women and children, including the lately widowed wives of the 1/24th soldiery killed at Isandlwana. The *Times of Natal* remarked as the faint-hearted left, 'The people whose fate it is to have to stay and face the Zulu crisis, are apt to be facetious at the expense of the runaways, but some are honest enough to say they would like to follow.'

Chapter 10

'I regret I have to report a very disastrous engagement ...'

Lord Chelmsford to Secretary of State

The dreadful and inexplicable news of Isandlwana had reached Pietermaritzburg long before Lord Chelmsford arrived in the city. Sir Bartle Frere had been awakened at 10 pm on the 24th by his private secretary, William Lyttelton, who had been raised from his bed moments earlier by Captain Wally Stafford and Lieutenant Harry Davies of the NNC. Both men had miraculously survived the battle. They had ridden hard, having barely drawn rein since crossing the Buffalo River and overnighting at Helpmekaar. Russell's NMP trooper, carrying Lord Chelmsford's despatch, would only reach Pietermaritzburg the following day.[1] Norris-Newman, of the *London Standard*, had ridden even harder, hoping to be the first to telegraph the news to Cape Town for onward transmission to St Vincent by steamer. From there it would be telegraphed to the British capital, scooping all others with the sensational news. However, his plan was to be foiled. Frere's official despatch, telegraphed a little earlier, was intercepted by the Reuters man at St Vincent. He undoubtedly bribed the telegraphist, and the *Times* was first with the news on 11 February.

By noon on the 24th many colonists were aware that something terrible had happened in Zululand and it was being widely rumoured that Colonel Durnford had been killed.[2] In view of these 'groundless and alarming' statements it was deemed prudent to issue an official announcement. At noon the following morning a despatch was displayed at the Pietermaritzburg Telegraphic Office. It was brief, uninformative and far from re-assuring:

> A heavy engagement has taken place ten miles from Rourke's [*sic*] Drift with Colonel Durnford's Column. Lord Chelmsford was also engaged. No news from Colonel Pearson.Further particulars will be published when received.[3]

Frere's most imperative duty was to contact London. He had to inform the British Government that without its authorization he had ordered the invasion of Zululand, and that in doing so the general to whom he had entrusted the mission had suffered a catastrophic defeat. Knowing that by now Chelmsford must soon reach the capital, Frere stayed his hand, pending his arrival. As for Sir Theophilus Shepstone, the third member of the conspiracy, he was safely out of the way in distant Pretoria where, as Special Commissioner to the Transvaal, he had resided for the last year and more. Shepstone need have no concern except, that by now, he would most likely have been aware that his son George had been killed at Isandlwana.

Chelmsford and his staff arrived worn and weary in Pietermaritzburg in the evening of Sunday 24th. They rode straight to Government House. The exchange of greetings between the High Commissioner and the General has not been recorded but their mutual emotion was undoubtedly that of the deepest consternation. Queen and Country would demand answers to many difficult questions.

The following morning, Frere was first with a telegraph to Sir Michael Hicks Beach, the Secretary of State for the Colonies.[4] The telegram commenced with the usual pompous greetings and recitation of titles typical of Victorian correspondence. Its lack of punctuation and irrational use of brackets perhaps indicating the writer's stress and concern.

From High Commissioner Natal 27 January 1879 from his excellency Sir Bartle Frere Pietermaritzburg Natal 27 January 1879 to the right honourable the Secretary of State for the Colonies Colonial Office Downing Street London SW [Lord Chelmsford wishes the following to be sent to the right honourable the Secretary of State for War] [from Lieutenant General Lord Chelmsford commanding Her Majesty's forces Cape of Good Hope Pietermaritzburg Natal 27th January 1879 – to the right honourable the Secretary of State for War Office Pall Mall London].

Lord Chelmsford then took over and dropped the bombshell:

I regret to have to report a very disastrous engagement which took place on the Twenty second January eighteen seventy nine between the Zulus and a portion of number three Column left to guard the camp about ten miles in front of Rorke's Drift the Zulus came down in overwhelming numbers and in spite of the gallant resistance made by five Companies first battalion twenty fourth and one Company second battalion of the same regiment two guns two rocket tubes one hundred and four mounted men and about eight hundred natives they overwhelmed them. The Camp containing all the supplies ammunition and transport of No 3 column was taken and but few of its defenders escaped.[5]

Chelmsford went on to count the number of officers and men lost, to advise that a Court of Enquiry had been assembled and that a full report would follow by mail. He speculated further that 'The troops had been enticed away from the camp as the action took place about one mile and a quarter outside it', making no reference to where or what he and his column were doing at Mangeni nor of the number of reports he had received informing him that the camp was under attack. He then stressed the need for reinforcements and detailed their composition.

Chelmsford next telegraphed Colonel Frederick Stanley who, young at 38 years, was ADC to Queen Victoria and the Secretary of State for War. The document was brief, outlining the contents of his earlier despatch to the Colonial Office but stipulating that the cavalry reinforcements requested should be prepared to act as mounted infantry, and also that they carry swords, shorter than the regulation pattern, fastened to the saddle.

Frere wrote directly to Field Marshal His Royal Highness the Duke of Cambridge, Commander-in-Chief of the British Army. Although a cousin of the Queen and having been long entrenched at Horse Guards, the Duke was no toy soldier. He had learnt his soldiering the hard way during the Crimean War twenty-five years earlier. Frere alluded to the 'sad disaster' and how he had collected what information that had come to hand from fugitives, often 'excited, exhausted and uneducated men'. He then made mention of Chelmsford:

Your Royal Highness will I am sure be delighted to hear that though greatly worn by all he has gone through he is well in health and a few days comparative rest will, I hope, quite set him up. He feels the calamity the more because he is naturally adverse, pending the result of the Enquiry he has ordered, to express any opinion as to who of the poor fellows who are gone was to be blamed for the undoubted neglect of orders which led to the disaster.[6]

Thus in a few lines Frere made plain that he supported Chelmsford and exonerated him from blame. Instead he implied that the guilty party was he who had disobeyed Chelmsford's orders, presumably either Lieutenant Colonel Pulleine or Brevet-Colonel Durnford. Frere alleged that both men had received written orders from Chelmsford hours before the battle commenced. It was implied he who had been given command was responsible for the disaster. These crucial instructions as to who was to command had, it seems, unfortunately been lost during the looting and destruction of the camp (except, it will be remembered, Henry Francis Fynn, on visiting the battlefield later in May stated he had found 'Lord Chelmsford's orders of the night of Tuesday 21st January, 1879, amongst the rocks close to Colonel Glyn's headquarter tent and sent them to Lord Chelmsford'). Of the two commanders it was Pulleine's reputation that was to

HRH The Duke of Cambridge, Field Marshal Commanding the British Army and cousin to Queen Victoria.

be protected. Pulleine had transferred into the 24th Regiment twenty-one years earlier, had seen service with the 24th from Rangoon to the Cape Frontier and was a tough but likeable officer. Not only that, he had died fighting with his men whose 'glorious' demise would evoke both the admiration and wrath of the Empire. Colonel Durnford, on the other hand, was not of a line regiment, nor a combatant officer in the true sense. He was a Royal Engineer. Furthermore, he had been in South Africa for so long he could almost be regarded as a colonial.[7] Yet due to the adverse remarks he had made in 1873 concerning the conduct of the Natal Carbineers, he was not popular in the colony. Both officers were dead but the choice was obvious. Durnford was to be the scapegoat. Frere continued: 'It will probably never be known how such a large body of the enemy got so close without being seen and their force earlier reported, nor why the main column with the General was not appraised and recalled earlier in the day.'[8]

Chelmsford, it would seem, had not confessed to Frere that there had been several sightings of a Zulu presence on the 21st in close proximity to the camp. Nor, it seems, had he mentioned the rumours and reports he had received at Mangeni. He either misled Frere or Frere decided, for the benefit of their mutual protection, to go along with Chelmsford's deception in an endeavour to keep him out of trouble. Then, suggesting how the disaster could have occurred, Frere went on to say: '… from all I can learn there was ample time after the enemy were discovered [word illegible] the detaching companies of the 24th more than a mile from the camp instead of concentrating them as was objected to by Colonel Pulleine, when Lieutenant Colonel Durnford took command'.[9] Then, in an effort to justify his unauthorized invasion, Frere vigorously appraised Cambridge that despite the disaster of Isandlwana, it was fortunate the initiative had been taken and that the menace of the Zulu Kingdom was being dealt with:

> I cannot describe the panic which this great misfortune has created in the colony among European as well as natives – and those who a week or so again were loudest in denouncing the necessarily large scale of the columns and [word illegible] that the Zulus were powerless as well as helpless, are now most aghast at finding on what a volcano they have been sleeping…. . but I feel assured that if H.M. Govt. will send the re-enforcements asked for and steadily resolve not to desist till the Zulus are subdued, there may be a lasting peace in South Africa which was hopeless as long as the Native Tribes in this and the other colonies looked on the Zulu king as invincible. I only trust that we shall not be obliged to hold our hands till the supremacy of Her Majesty is as clearly established here as in the Cape.[10]

Frere, further to the earlier telegram he had sent to Hicks Beach on Lord Chelmsford's behalf, penned a long despatch of his own.

> Sir, The telegrams which will reach you by the mail steamer leaving Cape Town on the 28th inst. will have given Her Majesty's Government the leading facts of the disaster which occurred to the camp of Colonel Glyn's (No 3) column, a day's march from Rorke's Drift, when it was surprised by an overwhelming force of Zulus, and Lieutenant Colonel Durnford, RE, who had just taken the command from Lieutenant Colonel Pulleine, 1/24th [the first direct accusation that Durnford had taken command], and the whole camp equipage and stores were taken and destroyed…. . there appears however to be no doubt that the Zulu force, which was composed of many thousand men of the younger regiments, the elite of the Zulu army, took the camp by surprise that in disregard of Lord Chelmsford's instructions, the troops left to protect the camp were taken away from the

defensive position they were in at the camp, with the shelter which the wagons, parked, would have afforded, that they were then surrounded and fairly overwhelmed by force of numbers... . Lord Chelmsford was not informed of the attack till late in the day; he immediately moved back to the camp but arrived after nightfall to find it destroyed and deserted.... I need not attempt to describe the extreme excitement caused in this colony by this misfortune. Its effects will, doubtless, spread throughout South Africa. The loss of such a large portion of one of the finest and best known of Her Majesty's regiments would be a grievous shock to this and to the Cape Colony; but among the Volunteers, Police and leaders of Native contingents, were over a hundred young colonists belonging to the best known and most highly respected colonial families... . The tales brought home by the survivors [NNC] who have escaped, will carry dismay and terror of the Zulu prowess to every native tribe and location, and spread to tribes far beyond Natal... . But there is no reason to doubt the ultimate success of his [Chelmsford's] plans for the defence of the British Colonies from inroads and for defeating the armies and putting down the military system of Cetshwayo, which is clearly incompatible with the existence of any civilized community near him ... for it is clear that nothing but the iron despotism of Cetshwayo keeps together his hordes of desperate gladiators; that when the rules laid down by military authority are followed those hordes are by no means invincible ... From other parts of South Africa I have received only uniform intelligence of the intense interest with which the contest with Cetshwayo is watched by every race and class, especially by the native tribes.[11]

During the morning of the 27th Lord Chelmsford resolved to write to the Duke of Cambridge, a person who could end his career and bring him back to Britain in disgrace – or even have him court-martialled or worse; after all, it was only 122 years since a British admiral, John Byng, when having lost Minorca to the French, was found guilty of 'failing to do his utmost' and was shot by firing squad. Chelmsford endeavoured to justify the invasion and avoid blame. He wrote:

Your Royal Highness, Sir, I cannot allow this mail to leave without sending your Royal Highness a few lines, although I can add no additional facts to the telegram and despatch I am sending this day to the Secretary of State. We have certainly been seriously underrating the power of the Zulu army

and it is fortunate for Natal that Cetshwayo never ordered it to cross the border when there was but one battalion in the colony and no Colonial defence worth mentioning. From our present experience it is evident that one year ago the Zulu army could have swept through Natal from one end to the other without any possibility of stopping it. The Zulus appear to have no fear whatsoever of death and although mowed down by hundreds at a time they quietly filled up the gaps and moved on. It is sickening to think of the terrible loss of life which has taken place and [word illegible] to consider the rich booty which the Zulu army has carried off. The garrison at the camp appears to have been scattered about one mile and a quarter in front of the camp it was ordered to defend, and of course fought at a very great disadvantage by not being together and by having both its flanks unprotected. It will be a melancholy satisfaction to your Royal Highness to know that the imperial troops fought in the most gallant manner and that their courage and determination is the theme of wonders and amazement amongst the natives who saw them fight, and who escaped to tell the tale …
I trust your Royal Highness will support my application for more troops. The crisis is a very serious one and I am in daily dread of hearing that some misfortune has happened to Colonel Wood's or Colonel Pearson's column. The disparity of numbers brought against our troops is so enormous and the difficulties of moving in a country without roads is so great that it is almost impossible to avoid giving an intelligent and very brave enemy some opportunities of striking a successful blow.[12]

Accompanying the despatches of the Commissioner and the General was an extraordinary yet influential letter. The Pietermaritzburg despatches went straight to Government House, Cape Town where they were received by Lady Frere, who was acting as her husband's ADC or private secretary, for onward transmission to London. On receipt of the documents in Cape Town they became privy, it would seem, to other members of the Frere family, certainly to Mary, the 33-year-old eldest and spinster daughter. Mary had spent many years in India and was a child of eleven when the Mutiny (now called the First Indian War of Independence) broke out. She was well aware of its many horrors. The present situation in South Africa suggested to her that an uprising of all the tribes was about to follow, accompanied by a fate for all too dreadful to contemplate.

Mary had decided – with or without her father's knowledge remains unknown – to write to Queen Victoria herself, albeit through the letterbox of Sir Henry

Ponsonby, the Queen's Private Secretary for the last nine years ('… the main source of communication between Her Majesty and those who wished to seek permission or opinion …'[13]), a man who undertook the great responsibilities placed upon him by the Queen. Mary's was a letter written in a racing and erratic hand, reflecting apprehension, indignation and her determination to protect her father and Lord Chelmsford. It was addressed from Government House, Cape Town 27.1.79. She began:

> Dear General Ponsonby. You will have heard by official Telegram the sorrowful tidings of our great sorrow … the General had advanced (it is here believed) to [the] support of [a] smaller force in advance who were in search of [a] large body of Zulus and when he was sixteen miles off the camp 1/24th and NNC were attacked by 15,000 or 20,000 Zulus who by sheer weight of numbers exterminated our men. The Zulus that night attacked the entrenched camp of the 2/24th but were repulsed. Gnl. Coming up to their support via the camp [Isandlwana] of 1/24th. The Gnl. returned to PMB wch. it was feared wd be immediately attacked and wch.is in a hollow in a circle of hills and quite indefensible. The object is to keep the Zulus if possible out of Natal itself. The fear is of the whole country being overrun, of its [native] population rising, of those with whom we were at war [the amaXhosa in the Cape, the 9th Frontier War] for seven months last year around Cape KWT [King Williams Town] and of a repetition at PMB [Pietermaritzburg] of the siege of Lucknow.

Mary continued and, tentatively, placed the downfall of the Isandlwana Camp on the shoulders of Colonel Durnford: 'Colonel Durnford RE commanding Natal Native Contingent was senior officer, I believe, in Natal … he was in the war agt. Langalebalele when his men were cut to pieces and himself escaped only and a sergeant survived.' A gross exaggeration: only three men and Durnford's native interpreter were killed out of a force of forty-five Carbineers, Durnford himself being wounded. Mary proceeded to mention various officers by name who had been killed at Isandlwana and then gave her idea of the reinforcements required:'The great need is for Mounted men to withstand weight and break masses of infantry [Zulus] and find out where they are. The Zulus travel nearly as fast as men on horseback. They are reckless of death for if they return home unvictorios they are put to death.' She then hammered home the wisdom and the merit of her father and Lord Chelmsford:

What my father foresaw has occurred. Our present struggle is for national as well as personal existence. There is entire confidence in my father and in the general who has already done miracles to reorganize the confusion arising from the loss, [at that moment Chelmsford had accomplished little other than organize the Court of Enquiry and pen his despatches] … my father is you may be sure doing in every way all that is possible to do to maintain confidence. The entire and absolute confidence felt in him – and [word illegible] is the one human strength we have in this time of trial. The strain is tremendous upon him but he trusts as you know in a higher strength than his own. But I must not disguise from you that the danger is very extreme. He may not be living when you receive this …, The enemies to be resisted are not only the Zulus and their Kaffirs but the Boers and English who have so cruelly ill-treated them; the gun runners, brandy smugglers and other lawless men who have made this rich and beautiful country a very volcano. The government must feel it has the national support of England [and the] backing of HM's govt. in sending in the aid so imperatively needed…. . I feel that it is impossible he [her father] should himself ask for support that can be given him in vain.

Mary then gave a brief resume of troop movements as far as she knew them, begged to be excused for an untidy letter, signed herself 'Yours very truly Mary Frere' and added a postscript: 'If the Queen should think good to send a message of sympathy to the poor women of the 1/24th they would I know feel deeply Her Majesty's gracious condescension.'[14] Judging by Queen Victoria's reaction when the news of Isandlwana reached London on 11 February, it would seem that Mary also sent her letter by telegraph. What would the Queen make of Mary's letter? Her Majesty would, of course, have heard of the incomprehensible news that one of her finest regiments had been destroyed whilst under the command of Frederic Thesiger, a favourite of the Royal Family. Chelmsford had enjoyed the Queen's patronage and would continue to do so. On his return to England seven months later he would be immediately summoned to Balmoral where the Queen would confer upon him the Insignia of the Grand Cross of the Bath. The Freres' were also well known. Sir Bartle had escorted the Prince of Wales during the Prince's visit to India in 1875. Lady Frere would shortly receive a comforting letter from the Prince: 'I cannot tell you how my thoughts have constantly been with you and good Sir Bartle during the last six weeks …'. And now for the Queen to contemplate was this letter from a brave and devoted daughter who, though clearly in peril, pleaded not for herself but for justice for her father, for the General and for Southern Africa. Yet at that moment the Queen had great concerns and grief of her own to contend with. Alice, her own dear daughter, who had been constantly at Prince Albert's side before he died in 1861, had now herself died of fever seven weeks earlier, on the seventeenth anniversary of her father's death. The Queen, broken hearted, had looked upon this coincidence as 'Almost incredible and most mysterious'. Possibly the Queen felt an empathy with Sir Bartle's daughter who, like Alice, was so devoted to her father in his time of need. The Queen would shortly dictate a response.

A week after her first letter to Ponsonby, Mary wrote again enclosing maps of Zululand, collected by her mother and which Mary begged Sir Henry to present to the Queen '… knowing that my father would wish a copy of such to be sent to her Majesty'. Mary continued: 'It appears to be, as we are told but not from Pietermaritzburg, too sadly true that the body of poor Colonel Durnford was decapitated and the head taken, it is presumed to Cetewayo [sic Cetshwayo] who would have known him as having surveyed the country. A price had been set by Cetewayo on his head – we fear this is true!' She then continued with a different version of the battle followed by, 'It appears there were printed orders that the camps were to be entrenched and that those left behind by the Genl. on this occasion were, I believe, ordered to act on the defensive in search of the Zulus … Many things will probably never be explained but when the result of the court of enquiry ordered by the general are published much will probably be known wch. is not so at present [Chelmsford would have been in possession of the court's findings for a week but had not disclosed them]. Durnford then came under scrutiny again. Mary wrote: 'The prevailing idea here at present is that Colonel Durnford coming up to the camp and not entrenching it engaged the Zulus and summoned those in the camp to his aid – others think he had apparently first reached the camp and subsequently quitted it.'[15]

Perhaps the first intimation that Durnford was responsible for the downfall of the camp inadvertently came from Lieutenant Davies' report to the press of 27 January. After Davies and his companion Captain Stafford had carried the dramatic news to Frere, it was realized that Davies was a local man, Pietermaritzburg born and bred. Not only that, he had as a lad been 'a much respected' staff member of the *Times of Natal* which, with the rest of the town, lionized Davies. Because Davies was with Durnford's column, his knowledge was more or less limited to Durnford's involvement. Consequently, the *Times of Natal*'s report of 27 January mentioned Colonels Glyn and Pulleine but once, whereas Durnford is mentioned again and again giving the impression that he was in command.[16]

Mary concluded by enclosing some newspaper cuttings '… which contained various matters regarding the past week'. It is doubtful, however, that the report from the *Cape Argus* of 1 February was included. Lord Chelmsford was also getting a bad press: '*Argus* publishes this morning a telegram from its special correspondent, who states he derives his information from Chief of Intelligence department, who is also special correspondent for *The Natal Witness*. Everything highly coloured: unfavourable to government: accuses Lord Chelmsford of culpable foolhardiness and gross blundering. Tendency to create unfounded alarm …'

Whatever the truth of the report, it was certainly mistaken in one aspect. The Chief of Intelligence and the special correspondent for the *Natal Witness* was, of course, the Hon. William Drummond who had, in fact, resigned as Special Correspondent due to the *Natal Witness*'s article of 30 January 1879, censuring Chelmsford, a portion of which read '… taking the disaster first, it is no use denying that it is complete and unmitigated. We have had, in the annals of our army, other instances of regiments being decimated, we have had other instances, even in South Africa itself, of disheartening losses of military material. But scarcely ever, if indeed, ever at all, have such losses remained unbalanced by some advantage.'

Chapter 11

'I have no desire whatever to shift any of the responsibility …'

Lord Chelmsford to Colonel Glyn

The despatches sent earlier on 27 January 1879 would arrive in London fourteen days later on 10 February, but the more detailed reports, travelling all the way by steamship, would take approximately thirty days.[1] While Frere and Chelmsford held their breath, wrestling with the anxiety of Whitehall's anticipated rebuke. Chelmsford, nevertheless, had been commendably energetic. He had ridden to Durban and the mouth of the Thukela and successfully opened communications with Colonel Pearson's No 1 Column, still under siege at kwaMondi. Writing on 2 February, Chelmsford hammered home how essential it would be to bring on the enemy and fight from behind entrenchments. 'Should the Zulus disappoint us and refuse to attack you, then combined arrangements will have to be concerted between your garrison and the lower Thukela [*sic*] force…'

Chelmsford went on to make light of the disaster of Isandlwana, especially his part in it: 'Altho- the misfortune of the twenty second was a very severe one, the Zulus suffered a very severe loss – we have beaten them five times out of six and humanly speaking we ought to have beaten them on the twenty second, but the forces instead of being kept together were scattered about, and at least a mile from the camp they were ordered to defend.'[2]

Chelmsford also gave thought to Colonel Glyn and the remnants of No 3 Column which were still enduring cold, discomfort, filth and fever at Rorke's Drift and Helpmekaar. After the mass desertion of the NNC, all of the cavalry and artillery – except for a few horsemen required for scouting purposes – had been moved up to Helpmekaar, leaving space for all within the temporary fort. Using whatever material that came to hand, the defences continued to be improved. Within a few days a search was made across the Buffalo for the bodies of Lieutenants Melvill and Coghill. It was known that at the height of the battle they had escaped the camp carrying the Queen's Colour of the 1/24th, had successfully negotiated

Fugitive's Trail, had swum the Buffalo River and had reached the Natal bank. Not only were their bodies found but after an extensive search along the flooded banks of the river, the Colour and its pole were dragged from the water. Later in the day, in a simple ceremony, the Colour was presented to Colonel Glyn who received it with tears running down his cheeks, so moved was the old soldier. Nevertheless, there was little cause for cheer for those at the Drift except there was now no shortage of food. However, apart from receiving new blankets, the garrison had little or no shelter from the elements, were unable to keep dry, had no change of clothing and were thus easy victims to disease and fever. Colonel Glyn fared no better. Clery wrote on 4 February, 'My present abode consists of a tarpaulin held up by some sticks and this I share with Colonel Glyn and the other Staff Officer. We have a little straw to lie on, but as this is the rainy season and the rains come down in torrents, our straw gets very soaky at times.' They were also constantly disturbed by a pack of twenty dogs, 'Newfoundlands, Pointers, Setters, and other notable breeds, all with collars'. Distressed survivors of Isandlwana? In fact, the pack attacked Captain Maxwell of the NNC '… making the most hideous noise …' then followed him'barking and howling for four hundred yards before running away'.[3] They soon returned, never allowing anyone to get near them. Their howling – and the likelihood that they were feeding on the bodies of the dead – became so disturbing that they were eventually shot. But most reprehensible of all were the floggings. Trooper Fred Symmons, as a Colonial and Volunteer, was immune from such treatment, no matter what, but the poor soldiers, to the shame of the British Army, were still being flogged on active service sometime after the barbaric punishment had been abolished in the Royal Navy and in British prisons. Symons relates how the troops, after their exertions of the forced marches to and from Mangeni and the night in the stricken camp, were '… thoroughly weak from the loss of sleep but, nevertheless, were almost worked to death …' reinforcing the barricades.[4] Consequently two unfortunates fell asleep on sentry duty. Next morning the garrison was summoned to witness the soldiers' punishment. The troops formed a square with a gun carriage in the middle. One after another the prisoners were tied across a carriage wheel and given fifty lashes with the cat-o'-nine-tails. Symons commented that he felt he could shoot the officer responsible but did not name him.

Conditions six miles away up the escarpment at Helpmekaar were equally bad. Having completed the Court of Enquiry, Colonel Hassard was then responsible for the fortification of the store now being structured under his direction. It was built in the worst spot anyone could have chosen, in a basin of ground receiving drainage from three sides. The troops were compelled to go into laager at night

Although flogging had been banned in the Royal Navy for some years, during the Zulu War there were numerous incidents of this brutal punishment. On 3 December 1878, Lord Chelmsford issued orders to his column commanders instructing them that any Imperial or native soldier transgressing orders would be liable to a flogging. (*The Graphic*, 5 April 1879)

and as Trooper Clarke remarked '… they had no option but to lay on the muddy ground, exposed to wind and rain, suffering the smell of the hot stench arising from rotting sacks of mealie flour and oats built into the wall of the laager'. Fred Symons remembered that '… if you looked into the enclosure on a stormy night you would see men sitting down in their wet clothes, unable to sleep and giving vent to their misery in deep groans'. It was a breeding-ground for fever and many who by a miracle had escaped the battlefield, had run the gauntlet of the Fugitive's Trail and the perils of the river crossing were within a few days to die of fever at Helpmekaar. Their lonely graves, whitewashed annually and blessed with a bunch of flowers, are still there.

    Less than three weeks after Isandlwana Glyn received a letter, dated 7 February, from Lord Chelmsford. It was not a personal letter as written to Colonel Pearson. Nor did it resemble the camaraderie of the correspondence between Chelmsford and Colonel Wood of No 4 Column. Glyn's letter came via the spiky pen of Deputy Adjutant General and Quartermaster General Colonel Bellairs, an experienced soldier and staff officer. Bellairs had fought in several major battles of the Crimea War, had served in the West Indies, Ireland, Gibraltar and recently in the 9th Frontier War. His letter, coming out of the blue, was accusatory and reproachful in tone:

Lieutenant Chard's report of the enemy attack of the 22nd ultimo on Rorke's Drift post has been received, but none from you of the movements of your column from the day of its leaving to the time of its retuning to Rorke's Drift, or the occurrence which took place in the interval. Please to be particular in the time of your taking up the position at Isandlwana. Furnish a sketch showing the formation of the camp; how the guards and picquets were disposed; where the alarm posts were placed; whether they were occupied in the evening and morning, the position of the wagon laagers, and etcetera. All with reference to the instructions on these heads laid down in Field Force regulations, paragaphs 16 and 21.[5]

The paragraphs referred to, 16 to 21, concerned details of 'formation of the camp' and 'guards and picquets by day'.

There is no doubt that Glyn saw through Bellairs' innocuous words, words baited to trap a scapegoat. It must have been salt in the wounds of his misery; his grief at the loss of his regiment, the humiliation of defeat and the present predicament of the survivors of No 3 Column. Glyn, however, sensed a trap and took his time. He responded on 14 February, merely quoting various regulations but adding that daily reports covering Bellairs' questions had been submitted earlier to Colonel Crealock; furthermore, Bellairs himself had already been sent details covering the events of Isandlwana. On 18 February, Bellairs testily responded snapping that Glyn's previous report '… as you will perceive by the minute referred to, is not as full as desired as to time, and does not enter into details enquired about. Be good enough to supplement your account as soon as possible.'[6]

Crealock also took the opportunity to lash out. Glyn having mentioned in his report of the 14 February that he had already been given the details sought, Crealock's hackles rose. He immediately dashed off a 500-word memorandum to Lord Chelmsford itemizing his objections.[7] Crealock's memorandum set Chelmsford to composing one of his own. Addressing Bellairs, Chelmsford began 'I have no desire whatever to shift any of the responsibility, which properly belongs to me, on the shoulders of the officer commanding no 3 Column … at the same time I am anxious to make it clear that, by accompanying no 3 Column, I did not accept the responsibility for the numerous details which necessarily have to be considered by an officer commanding a column in the field.' Then, like Crealock, he proceeded to itemise various aspects of contention stating that on joining the column he had explained personally to Glyn that he '… did not wish to interfere in any way with the command of the column';[8] however, with regard to the movement and reconnaissances, he, Chelmsford, was entirely responsible but, nevertheless, he had the right to assume that if Glyn considered any order given to him was likely to be injurious or hazardous to No 3 Column, he would at once have brought it to his notice. Furthermore, he considered Colonel Glyn was bound to inform him if, at any time, Glyn's own judgement dissented from his, he was bound to make such objection known, yet no objection was ever made and therefore he considered his orders had Glyn's approval; on the other hand, Chelmsford continued, had he interfered with the general running of the column, it would have been tantamount to his having taken over command of it, a position which he depreciated 'from the very first'.[9] Chelmsford concluded that he wished Glyn to reply fully to both his and Crealock's memorandums so that there might be no doubt regarding the relative positions occupied by himself and Glyn during the time he was with No 3 Column. Bellairs despatched a rider, carrying both memoranda, hurrying to Rorke's Drift.

Glyn was suddenly on very dangerous ground and out of his depth. Clery, vehemently believing Crealock was attempting to transfer the blame for Isandlwana from Chelmsford's shoulders to Glyn's, drafted his reply, dated 26 February. It was a masterpiece of counter-accusation but couched in 'the most decorous and respectful language'.[10] It began by Glyn referring to his previous responses and how, as far as he could see, he had complied with all that had been required of him. He then got down to business. Addressing Chelmsford's memorandum first, Glyn wrote:

I regret exceedingly that he [Chelmsford] should think from the manner in which the above information was conveyed to you that I sought to evade any of the responsibility devolving on me as Officer Commanding No 3 Column. I have no desire to do so, and I consider that during the time his Excellency was present with the Third Column, I was as fully responsible for the numerous details which necessarily have to be considered by an officer commanding a column in the field, as I was before his Excellency joined the column, and as I have been since he left it.... . As regards outposts and the ordinary precautions for safety of the camp, I consider for all these arrangements I was solely responsible. I lay as much stress as I am able on these different points, as I am anxious to remove from the Lieutenant General's mind the impression that I regret that he seems to labour under, that I seek to have sought to evade any responsibility that devolves upon me.... . I was certainly not aware that if I had been to consider that if any proposed movement of the Lieutenant General Commanding were in any way hazardous that I should have at once brought the fact to his notice, nor that if my judgement dissented from a movement the General had ordered I was bound to inform him of it. I was certainly not aware that my position called on me, or entitled me to do this, and indeed I was under the impression that it would have been presumptuous on my part to have done so. I might add that even had I understood this position towards his Excellency in this matter, as I appear not to have done, yet considering that the only Intelligence department on the force was entirely at the disposal and under the control of his Excellency and his staff and being aware that his Excellency was obliged to consider in all that he did the movements and interests of the other columns of the army, I certainly would always have been very diffident in volunteering an opinion at first to a movement decided on by his Excellency without having been referred to for an opinion on the matter. Though I am thus compelled to dissent from what his Excellency advances in these two paras I must express my great regret if the erroneous views I appear to have entertained in my position was due to a misunderstanding of mine, but having been ordered by his Excellency to reply on this matter I can only state what was the case, and greatly regret my error if I am answerable for it.[11]

Then Glyn cast the gauntlet of Pulleine's forgotten message into the fray:

I regret the omission made by me in the report on the occurrences of 22nd January in not mentioning the receipt of information during that day from the officer commanding the camp at Isandlwana. One communication only was received from the officer on that day. It is now before me, and the hour of its being sent from the camp is entered on it at 8.5am; the contents are as follows: 'Staff Officer. Report just come in that the Zulus are advancing in force from left front of the camp (8.5). Signed H.B. Pulleine, Lieutenant Colonel'. The hour of its reception is entered as 9:30 o' Clock with the initials H.P. {Hallam Parr).

   This memorandum was received by my senior staff officer, Major Clery. I saw him hand it at once to the Lieutenant General, who was close to him, before he showed it to me…. Further, my Senior Staff Officer, Major Clery, assures me that no answer was sent by him or with his knowledge to this memo. He adds that he is the more confident about this as when the Lieutenant General handed him back the memo above referred to, he asked His Excellency, 'Is there anything to be done with this?' His Excellency at once replied, 'There is nothing to be done on that.' I might also state that I have the distinct recollection of hearing His Excellency reply to this effect to either Major Clery or Lieutenant Colonel Crealock for I was close by all that time….'[12]

The reference to Pulleine's note, clearly disturbing to Chelmsford and his staff, was enough to squash any further attempt to hold Glyn accountable. Instead of responding to Glyn, Chelmsford addressed a subdued and defensive letter to Bellairs. Glyn appeared to be off the hook. But Chelmsford was far from finished with him. Soon the Duke of Cambridge was demanding answers to questions that Chelmsford was unable to answer truthfully, causing him to become so rattled that he, unthinkably, was sharp with the Duke:

I have done my best to obtain every snip of information regarding that unfortunate day which was procurable, and if it is not considered sufficient, the fault lies in its want and not in my desire to [not?] furnish it. As the evidence [the Court of Enquiry] is before your Royal Highness, I feel that I am justified in pointing out that it would be hardly fair to saddle me with the responsibility of any neglect of details connected with the command of No. 3 Column, for the performance of which the officer commanding the column was held accountable to me … When I ordered the troops to leave camp on the 22nd I entered into no details with regard to their reserve (regimental) ammunition, taking for granted, as I believe was the case, that it would be sent with them as a matter of course … This did not, of course, prevent me from drawing Colonel Glyn's attention to any points in his arrangements which appeared to me capable of any improvement … I have been thus particular in drawing Your Royal Highness' attention to the particular position held by me with regard to the command of No. 3 Column, as from what I can gather an attempt has been made to saddle me with responsibilities which did not properly belong to me. I have no desire to cast any blame upon Colonel Glyn. His evidence will be before Your Royal Highness and will speak for itself – all I ask is that, should it be considered that important column details were neglected, either before or after 22nd Jan., the fact that I was not in actual command of No. 3 Column may not be lost sight of …[13]

Yet in spite of Chelmsford's attempt to incriminate him, Glyn went on to command the 2nd Division at Ulundi, the final battle of the Anglo-Zulu War; was created a Commander of the Order of St Michael & St George (CMG) rose to the rank of Major General, and in 1887, at the age of 56, retired with the honorary rank of Lieutenant General.

Chapter 12

'Her Majesty places entire confidence in you and the troops, to maintain our honour and name'

12 February 1879

The telegram sent by Frere and Chelmsford on 27 January arrived in London on 10 February to be read and read again by Queen Victoria's incredulous ministers. Writing to Chelmsford, Adjutant-General Sir Charles Ellice, on behalf of the Duke of Cambridge, expressed the Duke's perplexity.

> His Royal Highness is well aware that your Lordship's despatch was written when many and grave affairs requiring your instant attention were pressing upon you and it was impossible a complete narrative could at that time be framed. His Royal Highness is in hope of receiving by the next mail the report of the Court of Enquiry which you ordered to assemble and which he trusts will elicit full information upon all those points which do not at present appear perfectly clear. But in case it does not cover the whole of the ground in regard to which information is sought by the Government and public opinion in this country, his Royal Highness thinks it right to draw your attention to the following points on which he would like full details …

Sir Charles Ellice went on relentlessly to demand answers to seven specific issues including: Why was the camp not laagered? Why was the enemy, so close to the camp, not detected? Why was no reconnaissance made? Why was Pulleine's message ignored? Were arrangements made for reserve ammunition to accompany the reconnaissance of the 22nd.? Ellice concluded: 'His Royal Highness has no doubt that upon all these points, your Lordship will be able to give most satisfactory replies.'[1]

But His Royal Highness was to be disappointed and further exasperated when the long-awaited details of the Court of Enquiry finally arrived. Both

Chelmsford and Frere could anticipate harsher words to follow. But both were saved by the immediate intervention by none other than Queen Victoria. She was informed of the disaster by Sir Henry Ponsonby during the morning of 10 February when Ponsonby passed her a copy of the Frere/Chelmsford joint telegram that he had just received from Colonel Stanley, the Secretary of State for War. At the time both the Queen and Ponsonby were at Osborne, the Queen's residence on the Isle of Wight. Ponsonby advised Her Majesty 'The disaster is a fearful one and will affect our arms everywhere as the enemy will exhort in declaring the British troops are vulnerable. With but few details it is impossible to offer any explanation to the nation ...'[2]

On receipt of such news it seems improbable that the Queen, fond of Chelmsford though she may have been would, without reference to her other ministers or the Duke of Cambridge, have impulsively instructed Stanley to inform Lord Chelmsford by telegram that 'The Queen has graciously desired me to say she sympathises most sincerely with you in the dreadful loss which has deprived her of so many gallant officers and men, and that Her Majesty places entire confidence in you and the troops, to maintain our honour and good name.'[3] That, however, was the case. Was it, in fact, merely affection held for Lord Chelmsford that evoked Her Majesty's response or was it Mary Frere's imploring letter that induced the Queen to write as she did? Not only that, the Duke of Cambridge, having been informed of Her Majesty's telegram, and despite the demanding letter that Sir Charles Ellice had already penned, could not contradict his Sovereign. Instead he also sent a supportive message: '... fullest confidence in regiments and satisfied that you have done, and will continue to do, everything that is right. Strong reinforcements to embark at once' (two regiments of cavalry, two batteries of field artillery, six regiments of infantry, three companies of the Army Service Corps and a detachment of the Hospital Corps, in all approximately 7,620 men and 1,600 horses).[4]

Lord Chelmsford was ecstatic. He replied: 'I cannot tell you with what feeling of pride and gratitude I received the gracious message from Her Majesty and from your Royal Highness saying that confidence in me as a commander was unshaken.' Chelmsford went on to remark that he had no hesitation in stating that the confidence of those under his command had also never wavered. However, as an advanced warning and to soften the blow when the opinion of the South African press reached England, he advised the Duke that a certain portion of the local press had commenced 'A series of violent attacks upon Sir Bartle and myself', which would undoubtedly influence public opinion in England. Chelmsford went on to explain that he had studiously avoided giving any opinion as to the cause of the Isandlwana disaster as he considered it 'more dignified to forward all the evidence … and allow the evidence to speak for itself'.[5] It was not what the Duke wanted to hear. Despite Chelmsford's prevarication, Cambridge, having reluctantly or otherwise underpinned the Queen's confidence in her general, would have to go along with the charade for the time being.

Equally ecstatic was Mary Frere. The Queen's message of confidence prompted her into composing a 22-page letter with two enclosures. It was unaddressed but like her previous letters was destined for Colonel Ponsonby. It was written from Government House, Cape Town and headed 'Private. Facts publicly known in Cape Town and in the Colony which answers some of the criticisms of English public opinion as expressed in the English press.'

Having expressed her approval of the Queen's 'most gracious and wise and courageous promptitude' in sending immediate telegrams of sympathy to Lord Chelmsford and her father, she lurched, as she had in previous letters, into a strident lambasting of Colonel Durnford. (Could this be a case of a woman scorned?) 'On receipt of the terrible tidings Isandala [sic] it should be noted that poor Colonel Durnford having been long in the colony and being in command of the Natal Native Contingent, was regarded by the colonists as a representative "Colonial" man. He was on very intimate terms with Bishop Colenso and I have been told much shared his views.' (Bishop Colenso and his daughters were strongly opposed to the invasion of Zululand and fearlessly expressed their sympathy with the Zulu people.) Mary then went on to give her own distorted version of the battle and who was to blame, dramatically comparing the catastrophe with that of an 'iron-clad going down in harbour'. But after eight pages Mary resumed her attack on Durnford

One thing told us regarding Colonel Durnford, if true, explains to me much I did not understand. We are told that after the loss of his men at the time of the war with Langalibalele (when he had called out 'Don't Fire!' to his men, 'till the natives [Langalibalele's warriors] had fired') he used to be called 'Major Don't Fire' by ill-natured, vulgar and ill-minded people, and was so stung by this that he said, in the next war, 'Orders or no orders, he should attack'. We have only heard this from people who knew him here [Cape Town] and have asked others who did not know of it. Whether my father and the General ever heard this I do not know. We never hear of such things till afterwards. If true, it is very strange and accounts for what occurred.

Mary finished her appraisal by expressing her approval of the reinforcements destined for Natal – especially the arrival of HMS *Shah* which she noted '… was known in Zululand almost as soon as here [Cape Town], news amongst the natives travels faster than our own telegraphic information'.[6]

However, back in England, the Queen was, no doubt, regretting her hastily-expressed confidence in Chelmsford and Frere, as Ponsonby had received another document. It had arrived, via Colonel Stanley, from Major-General Sir Archibald Alison, head of Army Intelligence. Before returning the document (replicated in full below), Ponsonby copied it in his own hand for the attention of the Queen. While the establishment fretted over the dearth of enlightenment in Lord Chelmsford's reports, Alison's paper gave, under the circumstances, a surprisingly accurate description of events leading to the destruction of the Isandlwana Camp.

THE ISANDLWANA DISASTER

January 22nd 1879. A memorandum from the Intelligence Department endeavours to describe what took place but as the chief officers are killed much must remain guesswork. Lord Chelmsford arrived on the 20th instant at Isandlwana. He sent out parties to clear the way for his advance on the 21st and when these met Zulus he went with his force on the 22nd to support his outposts.But he does not seem to have fortified the camp at Isandlwana. He did not keep up proper communications with his camp. He was led away by the Zulus who decoyed him from the camp. In the meanwhile the Zulus collected in thousands under the hills near the camp. Speaking was forbidden and they were not discovered. Why were not scouts sent to explore? When Lord Chelmsford left the camp he seems to have been anxious and sent to fetch up with Colonel Durnford from Rorke's Drift. He ordered Colonel Pulleine to draw in his men and defend the camp if attacked. But the Zulus soon appeared and Colonel Pulleine then called in the cattle and began to harness them so as to draw the wagons into a circle. Colonel Durnford arrived and in order to keep the Zulus off while this was being done went out to meet them. Colonel Pulleine refused to allow the 24th to go out but being ordered by Colonel Durnford to help him when beaten back he sent his men out. The Zulus now surrounded them, the native levies fled and the English soldiers attacked front and rear were massacred.[7]

More than likely the paper had been compiled by the Intelligence Department with information derived from one or a number of officers who had accompanied

Lord Chelmsford's reconnaissance and who later had the opportunity to question those survivors of Isandlwana who had pitched up at Rorke's Drift. It was no secret that General Alison had correspondents/informers scattered throughout the British Army; all were personally known to him and some had worked directly under him.[8] But how did the information reach London so soon? Norris-Newman would seem to be the obvious answer. On leaving Rorke's Drift on 24 January he later wrote '… I undertook to be the bearer of any despatches, messages, or telegrams, and received a great many from all ranks from His Excellency [Lord Chelmsford] downwards'.[9]

Norris-Newman could, of course, have been not only the postman but also an Alison informant. Could the Queen have been aware of Alison's report before she instructed Stanley to express her confidence in Chelmsford? It would seem to be unlikely. But having done so, she and the Duke of Cambridge were obliged to justify keeping Chelmsford at the helm of her forces in southern Africa. Despite the Intelligence Department's damning assertion that Chelmsford had been decoyed, and despite the evidence of others in a position to know – Captain Penn Symons '… that the cattle had been seen and retreating bodies of men were simply decoys to entice us away from the camp'[10] and The Hon. William Drummond: '… the General, however, did not, of course, at this time, imagine that the Zulus were carrying out a concerted scheme …'[11] – the Establishment never admitted to Chelmsford having been led away by a preconceived Zulu plan. It would, of course, have been unwise for the Government to do so, to let it be known that a British lieutenant general had been outwitted and out-generalled by native tribesmen. Many, if not the majority of modern academics, military men and battlefield guides, true to the old adage 'History repeats itself and historians repeat each other', adhere to the premise that Chelmsford was not decoyed into leaving the camp and embarking on a wild goose chase. For instance, Lieutenant Colonel Mike Snook, Royal Regiment of Wales: 'It will be obvious to all that I am implacably opposed to the decoy theory',[12] and Ian Knight, historian, '… there is no evidence to suggest this was the case [a deliberate ploy to lure Chelmsford away from the camp] … and it is extremely unlikely'.[13]

However, conversely, Professor John Laband and Geoff Mathews support the presumption that Chelmsford fell for a Zulu ploy: 'The question is whether the British had divided their army through their own carelessness or whether the Zulus had deliberately tricked them into making such a fatal mistake. On balance it would seem the British fell into a Zulu trap.'[14] If, then, having weighed the evidence, it is accepted that Chelmsford was lured away into the Mangeni Valley, what happened at Isandlwana Camp on 22 January 1879?

Chapter 13

'My dear fellow, the rear always looks after itself'

Lord Chelmsford's column marched out of Isandlwana camp at dawn on 22 January, heading east towards the rising sun and on towards Mangeni two and a half hours slog away. Lieutenant Charles Pope and his G Company of the 2/24th were the only men of the 2nd Battalion to remain in camp, due to their having been on picquet duty that night. They were still in position as the column came past, causing much banter and evoking considerable envy in those left behind. Little did Pope and his envious men know that within hours it would be they who would be fighting a battle, one in which every one of them and many more would die.

Hardly had Chelmsford's column disappeared from sight than Pope, in accordance with the instructions given to Colonel Pulleine 'to draw in your picquets and extend your vedettes', received orders to retire on the camp. It was a camp that in the eerie half-light and ground mist of dawn, held the aspect of a semi-deserted town of tents. A canvas town stretching almost half a mile across the western base of Isandlwana Hill which rose, Sphinx-like, 400 feet high, behind. Closer to the base of Isandlwana and overlooking the camp, stood the deserted tents of Lord Chelmsford and his staff above which, in the stillness of the morning, limply hung the Union Jack. To the south, Isandlwana Hill is connected by a saddle, or nek, to Mhlambankosi or 'Black's Koppie', as Chelmsford's column was to rename the prominence later in the day. Between the two mounts, over the nek, ran the road back to Rorke's Drift. With one's back to the camp, looking east, the Isandlwana plain fades into the distant eminences, twelve miles away, of Mdutshana and Magogo, Chelmsford's destination.

The plain, deceptively level and featureless in the early light was, in fact, beset with dongas, which in the rainy season became trenches of waist-deep water. To the south, eight miles away, rose the Malakatha and Hlazakazi hills, the location of Dartnell's reconnaissance of the previous day. To the north, on the opposite side of the Isandlwana the plain under a mile from Lord Chelmsford's tent, the Nquthu plateau, 250 feet higher than the British camp, dominated the plain for ten miles until it merged into the mist and distant hills.

Isandlwana. This painting by the late Jack Simpson clearly illustrates how open and vulnerable the British camp was to Zulu attack.

Pulleine was now responsible for the camp, the safety of its men, stores and the arsenal that the camp contained. Yet, against standing orders, no entrenchment or wagon laager had been formed. A month previously, long before Lord Chelmsford had decided to accompany No 3 Column, he had sent Glyn instructions as to how he should go about the defence of an 'advanced depot' as he called it. 'Wherever it may be finally decided to form a depot, it will have to be strongly entrenched and made as secure as possible against sudden attack, for we would not be able to afford to leave a large garrison behind.'[1] Thus Chelmsford had predicted the very situation that now befell Pulleine, except that no attempt had been made to entrench the Isandlwana camp: indeed, no order to do so had been given. On the contrary, when a few days earlier, Chelmsford, accompanied by his staff and Colonel Glyn, first decided on the base of Isandlwana Hill as his next depot, Glyn, as column commander, mentioned entrenching or laagering the camp, Chelmsford pooh-poohed the idea remarking in a jocular fashion 'Why? It would take a week to make one'[2] as indeed it would – that is – to make an entrenchment, as the ground, if not rock itself, was rock hard. However, a laager formed of wagons, an effective bastion as so effectively illustrated by the Boers forty years earlier at the Battle of Blood River, was a different matter. There were, at that moment, close to sixty vehicles parked on the nek between Isandlwana and Black's Koppie. With close on 800 oxen to hand ready to be yoked, and with 2,000 pairs of hands to push and pull, it would take no more than a few hours to form a barricade. Alas, however, it was out of the question: the wagons were required to trundle back to Rorke's Drift and return as soon as possible with the supplies that Chelmsford required in order to keep his army in the field. Only a few days earlier he had written an irate letter to Commissary-General Edward Strickland in Pietermaritzburg: '... This column will advance shortly and it will be a sad disgrace to the commissariat, if it is obliged to halt short of its destination for the want of supplies.' Chelmsford was later, on 11 April, to write to the War Office by way of an explanation for the want of a laager: 'The wagons which accompanied the troops to Isandlwana were under orders to return to Rorke's Drift on the 22nd January in order to bring up more supplies and were therefore not available for use as a laager. Owing to the bad state of the roads a good number of them did not reach camp till the 21st January.' Thus, the camp at Isandlwana was, as an officer recalled, 'as defenceless as an English village with the air of a racecourse on a public holiday'.

However, at that moment, Chelmsford was intent on his advance into Zululand and bringing the enemy to battle, so it is doubtful that he gave a moment's serious consideration to the possibility of a Zulu attack on his Isandlwana depot. Its location had been chosen, first and foremost, for its ability to provide wood and water for its garrison rather than as a natural stronghold. In any event, Chelmsford, like most of his officers, believed that the column possessed an impregnable shield in the form of 1,200 British infantry armed with the .45 Martini-Henry rifle, each soldier firing twelve man-stopping rounds in sixty seconds. Who could withstand that? Now, however, over half the column's strength having marched away to Mangeni, the garrison of Isandlwana camp had been reduced to a fighting force of 1,004 officers and men of whom only 424 were British infantry ... more than enough surely!

Yet, there were a few who were concerned, one no less than the adjutant of the 1st Battalion, 37-year-old Lieutenant Teignmouth Melvill, who only recently had fought throughout the 9th Frontier War. He had, in discussion with a fellow officer, criticized the slackness of the camp's defences stating 'these Zulus will charge home, and with our small number we ought to be in laager, or, at any rate, be prepared to fight shoulder to shoulder'.[3]

Inspector Mansel of the NMP, it will be recalled from an earlier chapter, on placing the cavalry vedettes on 21 January, had an altercation with Major Clery, Clery insisting that the vedettes that Mansel had placed on the Nquthu plateau were too far from the camp and those placed to the rear of Isandlwana Hill were of no use. Mansel had pointed out that the hill obscured much broken ground, ideal concealment for a stealthy enemy, but Clery, formerly an instructor in military tactics at Camberley Staff College, would not hear of it and patronizingly remarked 'my dear fellow, the rear always looks after itself'.[4] Mansel appeared to concede the point but left his outposts undisturbed until nightfall. The following day, the 22nd, there was no such problem, Clery having ridden off with Chelmsford's column – as, of course, had Mansel himself.

The placing of vedettes had now become the responsibility of Lieutenant Frederick Durrant Scott of the Natal Carbineers, who placed his men even further afield. Vedette duty was the most unpopular assignment to befall the Volunteers whose lot it invariably was to carry out this dangerous task. Usually no more than two men, vedettes were, as a necessity, positioned on high and exposed points far from the camp, where they could give early warning of an approaching enemy.

Having left camp in the half-light of dawn, Scott's vedettes had proceeded at the best pace the terrain would permit, cantering wherever possible, for five or six miles, in order to get to their allotted place soon after daylight. A vedette's postprovided great visibility. It also publicized the vedette's position. Thus, a stealthy foe, advancing through the tall grass that in January covered much of Zululand, could burst out upon a pair of slack or sleepy troopers. Only the previous day, Troopers Clarke and Green of the NMP, forming one of the vedettes that Mansel had placed on the Nquthu plateau, being exhausted from continuous duty, lack of sleep and the hot sun, had dismounted and were dozing when they were disturbed by the approach of an inspecting staff officer and his escort. Immediately awake but still prone, the troopers were at once reprimanded for having dismounted. Quick-witted Clarke replied they were lying down in order to be less conspicuous. Because of an unperceptive or kindly officer, the troopers got away without default. How different their fate would have been had their visitors been a marauding band of Zulus.[5]

That day Scott had decided to place his vedettes posts even further afield than had Mansel. He and his staff would take up a position out on the plain atop a small extinct volcano known by the British as Conical Hill (amaTutshane). From this eminence, a mile and a half out from Isandlwana Hill, Scott would command an unrestricted view of his lookouts and the camp. His most distant vedette was to be situated five and a half miles to the east, on a high point of the Nquthu plateau called Nyezi. It consisted of two Carbineers, one of whom, Trooper Whitelaw, was a Pietermaritzburg blacksmith in civilian life and also a fine shot having, the previous year, won the regimental trophy for marksmanship. His mate, Trooper Hayhoe, would later that day courageously lose his life in galloping a lone and futile warning of the camp's impending fate to the ears of Chelmsford's staff officers.

Closer to the camp, but situated on the plain away to the south of Whitelaw and Hayhoe's position, two Carbineers, having dismounted and having led their horses up the steep slopes of Qwabe, a flat-topped hill, had a 360-degree view. An ideal position. Both carbineers were youngsters, each no more than 20, and bosom pals. As their names – Villiers Caesar Hawkins and William Walwyn Barker – indicated, they were members of elite colonial families and as the day would later witness would not be intimidated by senior Imperial officers. The method of conveying an alarm from these distant positions back to Scott's command post on Conical Hill was simple. On sighting an advancing enemy, and depending on the numbers involved, the troopers, before hastening away to safety, would perform one or two simple manoeuvres, such as circling their horses at a canter or walking them backwards and forwards, depending on what the coding of these actions conveyed.

There would have been at least one additional vedette positioned on the Nquthu Ridge, most likely atop iThusi, the highest point east of Isandlwana, overlooking a notch, or ravine, in the plateau which sheltered the birthplace of the Ngwebini stream and gave access to the Ngwebini Valley to the rear. At the western end of the plateau, almost six miles from Whitelaw and Hayhoe's position on Nyezi, there was another outpost. A mile and a half and 600 feet above the Isandlwana plain, the Magaga Knoll (Mkwene) was barren, rock strewn, exposed, out of sight of the camp and a miserable place to be. Having been on duty all night at this cheerless spot, the morale of Captain Barry's picquet of No 5 Company NNC was low. It had been a disquieting night; indeed, at times alarming for Barry and his second-in-command, 28-year-old Lieutenant the Honourable Standish Vereker, a son of Lord Gort. Vereker, after studying at Agricultural College in England, had come to Natal to try his hand at farming but instead joined the FLH. Promotion quickly followed with a transfer to the NNC, although his knowledge of the Zulu language was negligible. As for Barry's men, approximately twenty-five in number of the amaChunu clan, led by Chief Gabangaye kaMancingwana, they had beseeched the ancestors to hurry the dawn. With only one blanket to arm themselves against the cold – their parade order being, 'Naked, blankets over the left shoulder'[6] and with only one rifle plus ten rounds per rifleman, the night, on occasion, had been both bitterly cold and frightening. Out of the darkness, for there was no moon, they had been called upon by Zulu voices. Gabanquaye knew quite well that the local population had long since departed. These disconcerting voices, he was convinced, shouting incoherent messages, could only be those of Cetshwayo's army.

Apart from Barry's company, there were five other NNC units in the camp. The two companies brought in the previous evening by Captain Orlando Murray were off duty. Despite Major Clery having pooh-poohed the idea of picquets to the rear of Isandlwana Hill, with or without his knowledge, a fifty-strong picquet, drawn from No 9 Company 1/3rd NNC, under the command of Captain James Lonsdale (not to be confused with Commandant Rupert Lonsdale) had been stationed there all night. These were *iziGqoza* men, some of the remnants and descendants of the late Prince Mbuyazi's warriors who had been defeated by Cetshwayo's *Usuthu* faction at the Battle of Ndondakusuka twenty-three years earlier. They, of all the NNC, were the only ones to relish an encounter with the Zulu army, taking revenge on the *Usuthu* and, who knows, with the grateful thanks of *Nkosi* Lord Chelmsford, perhaps establishing the *iziGqoza* as rulers of the Zulu Kingdom… .

No 6 Company NNC, commanded by Captain Krohn, were drawn up in front of the NNC lines where they would stand idle for some time awaiting orders. At the opposite end of the camp, in front of the British tent lines, the men of F Company 2/24th, commanded by Captain William Mostyn, were recovering from a gruelling twelve-day march. They had left Pietermaritzburg on 9 January and had been marching ever since. On arrival at Isandlwana, Mostyn had been heard to ironically exclaim 'Thank goodness, here we are at last!'[7]

There were now less than 440 officers and men of the 24th Regiment in camp, including Pope's company of the 2nd Battalion, going about their various duties. In addition there was one officer, seventy-eight men and two guns of the Royal Artillery that had been left behind. The European troops, except for the colonials, and those destined for road repairs, anticipated a fairly relaxed day until Lieutenant Vereker, hurrying down from Magaga Knoll, arrived in camp. The Zulu voices that had caused such constentation during the night had, with the dawn, materialized into an army of warriors.

Meanwhile, Lieutenant Horace Smith-Dorrien (destined to be one of Britain's most famous and controversial generals of the 1914–18 War), who had been selected to carry Colonel Crealock's orders to Colonel Durnford, was having an uneventful ride to Rorke's Drift. It was only later that he would reflect on how inappropriate his nonchalance had been. 'It ought to have been a very jumpy ride, for I was entirely alone and the country wild and new to me ... but the pride of being selected to carry an important despatch and the valour of ignorance, carried me along without a thought of danger.'[8] His only weapon was a revolver. Not only was it unloaded, he had no ammunition. He rode into Durnford's camp around 6 am to be welcomed by the warmth and steaming breath of the column's 300 horses and four times as many oxen. The camp was teeming with activity but Durnford was absent, he had already left to search for additional wagons that could be purchased, or commandeered, from farms along the Natal bank of the Buffalo River. Captain George Shepstone, however, was soon located and, as Durnford's staff officer, hurriedly tore open and read Crealock's orders which read: 'You are to march out to this camp [Isandlwana] at once with all the force you have with you of No. 2 Column. Major Bengough's battalion is to move to Rorke's Drift as ordered yesterday. 2/24, artillery and mounted men with the General and Colonel Glyn move off at once to attack a force about ten miles distant. PS: If Bengough's battalion has crossed the river at Eland's Kraal, it is to move up here.'[9] (However, as we know, later that day, having crossed and re-crossed the river, Bengough's NNC returned to Helpmekaar where they all but mutinied.)

Immediately all was action. No 2 Column set about dismantling the camp, ready to take the road to Isandlwana the moment Durnford gave the order. Lieutenant Alfred Henderson, a successful Natal farmer and a man of education, having attended Heidelberg University, but now an officer in the Natal Native Horse, was given Crealock's orders and sent galloping to find Durnford who, believing he and his horsemen had been doomed to a rearguard role in the invasion of Zululand, was overjoyed. 'Just what I thought,' he exclaimed to Henderson, 'There is an *Impi* eight miles from the camp which the General has moved out to attack.'[10] Now, perhaps, there would be an opportunity to redeem his reputation and rid himself of his insufferable nickname of 'Don't fire Durnford'.

The raising of Durnford's Horse, or the Natal Native Horse (NNH), can be found in a directive of Sir Henry Bulwer's instructing the magistrates of five different districts, whose areas ranged either along the border of Zululand or the Drakensberg mountains, that Colonel Durnford would be recruiting in their districts.[11] In a matter of three months Durnford had raised, mounted, equipped and armed over 300 men. All were horsemen of a sort who preferred to ride long-legged with an iron or rawhide ring for a stirrup. The type of horse/pony that they rode, ideal for the terrain and conditions that they would encounter, had been aptly described, several years earlier, by Durnford in a letter to his mother '... kaffir ponies for five pounds each. They are not much to look at, but they go fifteen miles a day for a week, and never require to be fed.' At the same time he described, just as he found them, the sort of 'Blacks' that he would recruit for the NNC and NNH. '… they are at least honest, chivalrous, and hospitable, true to their salt, although only barbarians. They are fine men, very naked and all that sort of thing, but thoroughly good fellows.'[12] Six troops, each approximately fifty strong, composed of men from different tribes or clans and each commanded by two white officers, were soon ready to ride.

No. 1 Troop – Zikhali's Horse, commanded by Lieutenant C. Raw.
No. 2 Troop – Zikhali's Horse, commanded by Lieutenant J.A. Roberts.
No. 3 Troop – Zikhali's Horse, commanded by Lieutenant V. Vause.
No. 4 Troop – Hlubi Troop, commanded by Lieutenant A. Henderson.
No. 5 Troop – Edendale Troop, commanded by Lieutenant H.D. Davies

The three Zikhali troops were also referred to as a squadron under the command of Captain W.B. Barton.

The Zikhali troops, who carried the name of their old chief who did not accompany his men, had good cause to hate their Zulu cousins. They were of the amaNgwane clan who had once occupied an area of Zululand along the banks of the White Mfolozi River. In the 1820s they had been set upon by King Shaka and driven south. Fighting much of the way with other tribes whom they encountered, a thousand miles later the Ngwane crossed into the Cape Colony. They were met by a British army led by Colonel Henry Somerset, who soundly defeated the invaders. In desperation, Matiwane, the Ngwane chief, decided he would return to Zululand and seek reconciliation with Shaka. But Shaka was dead, having been murdered by his half-brother Dingane who, upon receiving Matiwane, had his eyes put out. Matiwane was then taken to a small hill nearby that still bares his name, kwaMatiwane, where he was impaled. The amaNgwane, after furthering wanderings, were finally settled in Natal in the area of Spioenkop, close to the Drakensberg Mountains.

Amongst the amaHlubi troop, so named for its native leader, there were old acquaintances including Hlubi himself. They were men of the Batlokwa tribe, several of whom had ridden with Durnford at Bushman's Pass. Like the men of the Zikhali troops, they were of warlike disposition and non-believers. Not so, the mode of the remaining black volunteers, the Edendale Troop. They had adopted the white man's way of living. They were Christian converts of the Edendale and Driefontein missions, situated on the outskirts of Pietermaritzburg and Ladysmith respectively, who farmed and prospered to a modest degree. No

Men of the Natal Native Horse. The date of the photograph is uncertain as is the name of the unit. Note, two of the senior NCOs are sporting beadwork headgear of a style varying between a deerstalker hat and a military pith helmet.

A fine sketch of a Natal Native Horse trooper. He rides without stirrups and the curb with a long shank is severe. However, the manner in which he has pigtailed his pony's mane indicates his pride and affection for his sturdy mount.

strangers to Durnford, Elijah Kambule, who had met his death at Bushman's Pass, had been an Edendale man. Having provided their own uniforms – a slouch hat, corduroy jacket, trousers, boots and spurs – they were proud of their civilized way of life and Christian belief. They held themselves aloof from their more rugged comrades. There was yet one other troop, that of Jantze's men. Being under-strength it had remained at Kranskop.

Abandoning all thought of commandeering additional wagons, Durnford and his foragers set off for camp at a gallop. George Shepstone had already done much to see the Column packed and ready for departure. Ever eager to press on, and like Smith-Dorrien without a thought for danger, and despite Chelmsford's directive that 'the leading troops must not be allowed to outmarch the baggage wagons …', Durnford left the transport devoid of escort. Also lagging behind because of its unmounted escort of NNC, came Durnford's artillery in the form of what was regarded as by many as a new-fangled contraption, a rocket battery carried, together with its ammunition, on mule-back. Commanded by Major Francis Broadfoot Russell RA, and its NNC escort commanded by Captain Cracroft Nourse, it would contribute little to the battle that lay ahead.

Durnford was now in his element. No longer performing the job of a humdrum colonial engineer, he saw himself, as indeed he was, a rough-riding leader of irregular cavalry. Only a few days earlier in a letter home to his mother, he had described himself in the role he now relished:

> I wonder whether you would admire my appearance for the field? Boots, spurs, dark cord britches, serge patrol jacket, broad belt over the shoulders, and one around the waist – to the former a revolver, and to the latter a hunting knife and ammunition pouch. A wide-awake hat with a wide brim, one side turned up, and a crimson turban [puggaree] wound around the hat – very stage brigand!'[13]

Back at Isandlwana camp, Colonel Pulleine had commandeered Lord Chelmsford's tent, high above the town of tents, with an unrestricted view east across the Isandlwana plain – except, that is, for the obstructions of Conical and Qwabe Hills which, at that moment, were occupied by the vedettes of the Natal Carbineers. Pulleine, having taken charge of the camp, had relinquished command of the 24th to acting Major William Degacher. In addition, two 7-pounder guns, half the strength of No 3 Column's artillery, had also remained behind. Major Stuart Smith, who would have held command, had, at the last moment, accompanied Chelmsford's column leaving a delighted Lieutenant Henry Curling congratulating himself 'on having an independent command'.

Where, however, was the Zulu army that Major Dartnell had first encountered the previous day? The army that had bivouacked the same night, the 21st, to the rear of Isipezi mountain and whose rearguard were now about to decoy Chelmsford on a will-o-the-wisp chase amongst the Magogo Hills? It had, as has been revealed, headed for the Ngwebini Valley where a portion, but far from all, of Ntshingwayo kaMahole's warriors, spent the night. In 1966 Donald Morris published his book *The Washing of the Spears*, which contained this spellbinding description:

> The Zulu herders ran over the crest of the slope and disappeared, and the cattle slowed on the rise and stopped. One of the pursuers cantered up beside them, and in sudden alarm, pulled up his horse just in time to prevent a tumble over the edge of a wide, deep ravine that lay just beyond the rise. Then, in astonishment, he stared into the ravine itself. Closely packed and sitting in utter silence, covering the floor of the ravine and perched upon the steeply rising sides, and stretched as far as the eye could see in both directions, were over twenty thousand Zulu warriors. The main Impi had finally been located.[14]

Ever since the publication of Morris' book many historians and battlefield guides have doggedly maintained that the Zulu army bivouacked in the Ngwebini Valley on the night of 21/22 January, and was discovered, just as Morris described, by Lieutenant Charlie Raw, at 11:30 am on the 22nd. Not only that but, as also suggested by Morris and maintained by many since, that due to it being the 'Day of the Dead Moon', an inauspicious time in Zulu belief in which to undertake any important action, it was the intention of Ntshingwayo kaMahole not to attack that day but to keep his army in its Ngwebini Valley hideout. In a letter to Peter Quantrill, dated 10 November 2005, the late David Rattray described the time of the dead moon as follows: 'The moon phase in question is not New Moon. It is the last day of the last quarter of the Lunar cycle – i.e. before New Moon. On this day the moon is not visible because it is hiding in the glare of the sun. The Zulus call this "usuku olumnynmana" or the "Black Day". It was like a Sabbath for them. No burial of the dead, no marriage etcetera and there are numerous Zulu accounts which tell us that they were to avoid fighting on this day.'

But if that was indeed the case, who were the warriors who had intimidated the picquet of Barry and Vereker during the hours of darkness and were now appearing in considerable numbers to the left and front of their picquet? At about 6 am Lieutenant Vereker left Magaga Knoll and hastened down to the camp. Lieutenant Walter Higginson of the 1/3rd NNC took his report and Vereker returned to his post. Although seemingly unperturbed by Vereker's news, Higginson was nevertheless distracted by an officer of the 24th ordering him and his company to relieve another picquet that had been on duty for thirty-six hours. However, just as Higginson and his men were ready to depart, they were told to remain where they were. More Zulus had been seen on the extreme left of the camp, perhaps two miles or so to the north-east of Barry's picquet.

There was a further delay while another NNC officer, Lieutenant Adendorff, investigated Vereker's alarming news and duly reported to Colonel Pulleine. The details of Adendorff's report are unknown but soon afterwards Colonel Pulleine ordered Higginson, accompanied by Sergeant-Major Williams, to belatedly ride to Magaga Knoll and see what Vereker's sighting was all about. Higginson later reported that he had '… found Captain Barry and Lieutenant Vereker watching a large body of Zulu s on the extreme left of the camp, and they informed me that a large force of about five thousand had gone round behind the Isandlwana hill'.[15]

And what of the far-flung vedettes of colonial volunteers? What was happening five or six miles away to the south-east on Qwabe and Nyezi? The bosom friends, Troopers Barker and Hawkins, having climbed, leading their horses, 200 feet to the top of Qwabe, had hardly had time to familiarize themselves with distant landmarks and enjoy the view when '… we noticed a lot of mounted men [Zulus] in the distance trying to surround us'.[16]

By 1879, the horse, far from being regarded by the Zulus as the spawn of white man's wizardry and no longer an '*amaThakathi*', had become part of the Zulu way of life – that is, for those who could afford a horse. And now 'a lot' of Zulu horsemen were trying to surround Barker and Hawkins. Barker records that he and his friend 'gave the usual signal', by circling their horses. Possibly this was for the benefit of both Lieutenant Scott on Conical Hill and for the distant horsemen, the troopers at the time being uncertain whether or not the latter were friend or foe. But, as Barker later wrote,

… we had to retire off the hill in haste as we discovered they were Zulus. We retired to Lieutenant Scott, about two miles nearer to the camp [a ride of approximately two miles or more], and informed him of what we had seen, and he decided to come back with us, but before we had gone far we saw Zulus on the hill we had just left, and others advancing from the left [on the plain beyond Nyezi] and others advancing from the left flank where two other vedettes, Whitelaw and another [Trooper Hayhoe] had been obliged to retire from. Whitelaw reported a large army advancing, thousands I remember him distinctly stating, and he was immediately sent back to camp with the report. This would have been about 8 am. He returned with a message' [about 9:00 am?] from Lieutenant Scott that we were to watch the enemy carefully and send back reports of their movements.[17]

The vedettes and picquets were not the only ones to wonderingly observe the number of warriors advancing on the camp. Lieutenant Curling, up and about and in charge of the artillery, later wrote in a letter to his mother, 'At about 7:30 we were turned out as about one thousand Zulus were seen on some hills about two miles from the camp and I was congratulating myself on having an independent command. I had with my guns only twenty men, the remainder, fifty in number, stayed in the camp'.[18] Not far away, James Brickhill, a short-sighted government interpreter of many years standing, now attached to No 3 Column, was sighted enough to witness, as he later recorded, 'On the morning of the 22nd of January, between six and seven o' clock, the Zulus showed in considerable force at the south end [Brickhill constantly got his compass directions confused, he meant the north end], of the iNquthu [Nquthu] mountains. Shortly afterwards another force came into sight about the middle of the hill and the intervening space filled in.'[19]

At the same time, Lieutenant Charles Pope took a moment to write in his diary, which would later be found in the ruins of the camp, 'Alarm – three columns of Z's and mounted men on hill E, seven thousand more went around Lion's Kop [to the rear of Isandlwana Hill]'. If then the Nquthu Plateau and the Isandlwana Plain, up to a distance of five miles from the camp, was alive with warriors, how could the Zulu army be 'discovered', three hours later, four miles away from the camp, hiding in the Ngwebini Valley? There are, in fact, numerous Zulu accounts describing where the army spent the night of the 21st, and at what time on the 22nd the army began to deploy in preparation to attack the British camp. However, many Zulu reports are not only contradictory, but in other respects they appear biased one way or the other, for it is pertinent that every Zulu statement was taken down by a white interpreter, more often than not either the Hon. William Drummond or Henry Longcast of Lord Chelmsford's staff. Hence most testimonies, either prisoners, deserters or spies, reflect what the interrogator wished to hear and that which the witness, ingratiating himself, thought it wise to relate. Let us see what some had to say.

Perhaps the most significant testimony was that of Mehlokazulu, a most notorious Zulu in British eyes, he who by crossing into Natal and murdering his father's adulterous wives was seen as an instigator of the war. At the conclusion of hostilities in July 1879, Mehlokazulu surrendered but was later recognized and charged with a capital offence. He was imprisoned in Pietermaritzburg jail, there to await trial and a likely death sentence. While incarcerated he was questioned as to the location of the Zulu army bivouac on the night of 21 January. Mehlokazulu replied, 'in a valley rising from the Nquthu range and running eastwards towards the king's kraal. It abounds with scrubby bush and small stones.'[20] That is, the Ngwebini Valley. Subsequently, Mehlokazulu was brought before Mr. J.P. Symons, Justice of the Peace, for trial and sentencing but by that time the British government was enduring a clamour of censure from the British public. For instance, the Workers' Peace Association demanded '... that no feeling of revenge ought to be entertained with regard to Isandula [Isandlwana] as the Zulus were defending their country from foreign invasion'.[21] Consequently, after two hearings, Mehlokazulu was discharged, the bench asserting that ' ... as the Crown of England had obtained satisfaction for the violation of English territory [Natal] and did not desire to proceed further against the prisoner'.[22] A year or so later, General Sir Evelyn Wood, who had commanded No 4 Column, visited Isandlwana for the first time and got into a matey conversation with the locals, one of whom was none other than Mehlokazulu who, no longer under the threat of death, described to Wood how the Zulu army had deployed. Wood later annotated a military survey map of the country around Isandlwana (compiled by Captain Anstey RE and Lieutenant Penrose RE), indicating the deployment of the Zulu army as described by Mehlokazulu. 'The Zulu pointed out exactly the position of the Nodwengu [regiment] in bivouac – near a mealie garden and indicated generally the remainder ... The Zulus attacked exactly as they bivouacked all in a line of regiments ...'[23] All regiments were depicted as having bivouacked the night on the Nquthu plateau – not hidden in the Ngwebini Valley as Mehlokazulu had testified when in jail (Wood's map will be referred to again later).

What did other Zulu combatants have to say? A warrior of the uKhandempevu Regiment recalled 'just after the sun had gone to rest on the Saturday [warriors when giving testimony, constantly referred to Wednesday, 22 January as either a Saturday or Sunday] we left Nquthu and made towards Isandlwana, sleeping

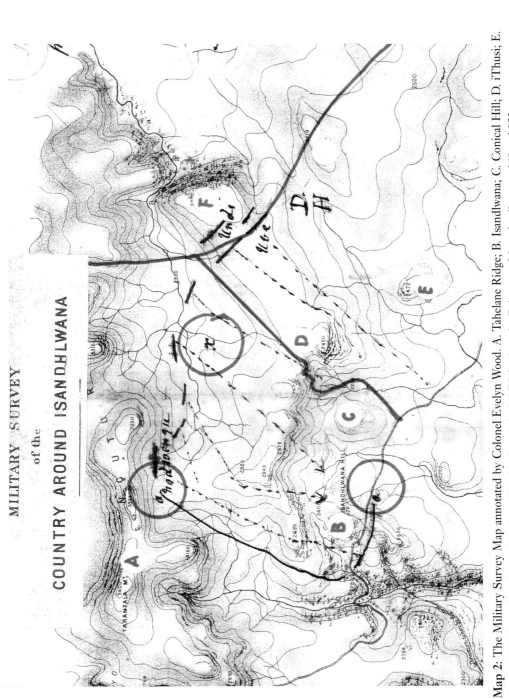

Map 2: The Military Survey Map annotated by Colonel Evelyn Wood. A. Tahelane Ridge; B. Isandlwana; C. Conical Hill; D. iThusi; E. Qwabe; F. Mabaso; The figure 'X' where Wood believed the NNH fired on the Zulu army. More details pages 140 and 153.

Mehlokazulu kaSihayo, troublemaker and gallant warrior, in captivity and awaiting trial.

that night on the side of the donga near the camp …'.[24] In 1939, a Mr. Hugh Tracey, travelling in Zululand, interviewed an old warrior of the 'iNgobamakhosi [*sic*] regiment':

> He told us that the whole Zulu army had arrived from the north on the previous evening [21 January 1879] and had lain down in the hills in the tall dry grass without fires, without food or water. They slept on the spot as they lay, and none of the men of the British army encamped below the head of the Isandlwana Hill was aware of their presence. Early in the morning, looking through the grasses as they lay, they watched the soldiers who had been left behind by the main army, wake up and get out of their tents, have breakfast and generally move around the camp …[25]

What, then, is the Zulu support for the theory that its army spent the night of the 21st in the Ngwebini Valley? The writer has found but few who remember bivouacking there on the night in question, such as: 'before sunset they had reached their objective, a rocky, bushy valley close under the north-east slope of the Nquthus':[26] 'on keeping away to the eastward, we occupied a valley running north and south under the spurs of the Nquthu hill, which concealed the Sandhlwana [*sic*] hill.'[27] The *Natal Witness*' fiftieth-anniversary issue of January 1929 mentioned there was evidence that elements of the Zulu army did not arrive in time to sleep in either location: '... I arrived [at Isandlwana], just before sunrise and we fought all day without food or water ...'

There are numerous interrogations, mostly recorded by either Drummond or Longcast, that make no mention of where the Zulu army spent the night of the 22nd but almost without exception adamantly state that the Zulu army had no intention of doing battle on the 22nd due to the inauspicious phase of the moon. So universally adamant are the Zulus in this respect, it is almost as though there was a universal collusion. The writer contends that there was indeed collusion but not between Cetshwayo's warriors but, instead, between Drummond, Longcast and the members of Chelmsford's staff, possibly including Chelmsford himself. Sir Charles Ellice, of the War Office, and the Duke of Cambridge's right-hand man, was to pointedly enquire:

As your Lordship [Chelmsford] had a considerable number of mounted men in Colonel Glyn's column, it should be stated what steps were taken on the twentieth and twenty first to reconnoitre and thoroughly search the country on your flanks. It seems difficult to understand how a large Zulu army could have massed itself to the north and within striking distance of your camp without some evidence of its proximity having been afforded.[28]

Chelmsford and his staff, Crealock in particular, urgently needed to furnish a plausible explanation where none existed other than their own negligence. Could it be that one was concocted? Such as, 'The Zulu army was not within striking distance of the camp, but was hidden in the Ngwebini Valley and due to the unfavourable phase of the moon, had no intention of revealing itself until the 23rd?'[29] A preposterous idea? Yet at the same time on the same day and not sixty-five miles away from Isandlwana, another major battle was fought. Colonel Pearson's No 1, the Coastal, Column, consisting of 2,780 officers and men, including cavalry and artillery, were in the process of crossing the Nyezane River. Strung out and vulnerable, *the column was attacked* (author's emphasis) by a Zulu army of 5,000 men commanded by Chief Godide kaNdlela. After a stiff fight the Zulus were routed, leaving over 300 dead to the British loss of less than thirty dead and wounded. Colonel Pearson had fought a successful battle and was not required to find answers for his conduct and, consequently, it would seem, there is no mention of the moon. In fact, Godide and his warriors, in initiating the battle, appeared to have been unaware of any such

Zulu superstition. In addition, one of Drummond's interrogations involved UMshololo, a Zulu well known to Longcast, who had been wounded at the battle at Rorke's Drift where Longcast found him on the morning after the battle. UMshololo would have been well aware that the British were killing Zulu wounded and was no doubt eager to ingratiate himself and hopefully survive. He willingly poured forth answers to many pertinent questions and went on to say that there was 'no intention whatever' of making any attack on 22 January 'owing to the state of the moon being unfavourable from a superstitious point of view'. Furthermore, he said the usual sprinkling of the warriors with the medicine previous to an engagement had not taken place, nor had the war song been sung or the religious ceremonies accompanying it been performed.[30]

UMshololo's statement would have us believe that the Zulu army, having been subjected to a rigorous cleansing ceremony (see above, page 48–9), only ten days earlier, was required to undergo the same ritual again: the slaughter of oxen, the forced vomiting and the singing of the war song by 20,000 Zulu voices, all within the confines of the Ngwebini Valley and within five miles of the British camp. Such seemed so implausible that Peter Quantrill, my colleague, (in our writing of *Zulu Victory*, London, 2002), sought an opinion of AMAFA (the KwaZulu-Natal Heritage Council). In reply, Prince Mangosuthu Buthelezi, great-great grandson of King Cetshwayo, and the acknowledged custodian of the Zulu nation's history and culture, replied 'The Zulu army was ritually strengthened at kwaNodwengu. Once this had been done, the army was despatched and ready to do battle. There would have been no further rituals performed for either individual regiments or the army as a whole.' Far from waiting until the unfavourable phase of the moon had passed – if, that is, the position of the moon had ever been an element of concern – *Nkosi* Ntshingwayo, having decoyed half the column to Mangeni, forthwith determined to destroy the enemy at Isandlwana before their Mangeni kin could hurry to their aid.

Chapter 14

'God save you, Sir, from ever seeing a camp or homestead sacked by Zulus'

The sighting of Zulu columns in great force was disquieting, particularly so as it was assumed the Zulu army was about to be brought to battle ten miles away at Mangeni. Allowing for a certain amount of exaggeration by his informants, Colonel Pulleine had, between 6:30 and 7:30 am, been told of '… a large body of Zulus left of the camp', of about 5,000 Zulus having gone around behind Isandlwana Hill and of yet more warriors massing on the Nquthu Plateau. Pulleine's orders were simple enough: he was to defend the camp. He had, however, been saddled with a camp that was, as far as fortifications were concerned, defenceless. Yet, even though the camp lacked any form of bastion, there was throughout an air of complacency – that is until the arrival of Trooper Whitelaw at about 7:30 am, reporting the sighting of '… a large Zulu army advancing in thousands'.[1]

By this time Pulleine, no longer at his position at camp headquarters, had returned to his own tent in the 1/24th's lines. Having listened intently to Whitelaw's alarming news and having conferred briefly with his adjutant, Lieutenant Melvill, Pulleine ordered a bugler to sound the imperious call of 'Column Alert'. The prospect of a relaxed day in camp vanished. Distant work parties and foot picquets, with their rifles at the 'high port', doubled into camp. All with the exception, that is, of Barry's amaChunu Company at their hazardous location on Magaga Knoll, and Captain James Lonsdale's *iziGqoza* Company tucked away behind Isandlwana Hill close to the base of the plateau. They were to remain firm as Pulleine's first line of defence. Meanwhile, the NCOs of the 1/24th yelled and chivvied their men into company ranks while Lieutenant Curling, delighted at the prospect of commanding the guns in action, watched impatiently as his gunners raced to harness the cannons. He was to later recall '… that the large bodies of Zulus seen above the camp '[on the Nquthu Plateau] 'were too far away to fire upon but close enough to be intimidating'.[2]

Within a matter of minutes the infantry had formed up in 'columns of companies', two ranks deep with a number of the mounted troops taking position on either side of the formation. The remaining cavalry trotted out into the plain, seeking the whereabouts of any hidden enemy. Great excitement. Were they, after all, to be the ones to do battle while the General's column sought for a Zulu army that was now poised on the doorstep of the camp? Most thought not: distant rifle fire clearly indicated that the General's column was engaged. If that was the Zulu plan, Pulleine was not about to take the offensive. His orders were to defend the camp. Let the enemy come to him. So the minutes ticked away until both officers and men became restless. Finally the order was given to 'Stand at ease', while Pulleine, commanding the battalion for the first time, wrestled in silence with the biggest quandary of his military career. What if the camp was attacked? There were no fortifications and certainly no time in which to dig any. But what of a barricade? 'Forty five empty wagons stood in the camp with oxen in. It was a convoy which should have already gone to Rorke's Drift for supplies … these wagons might have at any time been formed into a laager.' So wrote Smith-Dorrien.[3] If, however, Pulleine gave the order to use the wagons to form a barricade, there would be no prospect of bringing up the supplies from Rorke's Drift that Chelmsford so urgently required. In the same way that no officer would wish to be branded as a coward or a cad, Pulleine did not wish to incur the stigma of being an 'alarmist'. Instead, he would do nothing but pass the buck and let Chelmsford and his staff decide whether the innocuous note he was about to despatch would warrant their hasty return to the threatened camp. Pulleine wrote 'Staff Officer. Report just come in that the Zulus are advancing in force from left front of camp. 8.5am. HB Pulleine, Lt.Col.'.[4] The despatch was handed to a galloper of the NMP who delivered it to Lord Chelmsford's staff an hour and a half later. What would 'in force' convey? 500? 5,000? It did not, as we have already read, alarm Chelmsford in the least, especially so as he believed it was he who was grappling with the Zulu army.

Meanwhile, up on the plateau at Magaga Knoll, Barry and his second-in-command Lieutenant Vereker, with their No 5 amaChunu Company, NNC, were conscious of the precarious position they had been ordered to defend. Lieutenant Adendorff, who had been sent to assess the situation had been and gone. Adendorff was of German descent and, it seems, had a poor command of the English language, so perhaps his report had been confusing. Consequently, Lieutenant Higginson with Sergeant-Major Williams, had been sent to weigh up what was going on. The situation was alarming. A large stationary body of Zulus in two columns, situated above and to the left of the camp, was plain to see. Furthermore, Higginson was told, an *impi*, 5,000 strong, had earlier gone round behind the Isandlwana Hill.[5] Higginson and Williams stayed for three-quarters of an hour watching the distant warriors until Barry eventually sent a runner to Pulleine informing him that the Zulus had retired out of sight. On receipt of Barry's message, Pulleine, perceiving his restless garrison, and assuming that there was no imminent danger of an attack, gave the order to 'stand down', stipulating, however, that the men should keep their equipment on.

Lieutenant John Chard RE was amongst those in camp that morning. He had ridden over to Isandlwana merely to confirm an instruction he had previously received. Mission accomplished, as soon as Pulleine had dismissed him, Chard, who had just witnessed the Zulu column as seen by Barry and Vereker, was anxious to get back to his station at Rorke's Drift. Having hurriedly mounted, he had ridden little less than a mile when he encountered Durnford at the head of his native horsemen, all armed to the teeth, each with a carbine and quiver of throwing spears. For Chard, newly arrived in South Africa, it must have been a blood-stirring sight, romantic soldiering at its best. Durnford, unlike the majority of Imperial officers, respected his native troops, regarding them as members of his military family and as friends. He had recently written to his mother:

Colonel Anthony Durnford, Commander of No 1 Column.

My men are drawn partly from clans well known to me. The Putini clan sent three hundred Sikhali [*sic*] clan, three hundred foot and one hundred and fifty horse. Langalibalele's old clan [five years earlier Durnford's enemies], a hundred foot, all fighting men, as indeed I believe are all the others, but I know the first lot well, and what they can do. My horse [his mounted troopers] are my old friends the Basuthos under their Chief Hlubi ... he sends fifty; Zikhali [*sic*] a hundred and fifty, Christians from

Edendale send fifty, led by a brother of Langalibalele, John Zulu, Jantje (an old friend), fifty, all full of ardour.[6]

Chard was somewhat in awe of this Engineer officer who had, somehow, transformed himself from a plodding builder of moats and bridges to a dashing cavalryman. Chard was eager to relate his recent sighting of a Zulu army. Durnford listened keenly and then, adding to Chard's gratification, ordered him to instruct Major Russell, RA, commanding the column's rocket battery, who was coming along behind, to detach one company of his NNC infantry to escort and guard the column's transport. With the remaining company, Russell was to close up as rapidly as possible. With a nod in acknowledgement to Chard's salute, Durnford and his Zikhali troopers were off in a thunder of hooves.

***

Lieutenant Smith-Dorrien, who had long since delivered Clery's orders to Durnford's staff officer Lieutenant George Shepstone, decided to carry on to Rorke's Drift where he had been tasked to supervise the manufacture of 'riems' – rawhide strapping or reins for use in the harnessing of wagons. Having satisfied himself that the job was under control, he thought it as well to acquire some ammunition for his revolver. At first none was to be had but having successfully cadged eleven rounds from Lieutenant Gonville Bromhead, B Company, 2/24th, the officer commanding Rorke's Drift, Smith-Dorrien remounted his old 'broken-kneed' pony and headed back to Isandlwana camp where dozens of wagons stood empty, waiting to fetch the supplies that were ready and waiting at Rorke's Drift.[7] How the camp had changed since he had left it before dawn seven hours earlier! Durnford had just arrived and with Lieutenant Francis Dundonald Cochrane of the 32nd Regiment, a Special Service officer and the only Imperial amongst Durnford's mounted troops, had gone directly to Pulleine's tent. Awkward moments were to follow. Durnford was senior in service and rank to Pulleine thus, irrespective of the circumstances or any other consideration, would take command of the camp – that is if he could not rid himself of the obligation. Pulleine's actual orders, which Durnford now inherited, were:

You will be in command of the camp in the absence of Colonel Glyn. Draw in your line of defence while the force with the General is out of the camp. Draw in your infantry outposts in conformity. Keep your cavalry vedettes still well to the front. Act strictly on the defence. Keep a wagon loaded with ammunition ready to start at once, should the General's force be in need of it. Colonel Durnford has been ordered up from Rorke's Drift to reinforce the camp.[8]

These orders, according to the custom of the service, now applied to Durnford as though they had been given to him by Chelmsford himself. It would later be fraudulently stated that Durnford's orders, which were temporarily lost amongst the debris of the stricken camp, stated he was to take command of the camp rather than reinforce it. A significant difference. Nevertheless, whatever the implication between reinforce and command may have been, all the time Durnford remained in camp he was, irrevocably, the senior officer and therefore in command, a thoroughly undesirable role as far as Durnford was concerned. He was an independent column commander of irregular cavalry. His was an attacking role and, with the prospect of battle, he now sought the opportunity to redeem his reputation and erase the stigma of 'Don't Fire Durnford'; it was an opportunity not to be missed. Several hours earlier he had, no doubt, pondered what the situation at the camp would be and what role No 2 Column would play in the battle yet to come. On receipt of Clery's orders he had immediately exclaimed to Cochrane 'Just what I thought! We are at once to proceed to Sandlwana [sic] there is an *impi* about eight miles from the camp, which the General moves out to attack at daybreak'.[9] Durnford had made up his mind that somehow or another he would be in the thick of it.[10]

Arriving at Isandlwana at about 10:30 am, it had taken about two and a half hours for Durnford, and his advance guard of three Zikhali troops of the NNH, to reach the camp where they 'found everybody under arms'. Having gone immediately to Pulleine's tent, Durnford left his officers and troopers to make their way through the milling soldiers who gazed with curiosity at their tatty but fearsome-looking Zikhali brothers-in-arms. They dismounted on the open ground to the extreme left of the camp, just beyond the makeshift shelters of No 3 Column's NNC, but, as ordered, did not off-saddle. Cochrane remained with Durnford, acting as temporary staff officer and stayed throughout his discussion with Pulleine. Smith-Dorrien, who by this time had also arrived in camp, reported to Pulleine's tent and casually listened in to the conversation between the two officers. He later recalled: 'As far as I could make out the gist of the colonels' Durnford and Pulleine's discussion was that the former wished to go out and attack the Zulus, whilst the latter said his orders were to defend the camp and that he could not allow the infantry to move out.'[11]

At about the same time Lieutenant Higginson and Sergeant-Major Williams, fresh from their visit to Barry's picquet, also reported to Pulleine's tent. By then, it having been established who was in command, Pulleine ordered Higginson to report direct to Durnford who listened intently to what Higginson had to say. Durnford then ordered Higginson to take some men and climb to the top of Isandlwana Hill, a splendid lookout with a 360-degree view. Higginson and his men stayed on top of the hill for an hour, watching the movements of the distant Zulu columns, until Higginson, having decided for himself what the enemy were about, came down and reported the Zulus retreating. Durnford, taking Higginson's report at face value, exclaimed 'Ah! Is that so? Well, we will follow them up'.[12] Cochrane recalled the moment rather differently: 'Constant reports came in from the scouts on the left, some of the reports were … the enemy are in force behind the hills on the left … the enemy are in three columns … the columns are separating, one moving towards the left and one towards the General.'[13] According to Cochrane, Durnford assumed that the last-mentioned column was on its way to attack Lord Chelmsford's troops at Mangeni and take them in the rear. It was the opportunity Durnford had hoped for but, having briefly contemplated what he was about to undertake, he asked Pulleine to support his sortie by giving him two companies of the 24th. Pulleine immediately objected, reiterating that his orders were 'to defend the camp' to which Durnford replied 'Very well, I had better not take them, I will go with my own men', adding, however, 'If you see us in difficulties you must send and support us.'[14] Hurrying outside to where his troops, with their horses' feedbags on and girths loosened, were having a hasty breakfast of hard biscuit, Durnford called for Lieutenant Vause, commanding No 3 Zikhali Troop. Whereas it had not occurred to Durnford that the camp might be attacked, he suddenly realized his own unguarded wagons, still three to four miles back on the Rorke's Drift track, might well be. He ordered Vause and his troop, together with Captain Wally Stafford's Zikhali infantry, 120 strong, to hasten back and escort the wagons into camp.[15] Task completed, they were to catch up with Durnford wherever he might be.[16]

Durnford was now convinced that a Zulu column was about to attack Chelmsford.[17] He was further convinced that it was his duty to intercept it. He was not about to embark on a search for the Zulu army. Like Pulleine he had no doubt whatsoever that the Zulu army was hotly engaged ten miles away. As the particular enemy column was last seen heading east along the top of the Nquthu Plateau, Durnford was well aware that it would have to descend to the plain in order to grapple with Chelmsford. Thus, Durnford decided to split his force, sending No 1 troop, Zikhali Horse, under Lieutenant Charlie Raw, accompanied by Staff Officer Captain George Shepstone, onto the plateau, there to skirmish to the east. At the same time No 2 Troop, under Lieutenant Roberts, was also ordered to the plateau to '… skirmish the valley beyond the ridge taken by Raw'.[18] Both troops under the overall command of Captain William Barton, NNH. However, before the troops departed they were informed '… there was a company of Native infantry [Barry and Vereker's amaChunu] on duty on the ridge'. Barton was told he could take the company in support.[19] Thus, it would seem that Pulleine, regarding a Zulu attack on the camp to be implausible, had relented, offering to denude what was perhaps his key outpost. Either that or Durnford, without reference to Pulleine, had decided the picquet to be of little importance and without notice to Pulleine had commandeered it.

After the Zikhali troops had set off for the plateau, Durnford, with the remaining two troops, Henderson's No 4, Hlubi Troop and Davies's No 5, Edendale Troop (Vause with No 3 Troop was yet to return from escorting the wagons into the camp), set off across the plain in the direction of Conical Hill. The rocket battery, commanded by Major Francis Russell, with its weary escort of Zikhali infantry commanded by Captain Cracroft Nourse, gradually began to fall further and further behind the cantering horsemen.

An hour or so had elapsed since Durnford and his troops had, at 10:30 am, arrived at Isandlwana. Now that they had departed, the 1/24th, and Pope's G. Coy 2/24th, began to go about its business, the men, however, wearing their equipment whilst keeping an eye on the camp kitchens in anticipation of their dinners. Those off duty dozed in their tents or ambled about chatting to their mates. Nevertheless, and perhaps due to Barry's picquet on Magaga Knoll having left with Durnford's horsemen, Pulleine ordered E Company 1/24th, commanded by 29-year-old Lieutenant Charles Cavaye, up the Tahelane track to the top of the Nquthu Ridge, half-way to the now abandoned Magaga Knoll. Other than that, there was a general air of complacency about the camp.

Lieutenant Curling RA in a letter to his mother, later recalled 'We, none of us, had the least idea that the Zulus contemplated attacking the camp and having in the last war [the 9th Frontier War of 1878, in the Eastern Cape], often seen equally large numbers of the enemy, never dreamed they would come on.'[20] Captain Edward Essex of the 75th Regiment, a Special Service officer and the Transport Director of No 3 Column (Lieutenant Smith-Dorrien being his assistant), who earlier in the day witnessed the appearance of a Zulu column on the skyline, had returned to his tent after Pulleine had ordered the 'Stand Down'. Thereafter Essex busied himself writing letters until '… about noon a sergeant came to my tent and told me that firing was to be heard behind the hill where the company of the 1st Battalion, 24th [Lieutenant Cavaye, E Company] had been sent. I had my glasses [binoculars] over my shoulder, and thought I might as well take my revolver, but did not trouble to take my sword as I thought nothing of the matter, and expected to be back in half an hour to finish my letters.'[21]

By 11:45 am, Barton's command of Nos 1 and 2 Troops Zikhali Horse were riding east along the plateau where, the previous evening, Lieutenant Milne RN had, with a sailor's eye, compared the undulations of the Nquthu plateau with the swells of the ocean in which a vessel could effectively disappear from view. He had written '... the ground was very nearly level; there were slight rises, however, every now and again, which would prevent our seeing any men who did not wish it'.[22] Barton and his two Zikhali troops, together with the amaChunu NNC, were separated by two miles and 600 feet from Durnford and the remaining two troops of the NNH who, down on the plain, were spurring east towards Conical Hill and beyond. Durnford, in his eagerness to engage with the enemy, had left the rocket battery a long way behind and all but defenceless. It would have to get along as best it could. The column's ammunition supply was also a long way away, still in the wagons on their way to Isandlwana Camp.

Amongst the troops on the plateau, Durnford could claim old friends: Sergeant-Major Nyanda, of the amaNgwane, George Shepstone who, like Durnford had attended Cetshwayo's coronation, and Charles Raw who held a very special place in Durnford's esteem, for it was Raw, who with three others at the top of Bushman's Pass in 1873, when Durnford had desperately called 'Will no one stand with me?', had stood firm while the remaining troopers fled. Raw would now be the first to encounter the enemy who, strangely it seemed, turned and ran rather than gave battle. On giving chase, however, the NNH suddenly realized they were being lured to where the warriors waited in overwhelming numbers. Raw later wrote 'The enemy in small clumps retiring from us for some time, drawing us from the camp where they turned and fell upon us, the whole army showing itself from behind the hill in front where they had evidently been waiting.'[23]

The 'finding' of the Zulu army is one of the most controversial incidents of the Anglo-Zulu War: where exactly had ut been hiding? Certainly not in the Ngwebini Valley. In fact, it could be held, with some justification, that it had been found hours earlier by Trooper Whitelaw who, it will be recalled, had that morning reported 'a large army of thousands'. Or perhaps, the credit should go to Barry and Vereker who had encountered the enemy on top of Magaga Knoll before dawn. However, if it is accepted that Raw and his comrades were the first to happen upon the Zulu army, the writer suggests the encounter occurred at that point on the Nquthu Plateau, as indicated by Mehlokazulu to Colonel Evelyn Wood in 1880 (Map 2, page 141). Subsequent to his conversation with Mehlokazulu, Wood annotated a *Military Survey Map of the Country Around Isandlwana (13.11.79)*, as follows:

> The Zulu [Mehlokazulu] pointed out exactly the position of the Nodwengu in the bivouac – near a mealie garden and indicated generally the remainder, The thick line a.a [circled] shows the intended movement. The dotted lines that actually followed.
>
>   X [circled] <u>I believe</u> about where the Basuthos [NNH] fired on the Umcityn [*sic*]
>
> The Xulus attacked exactly as they bivouacked all in a line of Regiments except the Undi Corps and Zikasi battalion which was ½ a mile in the left rear of Ngobamakosi in bivouac and in action
>
> D.H. Approximate position of Colonel Durnford when Hlubi hearing the firing of the Umcityn [*sic*], and other contingents of Basuthos persuaded him to retire.

There are three primary-source accounts of the encounter: Raw's and one each from Hamer, a temporary commissariat officer who, as a friend of George Shepstone's, had accompanied the Zikhali troops that morning, and that of Sergeant-Major Nyanda. Although all three relate the same incident it is difficult to understand how the incident could be described so differently: Raw: '... they turned and fell upon us, the whole army showing itself from behind the hill in front where they had evidently been waiting'.[24] Hamer: '... they [the cattle] disappeared over a ridge and on coming up we saw the Zulus, like ants, in front of us, in perfect order and quiet as mice and stretched across in even line. We estimated these we saw at twelve thousand.'[25] Nyanda: 'We saw a handful (not many) of the Zulus, who kept running from us. All of a sudden, just as Mr. Shepstone joined me on the crest of a ridge, the army of Zulus sprung up fifteen thousand men ...'[26]

As the two troops were riding half a mile apart,[27] it is probable that Raw's sighting and those of Hamer and Nyanda, which are similar, were made from different positions. Let us presume, therefore, that Raw's troop, riding close to the edge of the plateau were faced with a hill. This would concur with the detail contained in the only other account describing the discovery which, although heresay, is pertinent: Henry Francis Fynn, in his 'Recollections of the Battle', wrote 'George P Shepstone and ... another officer of that staff went

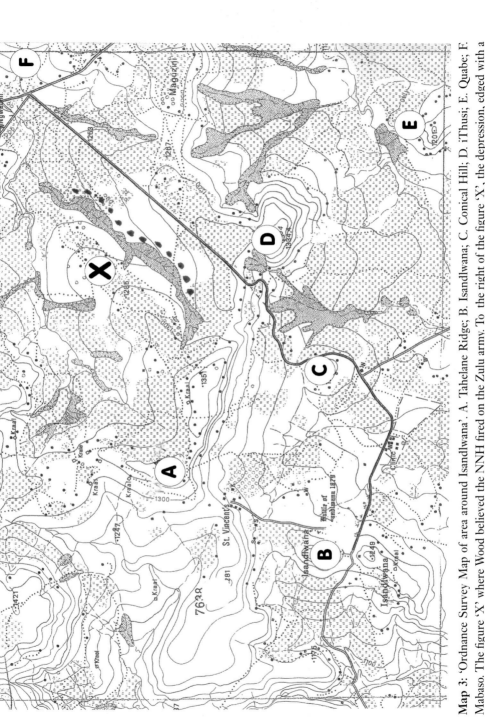

Map 3: 'Ordnance Survey Map of area around Isandlwana'. A. Tahelane Ridge; B. Isandlwana; C. Conical Hill; D. iThusi; E. Quabe; F. Mabaso. The figure 'X' where Wood believed the NNH fired on the Zulu army. To the right of the figure 'X', the depression, edged with a dotted line, deep enough to conceal an army of '15,000 men'.

northwards over the Nquthu Plateau main ridge reconnoitring. They observed
the Zulus showing over a cock's comb ridge side of a ravine ... and fired upon
them. It was the Zulu army there concealed ...'[28] .'A cock's comb ridge side of
a ravine'. There is only one feature on the Nquthu plateau that answers to that
description: iThusi (see photograph page 169) at about three-quarters of a mile
distant from where, it can be assumed, Raw first saw the Zulu army 'showing
itself from behind the hill in front'. If we are correct in that assumption, where
was 'the crest of a ridge', seen by Hamer and Nyanda? A half-mile north-east
of where I have calculated Raw's sighting to have been, there is a depression
of considerable size, the northern end of which descends into the Ngwebini
Valley where a portion of the Zulu army had spent the night. The depression
is two miles long (Map 3, page 154) and deep enough to conceal an army of
'fifteen thousand men'. Compare Map 3 with Wood's map (on which I have
superimposed the modern road) and it will be seen the depression corresponds
with where Wood believed the NNH 'fired on the Umcityn [sic uMcijo]' and
the position Mehlokazulu pointed out to Wood in 1880.

The horsemen, utterly stunned by the immensity of the army they now faced
were, for an instant, confounded, unable to move while in silence, both sides
stared at the other. Then, Shepstone, aware not only of the peril to himself and
his comrades, was taken by the danger to the camp, only three miles away and
unprepared. Shouting to Barton that he was going to warn Pulleine, he and
Hamer turned and at the best speed the terrain permitted, 'rode as hard as ever
we could back to the camp and reported what we had seen'. A different story is
told by Nyanda. He recalled Shepstone ordering him and his troop to '... retreat
fighting' and draw the enemy on towards the camp where, presumably, Shepstone
supposed the Zulu army would be mown down by the volley fire of the 24th.[29]

With the departure of Shepstone, Barton ordered both troops to dismount
and, at about a half-mile distant, commenced firing on the Zulus who returned
fire in good measure. Now the horsemen were hampered by the demoralized
and exhausted amaChunu infantry of Barry's picquet who, due to the horsemen
having come to an abrupt halt, had, after falling behind, caught up. Barry and
Vereker, like their men, were on foot and particularly vulnerable. As soon as the
amaChunu, outnumbered sixty to one or more, saw their Zulu foe rise up, they
turned and fled towards the camp.[30] Higginson and Sergeant-Major Williams,
who earlier had both been seconded by Durnford, had also accompanied
Barton's troopers to the plateau. Now recognizing the dismounted plight of
Barry and Vereker, Higginson requested Williams, '... a good shot, a good
rider and a very cool man under fire' to look after them while he, unaware that

Shepstone had already left to take warning to the camp, took it upon himself to do likewise. Higginson had not gone far when he caught up with Shepstone and Hamer. He later wrote:

> I was going along pretty quickly and soon overtook two officers riding into camp, one of them was Captain Shepstone who asked me where I was going. When I told him he said, 'Oh, I will make a report to Colonel Pulleine as I am going in, will you please ride back and tell my men not to be out-flanked'. Before I could say a word he was gone so I turned round and rode back, but as I came up, I found that they were out-flanked so I ordered them to retire on the camp.[31]

Barton and his Zikhali troopers had by then been keeping the Zulus at bay for a couple of miles and it is likely did not require Higginson's admonishment 'not to be out-flanked'. They retreated fighting, taking few casualties, to the crest of the Tahelane track above the camp.

Meanwhile, Durnford with Nos 4 and 5 Troops NNH, commanded respectively by Henderson and Davies, had bypassed Conical Hill and were riding, about four miles out from the camp, more or less parallel with the Nquthu Plateau, when Zulu elements were 'seen running away'.[32] Durnford, despite the firing that must have been audible from the ridge above where Barton was in retreat, nevertheless surmised that the Zulus 'in retreat' were in fact on their way to attack Chelmsford, exclaiming, 'If they are going towards the General we must stop them at all hazards'.[33] Having made that unfortunate decision, Durnford pressed on until he and his troops were overtaken, at a gallop, by two Carbineers, Troopers Whitelaw and Hayhoe. The men came

Captain George Shepstone of the Natal Native Horse, Durnford's senior staff officer.

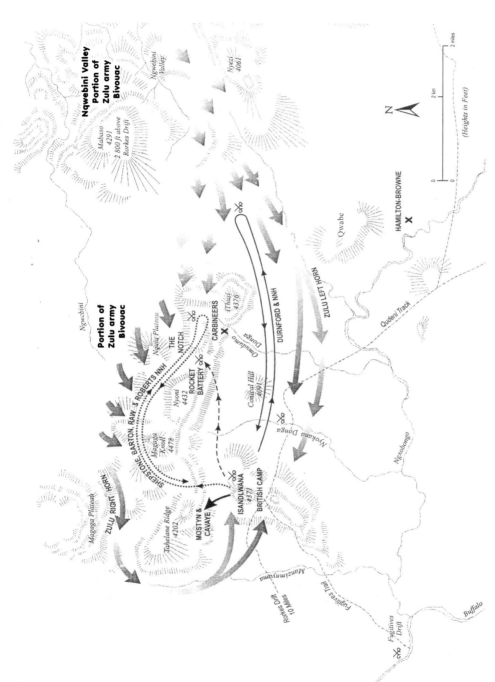

Map 4: The Isandlwana Battlefield, around midday, 22 January 1879.

with a message from Lieutenant Scott, warning Durnford that he was in fact being surrounded and that he had best return to the camp.[34]. Durnford replied,'The enemy cannot surround us, and if they do, we will cut our way through them'.[35] With that bombastic remark, he turned to Davies, asking: 'Where the rocket battery was; I told him a long way behind'.[36] Addressing the Carbineers, Durnford first ordered Trooper Hayhoe, at a gallop, to find Chalmsford and appraise him of the situation. Whether Durnford's message was a request for reinforcements or a warning that he, Chelmsford, was in grave danger, we shall never know. Durnford then turned to Trooper Whitelaw, ordering him to ride back to Lieutenant Scott and to tell Scott to support Durnford with the Carbineers and NMP that Scott had on picquet. To fuel Durnford's anger, Whitelaw forthrightly replied that, 'Lieutenant Scott would not leave his post on any account whatever, as he had strict instructions from Colonel Pulleine not to leave his post on any pretence whatever.'[37] Durnford responded 'I am Colonel Pulleine's senior, you will please tell Lieutenant Scott to do as I tell him.'[38] But a glance towards the Nquthu Plateau confirmed that Durnford and his men were, indeed, about to be encircled by the Zulu army.

There are many accounts detailing the number and names of the Zulu regiments whofought at the battle of Isandlwana, most differing in both respects: H.B. Finney's description compiled '… from the most reliable sources and published by direction of the Lieutenant General Commanding, November, 1879', lists no less than 33 different regiments of which, for practical purposes, no more than 26, totalling 40,000 warriors, were able to take the field. Of these 26 regiments, 32,500 men were between the ages of 20 and 40 and a further 3,400 under the age of 50. However, most sources agree that no more than 10 or 12 regiments, totalling approximately 20,000 warriors, fought at Isandlwana while the regiments most frequently associated with

A fine-looking Zulu elder; a man of authority.

the battle are those compiled by Keith I. Smith and briefly enumerated here as follows: [39]

Regiment	Maximum Number	Alternative Spelling
Nokhenke	1,800	uNokhene
uMbonambi	1,800	
umXapho	700	uMxhapho
inGobamakhosi	7,100	iNgobamakosi
uDloko	1,400	
uVe	3,200	
umCijo	3,200	uMcijo
isAngqu	300	iSangqu
uDududu	900	
uThulwana	2,300	
iNdlondlo	900	
Ndluyengwe	1,800	
TOTAL	23,600	

Barton's Zikhali NNH had, by its encounter, presumably triggered Ntshingwayo's attack: the Zulu latecomers from Mangeni were still to be deployed. But now the die was cast. The Zulu army came '... pouring down from the plateau steadily and quietly'.[40] A fearsome yet wondrous sight as the warriors deployed with bewildering speed into an encircling line of skirmishers, ten or twelve deep and three miles in extent. For Durnford there was no longer any chance of riding to Chelmsford's aid. At that moment it was clear that he and his men were in great peril, as was the camp he had been ordered to reinforce. For a moment they sat their horses, riveted by the abruptness of events and the speed of the approaching enemy: 'They [the Zulu left horn] opened fire at us at about eight hundred yards, and advanced very rapidly.'[41]

Two miles to the rear, close up against the face of the plateau and below the Notch, the birthplace of the Ngwebini Stream, Major Francis Broadfoot Russell and the fagged-out rocket battery encountered Barker, Hawkins and other men of the mounted colonial picquets. Since early morning they had been engaged with an ever-increasing number of the enemy.[42] So much so that the two friends, Barker and Hawkins, having recently reported back to the camp, had taken the opportunity to acquire more ammunition from the Carbineers' quartermaster, William London. Now, both had a full bandolier of fifty rounds. Russell asked if they had seen Colonel Durnford. He also enquired of the enemy's whereabouts. Having no knowledge of Durnford or his movements, Barker, anxious to be helpful, replied that there were Zulus fighting on the ridge above, whereupon Russell rode to the base of the Notch with the intention of getting his battery up onto the plateau and there to join in the action. However, Russell quickly realized the steepness of the ascent would be too much for his weary mules – but not so for his equally weary native infantry. He ordered the rockets to be unloaded and carried by hand to the top. But before committing the battery into action, Russell resolved to see for himself. Spurring his horse up the rocky and steep defile he arrived on the plateau moments after Barton's troopers had opened fire on the Zulu army. He was met by a wave of impassioned warriors. Reigning in, Russell about-turned and, with the Zulus close behind, plunged back down the notch shouting the command 'Action front!'. His astounded and disorganized Zikhali infantry, still unloading rockets, at the sight of the pursuing warriors prepared to flee. Captain Nourse and the battery's eight gunners – who were not gunners at all in the sense that they were soldiers of the Royal Artillery, they being but 'borrowed' privates of the 1/24th – reacted with commendable but futile purpose. They managed to fire one rocket but before they could reload, the warriors, in overwhelming numbers, were upon them. Captain Nourse recalled 'My company was immediately scattered, and my horse, having got away, I was not able to get up with them' [the fleeing infantry] ', in order to rally them. From that moment I saw no more of them with the exception of five men who remained with me ...'[43]

Private D. Johnson, one of the 1/24th gunners, remembered that as soon as the Zulus opened fire, the mules bolted and Major Russell, shot in the head, virtually fell into his arms and died. Johnson further remembered, horseless and on foot, how he turned and fled, finding temporary sanctuary in the donga still held by the colonial vedettes, Barker, Hawkins and their comrades. Another gunner of the battery, Private Grant, had, at the moment of the first Zulu volley been holding several of the battery's horses and despite the ensuing noise and chaos, had managed to sort out the jumble of reins, mount and gallop away taking two of the lead horses with him.[44]

Durnford, with his three white officers, Lieutenants Cochrane, Davies and Henderson, together with the Edendale and Hlubi troops, had ridden far since early morning. Some, including Durnford himself, had already covered twenty miles, and all had ridden close on twelve, mostly at a canter. They were now three and a half miles from the camp, with no reserve ammunition, and about to be overwhelmed. It was not the distance their ponies had already travelled that was cause for concern; the hardy animals could cover twice the distance and still keep going. As Durnford had noted years earlier 'kafir ponies … gave fifty miles a week and never required to be fed'. The NNH ponies, having been fed regularly for months past, could do fifty miles a day without distress. What was disquieting was the rock–strewn and broken terrain where the most sure-footed animal could take a tumble and also a nimble Zulu could outrun a horse. As for a rider having taken a tumble, there was no hope of survival; prisoners were not taken. Now with the enemy closing rapidly, firing as they came, Durnford ordered his men to take up a position in a donga where they were instantly in danger of being outflanked. Evacuating the donga as quickly as they had taken possession, Durnford and his men retired '… steadily in skirmishing order, keeping up a steady fire for about two miles',[45] until they came upon the remains of the rocket battery, little more than moments after its destruction. Indeed, hand-to-hand fighting was still going on with those that remained. Davies found Captain Nourse dismounted, fighting for his life but still loyally supported by a handful of his Zikhali infantry, the remainder having fled.[46] (Nourse was fortunate enough to find his horse again. He also survived the Zulu War and lived to join in the hunt for King Cetshwayo. When, months later, the monarch was hiding in the area of the Black Mfolozi, Captain Fitz-William Elliot, of the 93rd Foot, a Special Service officer, sadly noted that; 'the gallant little horse that had carried Captain Nourse through the Battle of Isandlwana to safety, and had never been sick or lame during the whole campaign was last night killed and eaten by a lion'.)

It would seem that Davies, even at this moment, was uncommonly conscientious regarding the preservation of government property. When there was fighting and chaos all around, Davies endeavoured to preserve two of the unfired rockets which, in any event, would have been of no practical use to the enemy:

> I saw, a little to our left, a mule with two boxes of rockets. I sent one of my men to get it: he had to go pretty close to the enemy to do so as the mule was between us and the enemy. He brought the mule, and we sent it off to the camp; we also saw here some boxes of ammunition or rockets. We made some of our men carry them, but had to abandon them after a while, the enemy being so close.[47]

Durnford, not far away but yet to see the remains of the rocket battery, came upon Private Johnson, still on foot, who was attempting to reach the donga still held by the Carbineers and NMP. If Johnson, at the sight of Durnford accompanied by his orderly, hoped for rescue, he was to be disappointed. Overtaking the stumbling soldier, Durnford, aware that Johnson was a member of the rocket battery, must have sensed what the sight of this lone and fleeing soldier foretold: an unprecedented disaster for which he would, at least, be held partly responsible. In his self-recrimination, Durnford turned on Johnson, demanding to know where the rocket battery was. On being told that it had been 'cut up' and Major Russell killed, Durnford maliciously retorted that Johnson had better go back and fetch Russell's body. The astonished man pointed out that they were all but surrounded. Ignoring Johnson's reply, Durnford and his orderly, leading a spare horse, spurred off towards the camp, leaving the dismounted soldier to his fate.[48]

***

Captain Alan Gardner, one of Colonel Glyn's staff officers, it will be recalled, had left Mangeni earlier that morning in company with Major Stuart Smith RA, Lieutenant McDowel RE, and Lieutenants Dyer and Griffith, both of the 2/24th. Gardner carried Lord Chelmsford's orders instructing Colonel Pulleine that the camp equipage and supplies of the troops camping out were to be sent to Mangeni while Pulleine and the troops at Isandlwana were to remain where they were. Also, almost as an afterthought, or the first indication of Chelmsford's mounting anxiety that all was not well, Pulleine was also ordered to entrench the Isandlwana camp.[49] It is strange that in his report to the Court of Enquiry, to be submitted seven days later at Helpmekaar, Gardner made no comment regarding his ride from Mangeni to the camp. In some miraculous way, it would seem, he and his companions had been able to avoid the Zulu left horn that, at the time, was not only engaged with Durnford and his troops but was also flooding across the Isandlwana plain. On arrival at the camp, Gardner immediately sought for Colonel Pulleine, who he eventually found in his tent, meeting on the way George Shepstone and James Brickhill the interpreter. They too were looking for Pulleine. Brief formalities over, Shepstone, agitated and eager to be the first to be heard, said with commendable Victorian cool, 'I am not an alarmist, Sir, but the Zulus are in black masses over there, such long lines that you will have to give us all the assistance you can: They are fast driving our men this way.'[50] Even as Shepstone spoke, the Zikhali NNH appeared on the skyline, keeping up a steady fire as they retreated on the camp. Shepstone, having delivered his appeal, delayed no longer. Mounting his horse he galloped back to support his retreating comrades.

Brickhill stayed with Pulleine and witnessed Gardner's presentation of Chelmsford's orders. Brickhill was to comment that Pulleine '… seemed thoroughly non-plussed as to what he ought to do'.[51] As well he might. On the one hand, suddenly and astonishingly his camp that he had been ordered to defend at all costs, had come under attack; on the other hand he had been given a direct order to dismantle half the camp and entrench what remained. There was yet another order, a standing order, that he had overlooked: when under attack, all tents, at a bugle call, were to be dropped to the ground by pulling out the centre pole. Pulleine's failure to carry out this simple order was, at that moment, leading Lieutenant Milne RN, with his telescope, ten miles away on Isipezi Hill, to believe the camp was in no danger. Gardner, as a staff officer, gave counsel: as the General was unaware of the prevailing circumstances, his order must be ignored. But Gardner also failed to recall that the tents, obscuring the oncoming enemy and blocking the infantry's field of fire, should instantly be dropped.

Lieutenants William Mostyn and Charles Cavaye, with F and E Companies 1/24th, were the first Imperial troops to engage the Zulus at Isandlwana.

Pulleine's first thought was to stem the onslaught of the warriors pursuing Barton and his NNH. Lieutenant Cavaye and E Company 1/24th, were already on the plateau. Lieutenant Mostyn with F Company, having arrived in camp the evening before, was ordered to the plateau in support, taking with him his second-in-command, Lieutenant Dyson. So serious did Pulleine perceive both the threat on the plateau and his obligation to Durnford to be, that he ordered Captain Reginald Young, a tall, handsome man who had seen much service in Burma, India and the Eastern Cape, to hold his C Company in support close to the foot of the Tahelane track. Taking a moment to reflect, Pulleine realized that his support for Durnford's NNH was more than an obligation, he was obeying yet another order, which in Durnford's words were, 'if you see us in difficulties you must send and support us'.

———————⊃●⊂———————

At 10:30 that morning, after Durnford and his column had arrived at Isandlwana, Lord Chelmsford later stated that the strength of the camp stood at:

Two guns of the Royal Artillery with their gun crews
One rocket battery with crew
Six companies 24th Regiment
204 mounted colonial Volunteers including a few Imperial Mounted
   Infantry
450 NNH
400 NNC
Total Europeans including officers – 772
Total NNH and NNC including officers – 851
Grand Total – 1,623 men[52]

Within an hour this force was scattered, as previously described, helter-skelter over an area of two and a half square miles whereas Pulleine had been ordered to 'draw in your line of defence … draw in your infantry outposts in conformity …'.[53]

———————⊃●⊂———————

Led by Ntshingwayo kaMahole, one of the great commanders of the Zulu army, Prince Ndabuko of the uMbonambi Regiment, his half-brother Shingana, both of whom had fought at Ndondakusuka, Prince Sitheku and Zibhebhu kaMaphitha, hereditary chief of the Mandlakazi, had taken up a position on a rocky platform known as iNyoni. From there they watched, with great satisfaction, as Durnford and his column met head-on with the regiments of the left horn, the iNgobamakhosi and the Mbonambi, 7,500 strong, the warriors of both in the prime of manhood, their reinforcements, the isaNgqu, a regiment of 50-year-old veterans, trailing behind the younger men. Further west, along the plateau above the camp but out of sight from below, elements of the Undi Corps, the right horn, swept past but encountered distant volley fire from Mostyn and Cavaye's companies ensconced amongst the rocks above the Tahelane track. The

The Zulu commander-in-chief, Ntshingwayo kaMahole.

Undi Corps would not engage in the unfolding battle but would jog on to Rorke's Drift where the enemy, perceived to be an easier target, barred the way to plundering Natal.

The regiments of the right horn, the Ndluyengwe, Nokhenke and the uDududu who, with little success, had chased Barton and his horsemen along the plateau all the way from iThusi, now turned upon Mostyn and Cavaye, engaging in a bloody melee with the veteran toughs of the 1/24th who were now running low on ammunition. Having heard the gunfire of both Barton's NNH and Cavaye's companies, Captain Essex, his letter-writing done with, and with no specific duties that day, decided on a ride to the plateau.[54] On reaching the summit, he found both companies of the 1/24th in extended order hotly engaged, at 800 yards, with the Zulu right horn. It was disquieting that the enemy was making no effort to close but, instead, was rapidly extending to the north-west so as to encircle both Mostyn and Cavaye. More alarming, Lieut. Melvill, coming up from camp, brought news '... that a fresh body of the enemy was appearing in force in our rear'.[55] The order was given to retire, whereupon the Zulus charged, and closing rapidly, inflicted severe casualties. In the months and years that followed a myth grew that both companies had disappeared without a trace, the myth fired, no doubt, by Lord Chelmsford's report to the Secretary of State for War, dated 27 January 1879: ' ... one company, sent off to the extreme left, has never been heard of since.'[56] However, there can be little doubt that Mostyn and Cavaye's companies were the first Imperial casualties of the battle. (In an undated pamphlet, written in the early 1950s, George Chadwick of the South Africa Monuments Council, after a visit to the Isandlwana battlefield, recorded 'At the same time a search was made for neglected cairns. Some 40 were found and fully documented ... they included those on the ridge [Nquthu Plateau] where the British regiments were stationed ... In view of statements that very few were killed on the ridge, it is interesting to note that buttons, boot protectors and bones were found where these cairns were dismantled, documented and rebuilt.')

Only a portion of the Nodwengu Corps would descend directly onto the camp; the 43-year-olds of the Nokhenke, the uDududu and the Mbonamisi regiments, would sweep down behind Isandlwana Hill to link up with the left horn and eventually encircle the British camp. (Thus making a mockery of Major Clery's remonstration of two days earlier that 'the rear always looks after itself'.)

From the centre of the plateau, down the Notch and at every other place that afforded a path of descent, the boss of the Zulu horns, the uMcijo and the uVe, poured onto the plain. As they advanced a warrior, seeing the distant glint of the British bayonets exclaimed '*Mbane, mbane, wezulu, Kuyagenwazi mula!*' ('Lightning of the heavens, see its glitter'),[57] his words immediately echoed by his comrades until, like an anthem, it was chanted by all. They came on in skirmishing order, a dazzle of colour, their shields, white, red, black and spotted presenting a confusing target. They carried, poised to strike low into an enemy's belly, or an exposed armpit, the broad-bladed *iKlwa*.

It was over forty years since the Zulu nation, its warriors armed mostly with spears and shields, had, at Blood River, done battle with a white army. At that time, 1838, as we have read, a Boer commando of 460 men, supported by 300 black servants, firing muzzle-loading muskets from behind a barricade of wagons, defeated a Zulu army of 15,000 warriors. Since that time the Zulu army had acquired an arsenal of firearms, mostly obsolete muskets. Nevertheless, now as the battle developed, Zulu firearms, despite their antiquity, were being used to good effect, driving the mounted troops back towards the camp. Other than the acquisition of firearms, Zulu weapons had changed but little since 1838: the cowhide shield, strengthened by a double row of hide lacing, had been reduced in height from five to four feet, and the central stick, now sharpened to a point, facilitated jabbing an opponent's foot. The throwing spear had, more or less, become obsolete as Zulu fighting strategy was to close with the enemy and to fight hand-to-hand using the *iKlwa* and knobkerrie.[58] On the other hand, British weaponry had changed significantly from the musket with its slow and tedious loading procedure, to a breech-loading rifle capable of delivering twelve rounds a minute. Thus, it was essential for the warrior to close quickly with the enemy where his hand-to-hand weaponry, agility, and overwhelming numbers, could be used to advantage.

In the camp, there was an air of astonishment: they were being attacked. It was hard to grasp. Captain Alan Gardner, despite having run the gauntlet, inexplicably made no mention to Pulleine of the oncoming Zulu army but later recalled: 'I delivered him [Pulleine] my order but the enemy were now in sight on top of the hill [the Nquthu plateau], on our left. Lieutenant Colonel Pulleine sent out two companies [those of Mostyn and Cavaye] and drew up the remaining companies on the extreme left of the camp, and facing towards the left, from which direction the enemy were advancing in great number.'[59]

Pulleine, as observed by Gardner, had ordered A, C and H Companies of the 1/24th, commanded respectively by Lieutenants Porteous, Hodson and Captain George Wardell, to take up a position, beyond the rustic shelters of the NNC, at the extreme left of the camp, facing the Nquthu plateau and the Tahelane track. They were shortly joined by Lieutenant Pope and his men of the 2/24th, wide awake despite their all-night stint on picquet duty, falling in on the right of the firing line, in admirable order, as if on parade. Pope himself confidently remarking that he and his men had already been 'warming them well out there and that they would get hotter directly'.[60] However, the first to be deployed were the two guns of the Royal Artillery, now commanded by Major Stuart Smith who, only moments before, had arrived in camp with Gardner. Lieutenant Curling, in Smith's absence, had jubilantly anticipated commanding the guns himself, now, philosophically reflected that Smith's return 'released me of all responsibility'.[61]

In his Court of Enquiry evidence, Curling related how Smith took command and trotted both guns (no mention of infantry support at this stage) to a position, about 400 yards, '… and at once opened fire on a large body of the enemy'. It was only then that, 'the 1st Battalion, 24th Regiment, soon came up and extended in skirmishing order on both flanks and in line with us … We were able to throw shells [each containing forty-two shrapnel balls] into a huge mass of the enemy that remained almost stationary. The Zulus soon split into a large mass of skirmishers that extended as far round the camp as we could see'.[62] Curling's evidence begs the question 'Who ordered Smith to advance?' Or did he do so on his own initiative? Indeed, a particularly valid question would be who on the British side was in command at that moment? Not Pulleine, he was a mile or more away outside his tent, in company with Gardiner. Was it, in fact, Smith? Being a brevet major, he was the

Lieutenant Colonel Henry Pulleine, commander of the Isandlwana camp on 22 January 1879.

most senior officer in the lower end of the camp, the most senior officer in the firing line. Had he assumed command? We will never know.

Pulleine and Gardner watched as the guns began to fire: 'for a short time, perhaps fifteen minutes, the Zulus were checked, but soon commenced to throw forward their left extending across the plain on our front'.[63] Now, acutely alarmed at the enemy's speed and deployment, Gardner, realizing that the right of the camp was all but undefended, received Pulleine's permission to round up all the mounted men in the camp. There were but few, no more than forty, a mixture of mounted infantry, NMP, Carbineers, Newcastle Mounted Rifles (NMR) and the Buffalo Border Guard (BBG), many of whom had sick horses or were themselves in poor health. Although many horses were suffering from sore backs, they were, nevertheless, reluctantly saddled up and put to duty. Gardner, with Captain Bradstreet of the NMR, galloped the little troop forward, taking up a position in a donga close to the camp. There they opened fire at the advancing left horn of the Zulu army.

Lieutenant Vause, with No 3 Troop NNH, having been ordered to escort the wagons of Durnford's column into camp, was returning with the transport when, two miles from his destination, he heard heavy firing coming from the direction of Isandlwana. Giving the order to trot, Vause arrived in camp just at the moment George Shepstone, having delivered his warning to Pulleine, was seeking to join up with Captain Barton. With the arrival of Vause, Shepstone now had 250 Zikhali troopers and 50 infantry with which to support Barton in his retreat from the right horn. Shepstone immediately advanced through the chaos of the camp – the wagon drivers and all types of camp followers already making for the Rorke's Drift track – on towards the companies of the 24th and the guns which, from the rising clouds of smoke, the crash of volley fire and the cannon's boom, were already fiercely engaged. Also to be perceived, but with difficulty, was the distant outline of Barton's horsemen. The amaChunu NNC, having deserted Barry and Vereker, were already halfway down the escarpment, their leaders racing through any gap in the firing line to the perceived safety that lay beyond. Now it was Barton's turn to descend, he and his men tackling the rock-strewn descent, their horses back on their hocks, as they scrambled and slid their way down.

The iThusi Ridge; there is no mistaking Henry Francis Fyn's description when he wrote '. . . they observed the Zulus showing over a cock's comb ridge side of a ravine … it was the Zulu army there concealed'. (By courtesy of the late David Rattray)

Even as Shepstone spurred towards the firing line, he and his native troopers were met by a rush of mounted men coming towards them, not in retreat or flight but hurrying to the camp for ammunition. The companies of the 24th had been firing continuously for almost an hour. No provision had been made for reserve ammunition and, worst still, there was no means of opening the ammunition boxes. Made of teak planking, dovetailed and reinforced with copper bands, the box's wedge-shaped sliding lid, its only means of access, was secured by a countersunk two-inch brass screws. Without a screwdriver, the box defied all means of opening other than smashing it apart by brute force. The regimental ammunition supply of approximately 400,000 rounds, would have followed the regiment from one posting to the next with its screwdrivers, it would seem, being mislaid along the way. Weeks earlier, while the 2nd Battalion was still at Greytown, a requisition for replacement screwdrivers was made. In reply, Quartermaster Bloomfield was informed: '... the articles applied for are not in store'. The letter continued with a comforting aside, assuring the applicant that: 'however useful and necessary such appliances' [screwdrivers] 'may be in European warfare, it is not expected that they will be required in a war such as the troops are about to enter upon.'[64]

Lieutenant Smith-Dorrien, having earlier listened in on the conversation between Durnford and Pulleine, had done little since. Now, however, having watched the enemy afar coming down onto the plain '... with great boldness', and having marvelled as they came on in '... lines upon lines of men in slightly extended order, one behind the other, firing as they came and bearing all before them',[65] Smith-Dorrien realized he must wade in and do something. He took command of all the convalescents, stragglers and idlers he could find and with Quartermaster Bloomfield, set about breaking open ammunition boxes. Even at that moment of crisis the parsimonious nature of all quartermasters revealed itself in Bloomfield. Smith-Dorrien, about to hand over a box to an ammunition carrier of the 1st Battalion, was admonished: 'For heaven's sake don't take that man, for it belongs to our battalion'. To which Smith-Dorrien heatedly replied 'Hang it all, you don't want a requisition now do you?'.[66] Bloomfield and his assistants actually managed to get some open boxes secured to a couple of mules but before they had gone far, the mules, terrified by the thunder of the guns and the chaos, bolted, bucking and careering, doing their best to be rid of their cargo.

Close by, bespectacled James Brickhill, having no weapon of his own, wisely saddled his horse and rode about the camp hoping to get a gun somehow or the other: 'In this I failed and betook myself to a fairly commanding position in front of the column's office', from where he could see, 'the whole [Zulu] army thrown out in battle array' and 'the whole four and a half miles of the iNgutu [*sic*] covered in Zulus'.[67] But what Brickhill, and the whole of the army for that matter, was unable to see less than a mile away but concealed behind Isandlwana Hill itself, was the Nokhenke and the uDududu, perhaps 3,000 strong, of the right horn, racing to encircle the camp.

The assortment of colonials and mounted infantry that Gardner had gathered together a while earlier, had latterly been reinforced by some of the mounted picquets such as Barker, Hawkins and Whitelaw. All had taken cover in what has become known as the Nyokana Donga or later as 'Durnford's Donga'. From that position they had kept up a steady fire, covering the retreat of Durnford's Edendale and Hlubi troops of whom but a handful would pause in support whilst the rest galloped on, making good their escape.

Captain J.M. Penn Symons of the 1/24th was at that moment with the rest of Chelmsford's column, futilely chasing shadows in the Mangeni Valley. Later, he would pass the night in the stricken camp and on the morrow arrive at Rorke's Drift where for days he would diligently question and record the experiences of the few who had survived the battle. His report, compiled from primary sources, is undoubtedly the most concise and factual account of the last moments of the 1/24th. Nevertheless, accurate as his account may be, it is nevertheless subject to the teller's imagination and exaggeration. Penn Symons himself questioned his compilation by stating 'whatever demerits this account may possess, however inaccurate it may be in the details and summaries … it has the advantage of having been written from notes made on the spot … it was most remarkable how their accounts afterwards varied. Men forgot what they saw and did … and mixed up what others told them with their own experiences.'[68]

A Zulu general. The leopard skin, visible below the shield, indicates a prince of royal blood. Note the size of the skull-cracking knobkerrie.

A fine study of a Zulu regimental commander. (The Local History Museum, Durban)

The firing line, now reinforced by the Zikhali horse and footmen, had been inflicting appalling casualties on Ntshingwayo's resolute warriors, seemingly an automaton compiled of brave men. Yet, as the lines of warriors passed, here and there, into the undulations of the plain, shielding them briefly from the hail of lead above, it was with reluctance, bordering on refusal, that they hesitantly emerged again out into the killing ground. The great Zulu commanders, watched the slaughter and hesitation of their regiments while individual *Nkosi*, by fearless example, striding back and forth, exposed to the onslaught, inspired their men to follow.

Barton and his Zikhali troops, having completed their hazardous descent but still hotly pursued, at about 400 yards from the firing line, encountered Vause and Shepstone. Immediately joining forces, the combination about turned and faced the enemy. Lieutenant Raw later recalled: 'about this time the enemy advanced in great force in front of the camp, or I should say more to the left, I turned my troop and engaged them, the troops in the camp [now re-enforced by Captain Younghusband's C Company 1/24th] firing over us.'[69]

Lieutenant Higginson, after delivering his admonishment 'not to be outflanked' to Captain Barton, had returned directly to his post with Captain Krohn, No 6 Company 2/3rd NNC. Krohn and his men, who had hardly changed position since early morning, now found themselves in the firing line mixed up with Barton's and Shepstone's horsemen who were again in retreat. Higginson remembered how Barton's men had brought in Barry, Vereker and the outlying picquets and how the

> … Zulus rapidly extended along the whole front of the camp and soon the battle became general. They came on in columns of skirmishers, and when the front rank was shot down the rear rank filled in their places. They very soon came to close quarters, and the bullets came dropping amongst my men. They stood it very well for some time till at last one man had a bullet through his shield. He jumped up and tried to run away and it was with the greatest difficulty we could get the others to stand … soon afterwards the soldiers began to fall back.[70]

Lieutenant J.A. Roberts, No 2 Zikhali Troop, NNH, killed by friendly artillery fire whilst in retreat on the Nquthu Ridge. (By courtesy of Lieutenant-Colonel Justin Hume)

Up to that moment, Smith and Curling had been firing shrapnel as fast as the gunners could load, a task that no gunner relished, it being tricky and highly dangerous: the fuse having been set in the nose of the shell, the gunner had to carry the missile, leaving any shelter that the gun's position may have provided and, with his back to the foe, making a target for every enemy marksman, ram the shell down the muzzle of the gun. Easier said than done: the shells had metal studs let into their sides that were required to be aligned with the rifling of the muzzle before they could be rammed home. No easy task in the heat of battle resulting, perhaps, in poor shooting to such an extent that the retreating Zikhali Horse came under fire, killing Lieutenant Joseph Roberts.[71] Now, with the enemy so close, Major Smith ordered case shot to be loaded, but at that moment the guns came under fire. One man was killed and five wounded. As if by a satanic miracle the earth had opened up revealing a maddened enemy but a few strides away. It was no miracle but, nevertheless, could be seen as such: the uMcijo, the uMbonambi and the iNgobamakhosi had erupted not from the cover of a donga but out of an undulation of the plain. In the 1980s, a plaque in memory of the Royal Artillery officers and men, was erected on the spot where the guns had fired in battle. At that time, in the 1980s, the author, standing at the guns' position, took a photograph, looking south (see below) of the battlefield with Conical Hill in background. In the foreground, no more than 120 yards from what had been the gun's position on the day of the battle, several heads are to be

The Isandlwana battlefield in winter with Conical Hill dominating the background. The photograph was taken by the author standing next to the Royal Artillery memorial, erected on the position taken by Smith and Curling's guns. Several heads can be seen emerging from the depression that concealed the 'chest' of the advancing Zulu army that overwhelmed the guns. The distance from the emerging heads to the memorial is no more than 120 yards.

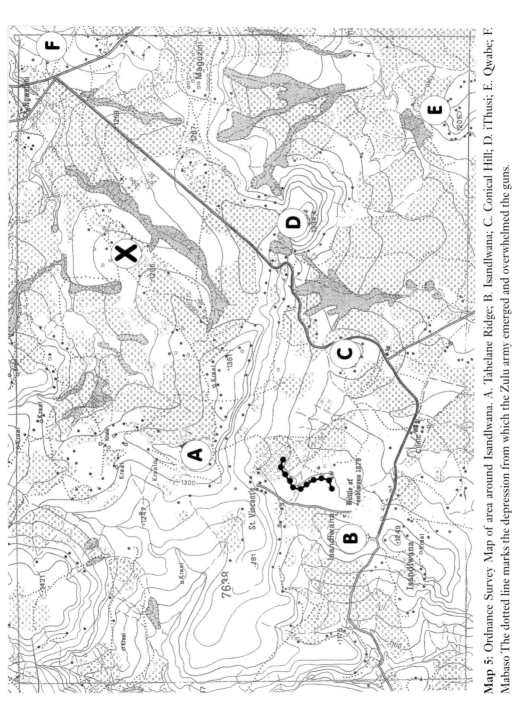

Map 5: Ordnance Survey Map of area around Isandlwana. A. Tahelane Ridge; B. Isandlwana; C. Conical Hill; D. iThusi; E. Qwabe; F. Mabaso The dotted line marks the depression from which the Zulu army emerged and overwhelmed the guns.

seen emerging from a depression in the plain. The depression is enormous in terms of providing concealment. In fact, today, it conceals a sizeable village and many scattered huts. On the day of the battle, it concealed part of the Zulu army that, having burst from cover, would have taken but little more than thirty-five seconds to reach the firing line. Curling's incredulity at the speed with which his gun was overwhelmed is patent: '… Of course no wounded man was attended to, there was no time or men to spare … we limbered up at once but were hardly in time as the Zulus were on us at once … one man was killed (stabbed) as he was mounting onto a seat on the gun carriage. Most of the gunners were on foot as there was no time to mount them on the guns …'. Curling galloped the gun away hoping to take up a different position … 'but found it in possession of the enemy who were killing the men as they ran out of their tents. We went right through them and out the other side losing nearly all the gunners in doing so…'.[72]

The speed and surprise with which the Zulus took the guns, clearly dumbfounding Curling and his men, is echoed in Penn Symon's account:

> In an instant, as in a flash, the enemy who had been creeping nearer and nearer, heedless of the hundreds falling around them, dropped their guns and rushed forward with their assegais shouting '*Usuthu Usuthu*'. The scene became one of wildest confusion. Many of the men had not time to fix their bayonets, but when mobbed, and loading and shooting was out of the question, in one's and two's and groups, they clubbed their rifles and died where they were caught and surrounded.[73]

Mhoti, a warrior of the uMcijo *amabutho* recalled how '… at a breath the whole British force rose from the ground and retired on the tents. Like a flame the whole Zulu force sprang to its feet and darted among them and a hand to hand conflict ensued amongst the tents …' Mhoti engaged in single combat with a soldier, one of the few to have fixed his bayonet with which he lunged at Mhoti, lodging the weapon in the warrior's shield. As the soldier tried in vain to pull the bayonet free, Mhoti stabbed him, his assegai lodging firmly in the white man's shoulder, who, despite the pain and encumberance of the assegai, dropped his rifle, grabbed Mhoti by the throat and threw him to the ground. Close to being throttled, and with his eyes about to burst, the Zulu succeeded in grasping his spear, still embedded in the redcoat's shoulder and, pulling it free, plunged it into the soldier's 'vitals'.[74] One officer, his revolver empty, drew his sword, a weapon more designed for ceremony rather than combat, and faced an advancing Zulu. The warrior came, weaving, springing from left to right until within striking distance he lowered his shield: a feint and the officer made to strike at the warrior's head: a thrust too slow. The blade stuck fast in the warrior's shield: an assegai thrust to the officer's chest quickly followed. Within the melee there were many other duels: one, a fight between Mathbula, a warrior of the iNgobamakhosi Regiment and a dismounted trooper of the Zikhali NNH. The trooper drew a throwing spear from the quiver on his back. Matebula describes the encounter: 'I approached him, he struck first with his spear. I lifted my shield to guard but unfortunately too high and it [the Zikhali spear] caught me on my forearm. I jumped upon him, and banged my shield in his face, and speared him. He fell down dead and I praised myself in the name of my regiment.'[75]

Here and there, groups of soldiers, perhaps as many as thirty in number, or as little as four or five, sought to fight back but were bludgeoned or speared to death. One group, the remnants of Younghusband's company, so legend has it, having found time to fix bayonets, rather than being overwhelmed and in a gallant show of defiance, charged the enemy, 'dying as British soldiers do'.

The movements of Colonel Pulleine and the part he played in the battle are obscure. Captain Nourse possibly mentions Pulleine's fate, not mentioning him by name, but by implication of rank: '… a company of the 24th, with their colonel in their midst, assegaied, just out of reach of their bayonets'.[76] Many of the much-maligned amaChunu NNC, as fleet of foot as any Zulu, had chosen not to run, a number of their bodies being later found intermingled with those of the 24th. The amaChunu tribe, once warriors of past Zulu monarchs, were now regarded by the Zulus as *amaMbuka* (traitors). When the iNgobamakhosi Regiment entered the British camp, and were fighting hand-to-hand, *Nkosi* Gabangaye kaPhakade was recognized and, as a gesture of disdain, Sigcwelegcwele Mhlekehleke, commander of the iNgobamakhosi, ordered him to be put to death by *uDibi* boys: they were to commit *inSeme*, to inflict death by throwing spears. In this way Gabangaye and his amaChunu were put to death.[77] Of all the black troops killed at Isandlwana, totalling 471 in number, over half were amaChunu.[78] There is a story, told to this day in the upper Thukela area of kwaZulu-Natal, relating the reason why Gabangaye did not flee the battlefield. As a young man and a warrior of King Dingane, he fought at the Battle of Blood River and witnessed a few hundred white men defeat a Zulu army of many thousands. This had so impressed Gabangaye that he believed, right until the moment of his death, that the white man's army that he fought for was invincible, thus that there was no need to flee.

In defence of those of the NNC who fled the battlefield, Mr. A.A. Allison, the Resident Magistrate of the upper Thukela Division, wrote, on 7 February 1879 to the Colonial Secretary in their defence, '… a large number of the Ngwabene footmen of Zikhalis Chieftain had been marched into action at Isandlwana armed only with assegaais which they had no opportunity of using … they had, therefore, been targets for the enemy.'

Sergeant-Major Nyanda of Raw's Zikhali troop recalled: ' …the Zulus drove in the right wing … and everyone who could save himself tried to do so',[79] as did Essex and many others. To be astride a horse's back was now the frenzied aspiration of every man and for a brief moment Lieutenant Vereker's luck changed for the better: having stumbled into the firing line with Barry and Williams, he had the good fortune to catch the reins of a riderless horse. Then, mounted and poised for flight, he was accosted by a Zikhali trooper who claimed the horse was his. A gentleman to the last, without argument, Vereker dismounted and watched Williams and it seemed every mounted man,

This picture clearly illustrates the chaos and brutality that prevailed at the last moments of the battle.

making his escape. Adjutant Melvill, of the 2/24th, saw it his duty to save the Queen's Colour, sacred to the Regiment: large, heavily embroidered, tassled, and attached to a weighty staff surmounted by a brass lion, it could only hinder flight. Gardner, also suddenly aware of large masses of the enemy already in the camp, completely surrounding the men of the 24th, decided to leave '… a few among us managed to escape …'.[80] Smith-Dorrien, still riding his 'broken kneed pony' that had had no rest for thirty-six hours, did his best to raise a canter as 4,000 Zulus appeared from behind Isandlwana Hill creating a scene of the 'wildest confusion'. Curling, his gun and limber having overturned in a donga, found the Rorke's Drift road in the hands of the enemy. He got behind '… a crowd of native camp followers',[81] who it transpired were about to flee by a path later to be known as 'The Fugitives Trail' that led to Sothondose's Drift (Fugitive's Drift) six miles away on the Buffalo (mZinyathi) River. Others of Curling's battery, farriers, saddlers and drivers, those lucky enough to have found horses, followed including Privates Johnson, Trainer and Grant, still astride horses salvaged from the rocket battery. Many more rode in their wake including Barton, Raw, Vause, Stafford, Higginson and others; in fact, as Sergeant-Major Nyanda had said, everyone who could save himself tried to do so.

At the other end of the camp, the south end, there had been but few Imperial troops, all noncombatants: storemen, clerks, the sick and the lame. However, when they saw their mounted officers and the colonials galloping pell-mell through the tents and had glanced in horror at what followed, they too, attempted flight. Some, in their mindless terror, sought to hide inside the tents.[82] Yet, not more than half a mile from Chelmsford's HQ, where the Union Jack hung limply in the sultry air, Durnford had just arrived with the Hlubi Troop, he and his men briefly joining in the defence of the Nyokana Donga, keeping the left horn at bay. It would seem, according to Molife, that the vindictive attitude Durnford had displayed in his encounter with Private Johnson, had changed to one of joviality. Durnford clearly did not intend to flee. He intended to stay and in death achieve honour rather than disgrace which would surely be his lot should he survive. Molife would later write: 'At last we came to a bad stony place and a little stream close to the camp [the Nyokana Donga], here we made a long stand firing incessantly. The Colonel rode up and down the line continuously, encouraging us all, he was very calm, and cheerful, talking and even laughing with us. "Fire! Fire my boys, well done my boys", he cried.' Molife and his comrades feared for their leader as he exposed himself to the enemy fire. They even remonstrated, begging him to take cover behind them but he merely laughed and called, 'All right! Nonsense!' As Durnford moved amongst his men, he assisted those with cartridge cases stuck fast in their guns, dismounting in order to do so. Molife and his troopers even considered binding Durnford and carrying him 'off with us as we had horses and the Zulus had none … If we had known what would happen, we would have seized him and bound him, no matter if he had fought us in doing so …'.[83]

Although Molife makes no mention of white troops, such as the colonials and IMI fighting with the Hlubi in the 'bad stony place', he is clearly referring to the Nyokana Donga. It is also clear that the Hlubi Troop, together with Durnford and Henderson, the Hlubi Troop commander, arrived not only ahead of Davies, Cochrane and the Edendale Troop, but also early enough to escape by the Rorke's Drift road and before the Zulu right horn overwhelmed the camp. Molife continued: '… We went back but on the outskirts of the camp we met Mr. Henderson who took us to our own wagon for more ammunition. The Colonel rode straight to the General's tent at the upper end of the camp. While we were refilling [their bandoliers] the Zulu army swept down on the upper camp, shutting us out, but our leader was within, and we saw no more of him.'[84] And with that, together with Henderson, the Hlubi troop escaped.

What else do we know of Durnford's movements once having reached the camp? Of the NNH officers, Henderson seems to have been the closest to him but Henderson left no account of the battle nor of his escape except to say, speaking of Durnford, 'If I had known what sort of man Durnford was (when he got into action) I don't think I would have gone with him. He was close to me during most of the fight and lost his head altogether, in fact he did not know what to do …'.[85] But then Henderson would not have had much to say as a description of his departure and his refusal to assist in the defence of Rorke's Drift would have done him no credit: Lieutenant Chard wrote, '… the officer [Henderson] of Durnford's Horse returned, reporting the enemy close upon us, and that his men would not obey his orders but were going off to Helpmekaar, and I saw them, about a hundred in number, going off in that direction …'[86]

On the other hand, however, Davies and Cochrane, described how they reached and joined in the defence of the Nyokana Donga. Davies: 'We continued firing until we got to the water course, about three hundred yards in front of the camp; we were here joined by some mounted men, suppose they were Mounted Infantry, Mounted Volunteers and Police …'[87] Davies went on to say that the group kept the enemy, the left horn, at bay for quite a while until he and his men began to run out of ammunition. Davies then took fifteen of the Edendale

Troop with him to the Carbineers' camp. Having secured 200 rounds from an open box, on attempting to return to the donga they found 'everyone was leaving it' and the Zulus very close. No mention of Durnford so far. Davies then describes the chaos of the camp, the Zulu right horn pouring in from behind Isandlwana Hill, cutting off retreat, and how he briefly saw Durnford with his mounted orderly 'standing before him with drawn sword, having taken up a position in the camp close to the General's tent'.[88] Cochrane's description of the engagement in the Nyokana Donga and his subsequent flight is similar in most respects to that given by Davies except that he makes no mention at all of seeing Durnford. He emphasises how the mounted men, the Carbineers and NNP, '... had been driven out of the donga'.[89]

What then are we to make of the beloved Victorian cameo of the Carbineers and NNP dying with their gallant leader, Colonel Durnford, their horses, the evidence of their resolve, by which they could have fled, killed alongside them still tied to their picquet ropes? Colonel Evelyn Wood set the scene when he eulogized:

> There comes a one-armed man, who, having shortly fallen back before the ever increasing foe is now determined to die. 'Save yourself. As for me, I shall remain.' He thus dismisses a staff officer and Hlubi's black soldiers, who vainly urged the great chief to seek safety with them. Recognizing his commanding courage, around him gather some twenty kindred spirits, who, nobly disdaining death, resolved to cover the retreat of the guns and die with him ... he himself was fully worthy of their devotion, and History will narrate the ring of dead white men that encircled him formed a halo round his and their own renown.[90]

It is clear that Durnford's 'stand', assumed by many to have been made in the Nyokana Donga which as late as the 1980s was still littered with empty cartridge cases, was made elsewhere, most likely in the vicinity of the present-day memorials to the Carbineers and NMP. But what evidence is there that some twenty 'kindred spirits' resolved to cover the retreat of the guns and die with Durnford? Curling's account strongly suggests that by the time his gun reached the south end of the camp it was out of control. Before retiring from the firing line two of his gunners had been killed, another badly wounded and 'most of the rest' left behind. Curling describes the fate of the few who were still aboard the carriage horses when he entered the camp and found it '... was in possession of the enemy who were killing the men as they ran out of their tents. We went right through them and out the other side losing nearly all our gunners in doing so.'[91] There was no 'retreat of the guns', rather an uncontrolled gallop through the camp, in one side and out the other. And what of the kindred spirits who, 'disdaining death', resolved to stay with Durnford? It has been suggested that those who died with Durnford did so as an act of atonement on behalf of those Carbineers who, six years earlier, abandoned Durnford at the top of Bushman's pass. That, however, seems improbable. More likely those Carbineers and NMP who stayed behind but could, being mounted, have attempted flight, were ordered to remain. On this occasion, Durnford would not forlornly cry, 'Will no one stand by me?' He ordered the men to do so.

Carbineer Barker who, as we have read, had retired on the camp to replenish his ammunition and on making his way back to the Nyokana Donga, encountered Durnford who shouted at him and his mates 'Carbineers, hurry up and follow me!' They did as ordered, accompanying Durnford back to the donga where they and the NMP, some eighty men in all, kept the Zulus in check, 'the donga being in direct front of the camp'.[92] Barker goes on to relate that even at that

Quartermaster William London of the Natal Carbineers, killed in action, was still opening ammunition boxes as the Zulus charged the camp.

Sergeant John Bullock, of the Natal Carbineers, a Pietermaritzburg chemist in civilian life, killed at Isandlwana.

stage neither he nor those about him had any idea that the camp was practically surrounded or that there was any likelihood of defeat. What Barker wanted was a fresh horse so that when the Zulus broke he would be in a position to pursue. On returning to the camp, where he had two spare horses, Barker found one 'shot in the side and kicking on the ground'. On mounting the second horse and attempting to return to the donga, he found that it had been overrun and the 'Zulus were advancing from the donga we had just left … the Zulus being busy now all over the camp stabbing soldiers'.[93] Barker had glimpsed Curling's gun carriage breaking through the Zulus before it overturned and Curling followed the rush of fugitives down towards the Buffalo River.

Trooper Francis Secretan of the NMP would be one of the 'ring of white men' later found encircling Durnford's body. Secretan had a brother, Archer, also a trooper with the NMP who, fortunately for him, was with Chelmsford's force in the Mangeni Valley. Later, in a letter home to his father, Archer recorded what he knew of his brother's death as recounted to him by a fellow NMP: '… I saw Francis mounting his horse. Colonel Durnford called out to him "What are you mounting for?" he replied, "I have no more ammunition, Sir". The officer then told him to stand his ground with his knife only and Francis replied, "'Yes, Sir, I will.'" This account of Francis's death was published in *The Standard* of March 1879 and contained the following extract: 'However, it is reported that one of these "last stands" was made by many of the NMP and Colonial troops around their leader Durnford, set somewhere back from the camp – many of whom could have escaped as their horses were found slaughtered close by still on their picquet rope.'

And what of circumstantial evidence? The *Daily Telegraph* of 15 August 1879 carried the following report:

It is stated that no fewer than twenty-three of the slain surrounding the body of Lieutenant Colonel Durnford on the field of Isandlwana – the total number being thirty-five – were recognized as members of the Natal Mounted Police. The strength of that Corps is one hundred and fifty and the portion of casualties, therefore, speaks eloquently for the courage and devotion of those who thus shed their blood at the call of duty.

Archibald Forbes, a famous war correspondent of the time, also wrote on the same day:

A group of Natal Carbineers prior to leaving Pietermaritzburg in January 1879. Of those present at Isandlwana, Captain Stirton and Trooper Clarence were with Lord Chelmsford's column at Mangeni, while Troopers Barker, Muirhead and Granger, escaped by crossing Fugitives' Drift.

On reaching the crest, I found the dead lying thick, many in the uniform of the NMP. In a patch of long grass, near the right flank of the camp, lay Colonel Durnford's body, a central figure of a knot of brave men who had fought it out around their chief to the bitter end. Around him lay fourteen Natal Carbineers and twenty NMP. Clearly they had rallied round Colonel Durnford in a last despairing attempt to cover the flank of the camp and had stood fast from choice, when they might have essayed to fly for their horses, which were close by at the picquet line.[94]

Yet had they stood by choice? As the camp had been overrun by that time there was no flank to cover. Could it be that the stigma of cowardice, cast upon the Carbineers by Durnford years earlier, still rankled the regiment to an extent that this handful of Carbineers were prepared to throw their lives away when clearly it was every man for himself? But what of the NMP who lay even thicker around? They had no stigma to erase. Is it possible that Durnford, already determined to die, orchestrated his own heroic death scene and by force of his personality, with perhaps an inference to Bushman's Pass, inveigled the colonials to die at his side?

Trooper Fred Symmons, who, we know, was a staunch Carbineer and well aware of Durnford's innuendo of cowardice against his regiment, on visiting Isandlwana battlefield in May 1879 had this to say:

We went all over the field and such a sight as met our eyes may I never see again. Oh, it was awful! Whichever way you turned your eyes there were dead men, dead horses, broken boxes and everything you can think of lying scattered about. The dead soldiers of the 24th were a great deal more scattered than we expected to find them but what struck everyone on the field was the way in which the Carbineers stuck to each other and to Durnford of all men.[95]

We shall never know the actual circumstances of 'Durnford's Last Stand'. Were the Carbineers and NMP prevailed upon to stay or did they, infected by Durnford's courage, scorn to flee?

Let Captain Barter who led the Carbineers at Bushman's Pass cast the final comment:

> And yet, on Isandlwana's plain
> between the slayers and the slain,
> at head of a Colonial band,
> he made a last and desp'rate stand.
> They fought and died, and sooth to tell,
> With those he scorned the hero fell.
> They rest alike in honour's grave:
> None can be braver than the brave![96]

Barter went on to write 'so ended the fateful day'. But the fateful day was far from over.

Cochrane's description of his return to the camp, the engagement in the donga and his subsequent flight is similar in most respects to that given by Davies except that he makes no mention at all of seeing Durnford. He also emphasises that the mounted men '… had been driven out of the donga'. Captain Nourse of the rocket battery, fifty years later, recalled a different story. Having survived the destruction of the rocket battery Nourse made good his escape back to the camp where he was accosted by Durnford wanting to know what had happened to Major Russell.

Chapter 15

Fugitive's Drift

Curling, having been perhaps the first of the Imperial and colonial fugitives to have observed the mass of fleeing camp followers plunging into the bush just beyond Black's Koppie, blindly followed. It was the only exit from the holocaust that was about to engulf the camp. Of the many non-combatants, native troops, Imperials and colonials, few would escape a brutal death and of those only a handful would leave an account of their miraculous survival.

The five Imperial survivors, Gardner, Essex, Cochrane, Smith-Dorrien and Curling, in their Court of Enquiry evidence, related the experience of their desperate ordeals in prosaic terms befitting both the occasion and British officers: Gardner '… a few of us managed to escape by riding down the hill on the right [Fugitive's Trail], but many were shot riding along a narrow valley, and more drowned and shot crossing the Buffalo'.[1]

Lieutenant Essex: '… the only space which appeared open was down a deep gully running south of the road into which we plunged in great confusion. The enemy followed us closely and kept up with us at first on both flanks, then on our right only, firing occasionallly, but chiefly making use of the assegai … the ground passed over on our retreat would, at any other time, be looked upon as impassible for horsemen to descend and many losses occasioned owing to horses falling and the enemy coming up with the rider. About half a mile from the nek, the retreat had to be carried on in nearly single file, and in this manner the Buffalo was gained at a point about five miles below Rorke's Drift.'[2]

Lieutenant Curling's evidence of his escape from the camp related his anguish and his horror at the guns being taken and as his gunners were put to death. Of his own survival, he simply said, 'I then left the guns: There was, as far as I could see, only one gunner with them [the guns], at this time, but they were covered with men of different corps clinging to them. The Zulus were in amongst them almost at once, and the drivers pulled off their horses; I then left the guns. Shortly after this I again saw Lieutenant Coghill, who told me Colonel Pulleine had been killed. Near the river I saw Lieutenant Melvill, 1st Battalion 24th Regiment, with a Colour, the staff being broken. I also saw Lieutenant Smith-Dorrien assisting a wounded man.'[3]

Neither Gardner or Essex, as far as the author is aware, ever elaborated on the experience of their escapes but what a different tale Curling related to his mother nine days after giving his evidence:

The road to Rorke's Drift that we hoped to retreat by was full of the enemy so no way being opened we followed a crowd of natives and camp followers who were running down a ravine. The Zulus were all among them stabbing men as they ran. The ravine got steeper and steeper and finally the guns stuck and could get no further. In a moment the Zulus closed in and the drivers who now alone remained, were pulled off their horses and killed. I did not see Major Smith at this moment but was with him a minute before. The guns could not be spiked, there was no time to think of anything and we hoped to save the guns up to the last moment. As soon as the guns were taken I galloped off and made off with the crowd. How any of us escaped I don't know, the Zulus were all around us and I saw men falling all around. We rode for about five miles hotly pursued by the Zulus when we came to a cliff overhanging the river. We had to climb down the face of the cliff and not more than half those who started from the top got to the bottom. Many fell down amongst the others and Major Smith. The Zulus caught us here and shot at us as we climbed down. I got down safely and came to the river which was very deep and swift. Numbers were swept away as they tried to cross and others shot from above. My horse fortunately swam straight across though I had three or four men hanging on his tail, stirrup leathers, etcetera. After crossing the river we were in comparative safety though many were killed afterwards who were on foot and unable to keep up. It seems to me like a dream, I cannot realize it at all. The whole affair did not last an hour from beginning to end. Many got away from the camp but were killed in the retreat. No officers or men of the 24th Regiment could escape: they were all on foot and on the other side of the camp. I saw two of them who were near the river but their bodies were found afterwards on our side of the river…. Altogether we lost sixty-two men and sixty-four horses just half the battery [the other half of the battery being at Mangeni with Lord Chelmsford's Column].[4]

Lieutenants Cochrane and Smith-Dorrien were equally uninformative in giving evidence to the Court. Cochrane: 'I found that the enemy had rushed into the camp from the left and were engaged hand to hand with the infantry who were completely overpowered with overwhelming numbers: I saw that "all was over".

I made in the direction which I had seen taken by the mounted men, guns, Royal Artillery and the natives on foot. I was cut off by the enemy who had now reached the line of retreat, but with a good horse hard riding and good luck, I managed to reach the Buffalo River.'[5]

Smith-Dorrien's evidence was so brief he came close to having said 'No comment' when he stated: 'I am Transport Officer with No. 3 Column. On the morning of the twenty second I was sent with a despatch from the General to Colonel Durnford at Rorke's Drift, the despatch was an order to join the camp at Isandlwana as soon as possible as a large Zulu force was near it. I have no particulars to mention besides.'[6] A more vivid recollection was to follow twenty-eight years later when Smith-Dorrien, at the request of the officers of the South Wales Borderers (the descendant regiment of the 24th), requested Smith-Dorrien to write an account of the Isandlwana battle. His account completed, Smith-Dorrien continued to describe his flight, mentioning that the Zulus assumed only those fugitives in red tunics were soldiers and that those in dark blue patrol uniforms were civilians. He went on to mention that it was coincidental that the only five officers to survive were all wearing dark patrol jackets. He continued:

I shall never forget for some four thousand had come in behind and were busy with shield and assegai. Into this mass I rode, revolver in hand, right through the Zulus, but they completely ignored me … I could see the Zulus running to complete their circle from both flanks, and alas their leading men had already reached the line of retreat long before I got there. When I reached the point I came on the two guns, which must have been sent out of the camp before the Zulus charged home. They appeared to me to be upset in the donga and to be surrounded by Zulus. Again I rode through unheeded, and shortly I was passed by Lieutenant Coghill, 24th, wearing a patrol jacket and blue britches.

Still some distance from the Buffalo, Smith-Dorrien was passed by Melvill, 'at least half a mile behind Coghill' wearing a red tunic and carrying, across the front of his saddle, the cased Colour of his regiment. Closer to the river, Smith-Dorrien relates '… I then came to Fugitives Drift, the descent to which was almost a precipice. I found there a man in a red coat badly Assegaied in the arm unable to move … I managed to make a tourniquet with a handkerchief to stop the bleeding and got him half way down when a shout from behind said "Get on man the Zulus are on top of you" I turned round and saw Major Smith, RA, as white as a sheet and bleeding profusely, and it seemed we were surrounded.' Major Smith, the wounded soldier and Smith-Dorrien's poor old knock-kneed pony were all slain. But Smith-Dorrien, leaping into the river and grabbing the tail of a swimming horse, gained the Natal bank but not safety. He was pursued for several miles by 'a lot of Zulus who had crossed higher up and were running to cut me off'.[7] He finally reached Helpmekaar early next day.

Of the colonials only Captain Nourse was singled out to give testimony at the Court of Enquiry, he being the only officer to witness the loss of the rocket battery. Although he gave no account of his escape from the camp he mentioned meeting up with Privates Trainer, Grant and Bombadier Gough who seem to have rescued the horse he had lost earlier and on which he eventually rode to safety.[8]

Davies, like the other colonials not having given evidence, later made a statement on how, attempting to flee the camp, he was attacked by warriors of the iNgobamakhosi Regiment, one of whom assegaied his horse. Fortunately the wound was in the fleshy part of the animal's leg. Nevertheless, on proceeding a few hundred yards, at a pace little better than a walk, the ground being so bad and his horse bleeding profusely, Davies was overtaken by two warriors, one grabbing the bridle. Fortunately, Davies had already fixed his issue bayonet-knife to his rifle and with it attempted to stab the Zulu but '… he got hold of the rifle and pulled it out of my hand as if I had been a child. My horse reared and shied, which saved me from an assegai thrown at me by the other fellow. I here used my revolver to advantage.'[9] The remainder of Davies' ride to theriver was fairly uneventful, relative to the circumstances, but on reaching the Buffalo he was attacked by local 'friendly' natives. These could well have been Gamdana's people, Gamdana being *Nkosi* of the area surrounding Fugitive's (Sothondose's) Drift. Davies stated:'My natives [NNH], tell me that the Zulus who were left in the kraals as loyal men did more harm at the river than the men we were fighting with'. On the way to the river Davies had taken up a wounded NNH trooper and, despite everything, managed to get the man across the river to safety.[10] Finally, as we have read earlier, Davies, having reached Helpmekaar in company with Captain Stafford, rode practically non-stop to Pietermaritzburg to deliver the news of the Isandlwana disaster.

And what of the two chums of the Natal Carbineers, Troopers Barker and Hawkins? In the confusion, after evacuating the Nyokana Donga, they had got seperated. Barker later related 'I mounted my horse, the Zulus being busy now all over the camp stabbing the soldiers, and made in the direction of the Nek'. On the way Barker was joined by another Carbineer, Trooper Tarborton, but both were '… obliged to retire back towards the camp which was now a mass of Zulus. We then went in the direction we had seen an artillery carriage go.' Nevertheless, they managed to get through but having ridden a half-mile or less, Tarborton became concerned for his brother, also a Carbineer. Tarborton determined to about-turn and find him. Together with Barker, who was equally concerned for Hawkins, both started back in the direction of the camp, neither realizing they were in the midst of a total cataclysm. Barker later wrote:

> Up till this time I never thought of disaster, but only that we were retiring on a point to rally; but the defeat was only too palpable and we had to spur and hurry our jaded horses over the most awful country I had ever ridden. Riderless and wounded horses were galloping past and tumbling down precipices and gullies. Here I heard for the first time and only time the awful scream of a terrified horse. He was a black horse with a saddle turned round and as he went past us he went crash against a mounted man in front of us and rolling over the krantz, this awful scream was heard. The Zulus seemed to be behind, before, and on each side of us, and as we hurried on we had to leave poor fugitives crying and begging us not to leave them.[11]

As Barker and Tarborton neared the Drift they caught up with Charlie Raw and his men of the Edendale Troop, the only unit to leave the battlefield as a cohesive and disciplined force. Barker later stated '… and well it was for us two, as his men, mounted Basuthos [from the Edendale Troop] were already on the Natal side of the river, and had it not been for these Basuthos I doubt if a single white man would have escaped by Fugitive's Drift, as they kept the Zulus in check while the few escaped'.[12] So impressed was Queen

The Colour of the Edendale Troop, NNH, presented to the unit in 1881, was aquired for safe keeping by the Killie-Campbell Africana Library in 1959. Alfred kaMhulo, whose father fought at Isandlwana, was present at the handing-over ceremony. (By courtesy of the Killie-Campbell Africana Library)

Victoria with the conduct of the Edendale men that she ordered the Royal School of Needlework to furnish a Colour, emblazoned with the Union Jack and the battle honours of the troop, while Sergeant-Major Simeon Khambule was later awarded the silver Distinguished Conduct Medal.

Although Raw ran the gauntlet with the rest, he had remarkably little to say: 'The artillery poured through the camp and finding the road full of the enemy tried to go along the road of retreat but the guns were upset and most of the men killed. We crossed the Buffalo about five miles below Rorke's Drift, arriving at Helpmekaar about eight in the evening.' Could it be that Raw, having 'stood by' Durnford at the top of Bushman's Pass, now remained silent, merely marvelling at his twice good luck!

James Hamer, the civilian Assistant Comissariat Officer and friend of George Shepstone, had been close to Raw during much of the battle but when all was lost and '... the scenes at the top of the camp baffled all description, oxen yoked to wagons, mules, sheep, horses and men in the greatest confusion, all wildly trying to escape'. Hamer followed the lead, shooting his way out of the camp and down the Fugitive's Trail. He related that his horse, by the name of 'Dick', was so done in that, 'a man of the rocket battery galloped up with a lead horse and let me have it. I had just taken the saddle off poor Dick when a bullet struck him dead and the poor fellow who gave me the horse had only ridden two yards when I saw him fall killed from his horse. The animal I was now on was a splendid beast but the girth of the saddle was not strong enough and when I galloped another two miles it broke and I came down on the stones, luckily I stuck like mad to the bridle and quickly rigged up a girth by passing the neck rein through the 'D' of the saddle and thereby saved myself, for the Zulus were by this time close upon me.'[13] Not only did Hamer have the good fortune to cross the Buffalo and get to Helpmekaar. Two days later he was allowed to accompany Lord Chelmsford and his staff to Pietermaritzburg.

Lieutenant Higginson left two accounts of his escape: one, handwritten, dated 17 February 1879, and the other the official War Office statement, dated the day following the battle. However, his acounts not only differ on several salient points, they are in serious conflict with Trooper Barker's description of his encounter with him. During Higginson's ride to Fugitive's Drift, he later related how he met up with Melvill and Coghill and how on reaching the river, with Melvill still carying the Colour of the 24th, the emblem was lost in the river as were all their horses. Nevertheless, having made the Natal bank and a degree of safety '... we saw two Zulus following us. When they got within thirty yards, Melvill and Coghill fired and killed them both.' In Higginson's official report this incident is related as 'we got out' [of the river] ' all right and as we were going up the other side, Coghill called out, "Here they come", I turned round and saw two men close to us and, turning to Melvill said, "For God's sake fire, you both have revolvers". I saw both the Zulus drop!'[14] Higginson goes on to relate how, having disposed of their pursuers and climbed the bank, Melvill and Coghill could go no further. Higginson, however, being of the opinion that both men believed themselves to be safe, ran on encountering four Basuthos 'with whom I escaped by holding onto a horse's tail'. The first account of Higginson's escape ends at that point. His second version is more detailed: 'I ran on, past them [Melvill and Coghill] and got to the top of the hill, where a few Basuthos on horseback had stopped … When I got to them I got hold of a horse's tail and ran on; I could see nothing of the poor fellows behind me, so I guessed that they [had] been overtaken.' Then, still holding onto the horse's tail, Higginson runs for three miles until he sees a mounted Carbineer approaching who informs him that other Basuthos have off-saddled two miles further on. Higginson then tells the Carbineer, who happened to be Trooper Barker, that he had been injured in the river, 'he let me ride his horse to where the men [the Basuthos] were'. Very different from Barker's version, collaborated by Raw and others. After Barker and Tarborton had crossed into Natal, they waited a while in hope some of their comrades were not far behind. Barker recalled:

> I fancied I saw a man who I thought was Hawkins some way down the hill, I rode back, but it turned out to be Lieutenant Higginson, so he informed me, of the Natal Native Contingent, and had got hurt in the river where his horse was washed away. As my horse was too tired to carry two, I assisted him to mount and he rode away leaving me to follow on foot. Tarborton, Henderson, and Raw, recognizing him on my horse, took the horse from him and came back to meet me with it, of which I was right glad, as I had ran for about three miles. Higginson told them he could not have walked any further, and he knew I was fresh, and that he was sending the horse back for me. Raw obtained a horse for him by dismounting one of the Basuthos. We gave our horses a rest here for about an hour, I can tell you that they needed it, as we (the Carbineers) had been in the saddle since 4am, and had had a lot of galloping about. My poor horse had come down twice with me along the Fugitive's Track.[15]

Barker and Tarborton reached Helpmekaar at sundown, not knowing that Hawkins and Tarborton's brother were long dead on the battlefield.

Captain Stafford, on the other hand, attempted to save another man's life at the likely expense of his own. Fifty-nine years after the battle, and when in his eightieth year, Stafford was persuaded to dictate the tale of his adventures. Of his escape down the Fugitive's Trail he stated 'Thanks to the noble animals we rode to which terror seemed to impart strength and speed, we fought our way through and then commenced a race for life. The fleet-footed Zulus kept at our heels and a small distance gained was temporarily lost owing to the fact that at one of the dongas I came across a wounded man and, after several attempts to get his foot into the stirrup iron of my saddle, I eventually pulled him up behind me. He had an Assegai wound under his arm and was already so weak from loss of blood that I could hardly feel his grip on me.' However, all went well for a few hundred yards and then attempting to leap a gully, twelve feet in width, Stafford's wounded passenger fell from the horse, never to recover. The man was left behind and pressing on Stafford and others came upon another wounded fellow, Lieutenant Erskine … 'who was lying against a rock with an Assegai wound through the calf of his leg, quite exhausted and unable to proceed further, opportunely I was able to get Erskine up behind me just in the nick of time. Fortune favoured us now as a large white horse with a rein round his neck came up alongside us evidently instinct prompted him to seek protection and we were able to catch the charger. The rein was twisted round the lower jaw, as all youngsters who are brought up on a farm learned to do, and Erskine was placed on his brave back.'[16] Erskine's safe arrival at Rorke's Drift the next day is confirmed by an entry in trooper Symons' diary: 'We heard also that Wally Erskine and six Carbineers were safe.'

Of all the accounts of successful survival, the frankest testimony must be that of James Brickhill, the civilian interpreter, a man brave enough to admit his cowardice.

Our flight I shall never forget: no path, no track, boulders everywhere … our way was strewn with shields, Assegais, blankets, hats, clothing of all description, guns, ammunition belts and saddlery … our stampede was composed of mules, oxen and horses in all stages equipment and flying men all struggling intermingled, man and beast all apparently impressed with the danger which surrounded us … how one's heart steels itself against pity at such time. I came across poor Band-Sergeant Gamble, tottering and tumbling amongst the stones; he said 'For God's sake give me a lift', I said 'My dear fellow, its a case of life and death with me', and closing my eyes, I put spurs to my horse and bounded ahead.

Moments later Brickhill came upon a soldier who, like the Band-Sergeant, could go no further but instead of pleeding for rescue merely remarked 'I am done. The Zulus can just come and stab me if they like',[17] and with that the man quietly sat down on a stone to await his death. Brickhill rode on and despite losing his spectacles whilst floundering through a swamp, reached the Natal bank where his heart again steeled itself: he saw Melvill in difficulties but '… resisting the impulse', to go to his assistance Brickhill 'hastened on'.[18]

A few other fortunate, dogged and no doubt terrified men reached the Natal bank: Privates Grant, Johnson and Trainer of the rocket battery, one, or possibly all, riding bareback, escaped, as did another twenty-five Imperial soldiers of whom approximately half were of the Royal Artillery. The white colonial troops were a little more fortunate, with twenty-nine, including those already mentioned, successfully running the gauntlet.

James Brickhill, a civilian interpreter attached to No 3 Column. As the Zulu army charged the camp, Brickhill thought to find a gun and a fast horse. He later successfully escaped across Fugitives' Drift.

But who was responsible for this British catastrophe, this dumbfounding Zulu victory, perhaps the worst disaster in the history of Victorian colonial warfare? Who would be blamed for the loss of 1,439 Imperial and colonial troops, two guns, a thousand Martini-Henry rifles and 400,000 rounds of ammunition plus the equippage of a modern army? And many would ask what was Britain doing in Zululand in the first place? One local newspaper thought it had at least part of the answer, commenting: 'It is not Lord Chelmsford only who has found out that the Zulus are a match for us in generalship, and more than a match for us in cunning.'[19]

In 1880, one armchair officer, Major Waller Ashe, late of the King's Dragoon Guards, writing from London and destined never to visit Natal or Zululand, came to the astonishing conclusion that it was the soldiers who were to blame. Ashe published an authorative book, *The Story of the Zulu Campaign* in which he expressed the following opinion: 'The cause of our failure – and there were several of a palpable nature – are not to be found in want of Generalship, want of organization, or want of transport. They were due undoubtedly to the sending out of raw, sickly, unseasoned and untutored boys who, being the sweepings of

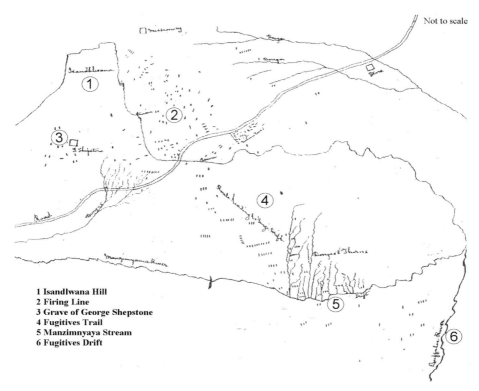

1 Isandlwana Hill
2 Firing Line
3 Grave of George Shepstone
4 Fugitives Trail
5 Manzimnyaya Stream
6 Fugitives Drift

Map 6: A rather confusing map, circa 1883, it being a mixture of perspective and tabletop. It is, nevertheless, an interesting and revealing document in that each tiny fleck depicts a grave of one or more men, thus silently, but eloquently disclosing not only the scattered nature of the battle but also the surprising number of fugitives.

half the regiments in Her Majesty's Service, could not possibly have any feelings of communion, or traditional sympathy, within the corps into which, before a formidable enemy, they found themselves pitchforked.'[20] Likewise, Chelmsford also found fault with the men he had commanded. Apart from attempting to offload blame on Colonel Glyn and Colonel Durnford, Chelmsford indicated that both the officers and men of the 24th had been found wanting. Writing to the Secretary of State for War five days after the disaster, Chelmsford reported:

> … As regards to the proceedings of the six companies of British infantry, two guns and two rocket tubes, the garrison of the camp, I can obtain but little information. One company went off to the extreme left and has never been heard of since, and the other five, I understand, engaged the enemy

to the left front of the camp and made there a most stubborn and gallant resistance. So long as they kept their faces to the enemy the Zulus were, I am told, quite unable to drive them back, and fell in heaps before the deadly fire poured into them … When, however, the Zulus got round the left flank of these brave men they appear to have lost their presence of mind and to have retired hastily through the tents which had never been struck. Immediately the whole Zulu force surrounded them, they were overpowered by numbers, and the camp was lost. Those who were mounted ran the gauntlet and some small portion managed to reach the river, which, however, at the point of crossing was deep and rapid … Had the force in question but taken up a defensive position in the camp itself and utilised the materials for a hasty entrenchment which lay near to hand, I feel absolutely confident that the whole Zulu army would not have been able to disodge them. It appears that the oxen were yoked to the wagons three hours before the attack took place so that there was ample time to construct that wagon laager which the Dutch in former days understood so well. Had, however, even the tents been struck and the British troops been placed with their backs to the precipitous Isandlwana Hill, I feel sure that they could have made a successful resistance. Rumors have reached me however that the troops were deceived by a simulated retreat and, in their eagerness to close with the enemy, allowed themselves to be drawn away from their line of defence.[21]

But despite the decoys Chelmsford attempted to deploy in order to divert blame from himself, he failed to deceive the Duke of Cambridge. The Duke not only admonished Chelmsford, he impartially commended the ability and bravery of the enemy. General Sir Charles Ellice wrote:

The Field Marshal Commanding in Chief has very carefully considered the evidence taken before the Court of Enquiry on the Isandlwana disaster, the supplementary evidence afterwards sent home and the answers transmitted by Lord Chelmsford to certain questions addressed to him upon the subject by the Adjutant-General.

HRH has come to the conclusion that the primary cause of the misfortune, and that which led to all the others, was the underestimate formed of the offensive fighting power of the Zulu Army. This was not unnatural as nowhere within Southern or Central Africa did such a powerfully organized, well disciplined and thoroughly trained force of courageous men exist as lay at the disposal of the Zulu King.[22]

Chapter 16

The Aftermath

In the nineteenth century, following a military disaster, it was customary, after the condemnation of the officer responsible, to award the Victoria Cross to those who had been seen to perform an outstanding act of valour. For instance, in 1852, after the Charge of the Light Brigade, ('a mission of breathtaking futility'),[1] at Balaclava, five VCs were awarded, each in respect of the recipient having gone to the assistance of an endangered comrade.[2]

During the flight to and the crossing of Fugitive's Drift, there were no less than seven acts of outstanding valour, six of which have been mentioned in the previous pages:

1. Sergeant-Major Williams gave up his horse to Captain Barry and Lieutenant Vereker.
2. Lieutenant Smith-Dorrien stopped and attended to a wounded man and later, on the Natal side of the drift, gave up his horse to Commissariat Officer Hamer.
3. Captain Stafford took up behind him wounded Lieutenant Erskine.
4. Lieutenant Davies took up behind him a wounded man.
5. Trooper Barker gave up his horse to Lieutenant Higginson.
6. Sergeant-Major Simeon Khambule stopped to rally his men to cover the crossing of Fugitive's Drift.
7. Private Samuel Wassall, not mentioned previously, having successfully reached the Natal bank, recrossed the river to rescue a drowning comrade.

However, there was a difference between the battles of Balaclava and Isandlwana. Although both engagements were monstrous calamities, Balaclava could be seen by some as a dashing, even a glamorous affair, whereas Fugitive's Drift was regarded as a scandalous rout. Furthermore, as the world's press had watched The Charge take place, the consequences could not be denied, unlike the calamity of Fugitive's Drift that was witnessed by none but the fugitives themselves.

Thus, as Chelmsford and others were anxious to sweep Isandlwana and the rout under the carpet, it was deemed unwise to publicize either event by the award of Victoria Crosses; and so no awards were made except one and then only due to the persistence of the officer who had witnessed Wassall's deed of valour.

On 11 February 1879, Captain Barton of the NNH wrote a statement, addressed to Lieutenant Walsh of the IMI, which read in part:

> As I approached the river, a man of the mounted infantry was riding in front of me, and I also saw at the same time another man of the mounted infantry struggling in the river and he called out his comrade's name; he was apparently drowning. The Zulus were at this time firing at our people from above us, others were down on the bank of the river stabbing others of our people on both sides of where I was. The man of the mounted infantry, who rode down in front of me, dismounted, left his horse on the Zulu side and sprang into the river to save his comrade. I consider this man to have performed a most gallant and courageous act, in trying to save his comrade at the almost certain risk of his own life. I crossed the river myself, about the same time and I did not think it possible that either of these two men could have escaped alive; Indeed I spoke some days afterwards to Lieutenant Walsh of the Mounted Infantry, of the circumstances which I had witnessed and I spoke of it to him as evidence of my having seen two of his men lost at the Buffalo River.[3]

So initially, Barton had informed Walsh of the incident in the belief that he was merely reporting the certain deaths of two of Walsh's men. However, a few days later when Barton was visiting the makeshift hospital at Helpmekaar, by a remarkable coincidence a Private Westwood, ill in bed, overheard Barton describing the gallant conduct of the unknown man and immediately cried out identifying himself as he who had been rescued and named a Private Samuel Wassall of the 80th Regiment, attached to the Mounted Infantry, as his saviour. It was then that Barton decided to write his report of 11 February.

The day following Barton's report, Lieutenant Walsh decided to obtain collaboration of Wassall's gallantry by interviewing Private Westwood in hospital. Westwood made a statement which Walsh took down in writing:

> I wish to bring to the notice of the Commanding Officer the gallant conduct of Private Wassall, 80th Regiment, who saved my life and nearly lost his own in doing so. In attempting to cross the river I got exhausted

and cried out for help. I saw Private Wassall on the bank of the river on the Zulu side. On seeing me he jumped from his horse and getting into the river seized me and dragged me to the bank on the Zulu side, advising me to cross by the other ford which I did. The enemy, at the time Private Wassall got into the river, were keeping up a heavy fire on us, the bullets striking all around. Others were stabbing wounded men. Had it not been for Private Wassall I must have lost my life, and in saving it, he was placing his own in very grave danger.[4]

On 12 February Walsh submitted Barton and Westwood's statements, together with one of his own, to Lieutenant Edward Browne, 1/24th Regiment. Browne in turn, on the same day, fowarded all three statements to Lieutenant Colonel John Russell, Officer Commanding 1st Squadron Mounted Infantry, commenting:

I have the honour to forward the accompanying reports for submission to HE the Lieutenant General Commanding … as the identity of the man mentioned, viz. Private Wassall, 80th Regiment, 1st Squadron Mounted Infantry, has in my opinion been fully established, I now respectfully submit for the consideration of HE the Lieutenant General Commanding, the circumstances of the case and hope that he may deem the gallant action performed by Private Wassall worthy of being rewarded with the decoration of the Victoria Cross.[5]

Russell, two days later, on 14 February, following the correct procedure up the ladder of the military hierarchy, wrote to Colonel Richard Glyn, the commander of No 3 Column, who was still entrenched in appalling conditions at Rorke's Drift with what was left of his shattered command:

Sir, I have the honour to forward to you a letter and correspondence I have received from Captain Browne commanding 1st Squadron Mounted Infantry, with reference to the gallant conduct of the man mentioned in the margin. [Wassall] This man appears to have behaved in an exceptionally brave manner, in saving the life of his comrade, and I trust that it may be considered right to bring his name forward for a special mark of distinction …[6]

But it appears Glyn was not interested. Was it because Wassall, despite being attached to No 3 Column, was not a soldier of the 24th? Without comment Glyn bundled all the correspondence together and on the 18th sent it off to Pietermaritzburg addressed to the Asssistant Military Secretary. However, notwithstanding Glyn's apparent disinterest in brave deeds, when it came to acts of gallantry performed by men of his own regiment he was effusive. Writing to Lord Chelmsford ten days later, he brought the saving of the Queen's Colour by Melvill and Coghill, to the General's attention. '... In conclusion I would like to add that both these officers gave up their lives in the truly noble task of endeavouring to save the Queen's Colour of their regiment, and greatly though their end is to be deplored, their deaths could not have more noble and full of honour [at that time their was no posthumous provision for the award of the Victoria Cross]'.

Private Samuel Wassall, who won the Victoria Cross. (By courtesy Royal Archives, Windsor Castle)

As an example of the acrimony that still prevailed between Chelmsford and Glyn, on receipt of Glyn's uncommented submission of the various statements regarding Wassall's valour, on 26th February Chelmsford, without bothering with a formal reply, merely scrawled a reprimand to Glyn across the bottom of Russell's statement: 'In cases like the one under reference it is absolutely necessary that you should yourself enquire into the matter and express an opinion as to the accuracy to the statements made.' Chelmsford's secretary added 'Please return without delay'.[7] But Glyn proved to be obstructive and cantankerous: furthermore circumstances had changed somewhat – the Mounted Infantry was no longer attached to Glyn's command. A few days earlier it had been transferred to No 4 Column, commanded by Colonel Evelyn Wood. So with no further ado Glyn scrawled under Chelmsford's comments: 'Officer Commanding No. 4 Column. Passed on to you as the Mounted Infantry is under your command' and sent the papers off to Wood on 2 March 1879. But Wood, no doubt, deeming it best not to get too involved, passed at least part of the buck back to Glyn. On 9 March Wood wrote: 'It would appear that Private Westwood is still serving under your command – perhaps you will enquire to his statement, and forward your remarks direct to the Military Secretary. I have ordered the attendance of Lieutenant Walsh and Private Wassall at this camp, and will forward the result of my enquiries to the Military Secretary.'[8] Nineteen days later, Glyn taking his time and seeming indifferent as to whether or not Wassall's act of gallantry be recognized, scribbled on the bottom of Wood's letter: 'Full enquiries have been made about Private Westwood but cannot be traced in connection with any corps in this command.'

Thus, it seemed, the quest for Wassall's VC was lost – but not quite. Brief, and clearly tiresome notes, continued to pass back and forth between No 3 and No 4 Columns until finally Private Westwood was discovered, still very ill, in Pietermaritzburg hospital. He was eventually brought before the Pietermaritzburg District Magistrate where he made another statement. This time it was recorded verbatim and not transposed into a formal style as had obviously been the case with his initial evidence. The straightforward simplicity of his new evidence both underlined his honesty and Wassall's bravery. It convinced the Officer Commanding Troops Pietermaritzburg, who witnessed the testimony, to write '... he [Westwood] made the statement clearly and without hesitation and without any leading questions being put to him. From the way in which the man made his statement I should say he was not in any way exaggerating the circumstances.'[9] It was enough. In May, Queen Victoria gave her approval, and the award of the Victoria Cross to Private Samuel Wassall was gazetted on 17 June 1879. Others who had been put forward for the award were not so lucky. Smith-Dorrien wrote: 'I was recommended for the Victoria Cross for two separate acts that day. These recommendations drew laudatory letters from the War Office, with a regret as to the proper channels for the correspondence not being observed, the statutes of the Victoria Cross did not admit of my receiving that decoration, and, having no friends at court, the matter was dropped.'[10]

Likewise, in 1882, Trooper Barker was recommended for the decoration by no less a person than Major General Sir Evelyn Wood VC, but the War Office replied '... while Trooper Barker's conduct on the occasion referred to is deserving of every commendation, there does not appear to be sufficient ground, according to the terms of the statute, for recommending him for the distinction of the Victoria Cross'.[11] Thus, minimal publicity was achieved to the detriment of brave men.

For several weeks Natal shuddered in the expectation of a Zulu invasion. The fear was well founded for had it not been for the Zulu reverse at Rorke's Drift, there is little doubt that Prince Dabulamanzi kaMpande, King Cetshwayo's brother, who had led the Zulu attack, would have taken an army into Natal. Such was the claim of Dabulamanzi himself: a few years after the conflict, Walter Stafford, late of the NNC, was running a small store, close to the town of Vryheid, when he heard Dabulamanzi was visiting close by. Stafford sent Dabulamanzi a message informing him that a white man who had fought at Isandlwana, would like to greet him. A meeting was arranged and Dabulamanzi's first reaction was to call Stafford a liar, saying that no white man had escaped from the battlefield. However, later Stafford recorded

> … After I had spoken to him for some time he handed me a pot of beer and said '*puza*' (drink). I asked him if it had been his intention to invade Natal. He said 'No', that Cetywayo [*sic*] told him that the flooded rivers were bigger kings than he was. I said why did your men shout out, both at Isandlwana and at Rorke's Drift, 'Nina Manga', which means you are killing yourselves, tomorrow night we will sleep with your wives and sisters in uNgungumhlobu [*sic*] (Pietermaritzburg). He said 'It was only bravado but should Rorke's Drift have fallen I should certainly have taken my army into Natal.'

Stafford added the comment, 'Had that happened all the Natal Natives and the Cape Natives would have joined him as a matter of policy to save their own skins. It is too awful to contemplate what the result would have been.'[12]

<hr />

But Rorke's Drift did not fall and although Natalians slept ill at ease, evacuating women and children to the Cape, the Zulu army, having taken a thousand casualties and with its King, perhaps hoping the British would not seek retribution, did not cross the Thukela. Reinforcements rapidly began to arrive and Chelmsford set about invading Zululand for a second time. His first priority was to relieve Colonel Pearson and his No 1 Column that had been besieged in Eshowe for over three months. But before making the attempt, Chelmsford was anxious that in doing so he would not blunder into a Zulu army. Therefore, towards the end of March, he requested Colonel Wood, with

No 4 Column, to make a 'demonstration' that would draw the enemy's attention in the direction of the Disputed Territories. Wood's subsequent attack on the mountain stronghold of Hlobane on 28 March 1879 was a disaster. Wood's force, consisting of 700 mounted men, mostly white colonials, supported by 800 native mercenaries, having reached its objective was attacked by overwhelming numbers of the abaQulusi clan and put to flight. Worst still, at the height of the engagement the Zulu army, 20,000 strong or more, was suddenly observed on the plain below racing to the aid of their Qulusi kin. However, the Zulu army's assistance was not required. Wood and his horsemen, in disarray, were heading back to their Khambula camp with all possible speed.

With the survivor's return to camp bringing the alarming news that the Zulu army was not far behind, a tense night followed at Khambula. But Khambula was more than a camp, it was a rustic fortress standing on an open plain. Two laagers, formed by 200 chained wagons covering five acres, sheltered the garrison. Trenches with turf and soil forming parapets encircled the camp while the near approaches had been strewn with broken glass and other devices. Additional turf had been dug and piled into and under the wagons to form two-tier firing positions; thorn tree branches had been rammed between the wagon wheels and into any aperture that might admit access to a determined warrior; hundreds of ammunition boxes had been opened and dispersed inside the laagers; water buckets had been strategically placed; range markers had been located in all directions; and breakfast had been served.

The first of the King's warriors came into view at 10 am, 'We were able to see dense masses of the enemy advancing in perfect order in four separate columns; their end seemed never to come ...'[13] It was the Zulu army at the height of its power, rampant with courage and folly. Despite the lesson of Rorke's Drift and their King's admonishment never to attack a fortified position – or as the King had put it, on no account was the army 'to stick its head into the den of a wild beast', for five hours the warriors continued vainly to attack, '... still they came on with the ferocity of tigers, never halting, never wavering ... no soldiers in the world could have been more brave than the Zulus on that day'.[14] Near dusk, leaving a thousand dead around the circumference of the camp, the Zulu army turned its back on Khambula camp and, as one, dejected and defeated, began to jog away. But it was not over. The horsemen, the vanquished of the previous day, mounted up and, executing fearsome vengeance '... we raced helter skelter after the flying Zulus ... they became exhausted, and shooting them down would have taken too much time; so we took the assegais from the dead men and rushed amongst the living ones, stabbing them right and left with fearful revenge ...

the slaughter continued as long as we could discern any human form before our eyes …'[15] The Zulu killed and wounded were estimated at over 2,000. British casualties, killed and wounded, seventy-seven.

———————◦◦◦———————

On 29 March 1879, at the same time as the Zulu army commenced its attack on the Khambula camp, 120 miles away to the south Lord Chelmsford was crossing the Thukela en route to the relief of Eshowe. The column that Chelmsford now directly commanded, the Relief Column, was vastly different from that element of No 3 Column that had fought the Zulu army at Isandlwana, it having consisted of approximately 1,700 men, whereas the Relief Column numbered no less than 6,600.

The Thukela safely crossed, the column, several miles in length, pushed on in pouring rain reaching the banks of the Nyezane River three days later. 'Tents there were none, so we had to pick out the driest spots under the wagons, the General [Chelmsford] doing the same as the others. There was no distinction and no grumbling, and we were all most thankful for something to eat.'[16]

John Dunn, the White Zulu, it will be remembered, had thrown in his lot with the British. Now, with 150 of his native horsemen, Dunn had been given the role of Chief Scout to the Relief Column, and believed a Zulu army lurked nearby. Crossing the Nyezane alone, he returned to report that there were Zulus in the vicinity on the opposite bank. That night the wagons were laagered. At dawn the following day, 2 April, a mounted patrol returning to the camp at a gallop, reported Zulus in force fording the Nyezane. Chelmsford, mindful of past blunders, had earlier instructed 'each wagon and cart must have some ammunition boxes placed on it in such a position as to be easily got at. The Regimental reserve boxes must have the screw of the lid taken out, and each wagon or cart will have a screwdriver attached to one of the boxes so that it may be ready for opening those in which the screw has not been taken out.'[17] The Zulu commander, Somopho kaZikhale, faced as formidable a fortress as had his counterpart faced only days before at Khambula. And, whereas Chelmsford was now a disciple of the Rorke's Drift lesson, Somopoho irrationally ignored it. Numerically the odds were more or less even, roughly 6,000 men a side. Weapon-wise, however, the Zulus were pitifully outclassed; the British armoury consisted of four 9-pounder guns, a 24-pounder rocket battery, two Gatling guns and 2,500 breech-loading Martini-Henry rifles whereas the Zulus had, perhaps, a thousand black-powder, muzzle-loading muskets (their kin who fought at

Khambula had confiscated all the Martini-Henrys captured at Isandlwana) and 6,000 assegais. The British square, large enough to shelter the column's oxen, to provide a firing position for every soldier along its entire length, and with either artillery or Gatling guns at each corner, confidently waited for the Zulu attack.

At 6.30 am, or thereabouts, the Zulus came and a Gatling gun, to test the range, opened fire: it was later recorded that having fired two bursts '… there was a clean lane cut through' the advancing enemy. During the next hour, the warriors charged again and again, failing repeatedly, despite their courage, to force the British laager. However, on occasion, it was a close run thing. One officer recalling that 'In spite of our steady fire the Zulus continued their advance, nothing daunted, … the donga to the right of my company appeared to be full of Zulus, who by groups of ten or fifteen began to make rushes for a clump of palm bushes ten yards from us.' [18] One officer, clearly distressed when his men began to waiver, later wrote: 'Our men were awfully nervous at first, could not even speak and shivered from funk …'[19] But within the hour the Zulu army, riddled with shot and shell, could withstand the massacre no longer and almost as one they turned their backs and hurried north. It was now the turn of the mounted infantry, each man recently equipped with a cavalry sabre. The chase was on and as the horsemen closed with the fleeing warriors, they hacked them down without mercy. The casualties occurred at the battle of Gingindlovu British: two officers and eleven men killed plus four officers and forty-four men wounded Zulus: conservative estimate, 1,110 killed or wounded.[20]

The British had scored a substantial victory but in doing so had earned the contempt of the Zulu army. The manner in which the white men fought, cowering, as the Zulus saw it, behind their barricades, was to be despised. 'They are continually making holes in the ground [trenches] and mounds left open with little holes to shoot through. The English burrow in the ground like wild pigs. Fight us in the open!' they cried.[21] Three months later Chelmsford accepted the Zulu challenge.

For the British the road to Ulundi an area of the Mahlabathini plain, a few miles west of King Cetshwayo's royal homestead of oNdini, had been a hard one. The terrain, adverse weather and disease ensuring sickness and extreme discomfort, had, on the line of march, been constant companions of all with no exception. Further reinforcements, artillery and two regiments of British cavalry, had swelled the ranks of Chelmsford's column to 5,000 officers and men.

At 5.15am on the 4 July 1879 the call of 'reveille' had awoken the British camp. By 8.30am the combined columns, having crossed the White Mfolozi River, had been drilled into the formation of a massive 'square', nearly nine acres in extent, unprotected by laagered wagons or any other form of barricading. Earlier, an officer had suggested an entrenchment to which Chelmsford had sharply replied, 'No, they [the Zulus] will be satisfied if we beat them in the open. We have been called ant-bears long enough.'[22] The column having reached a knoll, a feature selected by a reconnaissance of the previous day, Chelmsford took personal command, ordering the 'square' half right, so as to face the Ulundi kraal. There the column halted. With bayonets fixed and ammunition boxes open they waited: the two front ranks kneeling and the remainder standing.

The Zulu army, containing elements of all its regiments, with the exception of two who guarded the King, began to deploy. General Ntshingwayo of Isandlwana renown, supported by brothers of the King, took command. Fifteen thousand strong, with 5,000 in reserve. '… they advanced in beautiful order, covered by skirmishers, their object to surround us, with their largest force in the rear to cut off our retreat; it was a grand sight'.[23] Then, as the Zulu army closed on the British 'square', 5,000 'wild pigs' caught in the open, and as British officers drew their swords in apprehension, Chelmsford raised a barricade, a barricade of flying lead mowing the warriors down. But still they came causing Chelmsford, as the Zulu vanguard surged closer and closer, to shout in alarm 'Men fire faster! Cannot you fire faster?', with some brave warriors falling within yards of the British guns. But, inevitably despite Zulu valour, it was to be a repetition of Khambula and Gingindlovu. By 9.30 am, the battle having lasted little more than thirty minutes, the horsemen were in pursuit of the fleeing Zulu army, an NCO of the 17th Lancers, in a letter home, compared the pursuit to 'pig sticking, just like tent pegging at Aldershot'. One officer commented that the Lancers 'did well' spearing the enemy 'whether wounded or not'.[24]

Lord Chelmsford came in for a great deal of criticism on his return to England. Here in a cartoon of 1879, looking youthful and carefree, Chelmsford's handling of the campaign is held to question by an enquiring public.

Having burnt every barracks, building or homestead within easy ride, and having had coffee and a late breakfast provided by the ration wagons, the British army turned its back on Zululand and marched back into Natal. The casualties, British: thirteen killed and sixty-nine wounded. Zulu: estimated 1,300 killed, wounded unknown.

With the fight over, the Honourable William Drummond, Chelmsford's Civilian Intelligence Officer, was last seen galloping towards some burning buildings. He was never seen again nor was his body ever found. What happened to Drummond remained a mystery until very recent times. Two years ago, Prince Shange of the Royal Zulu family, was in London attending a lecture when he overheard two gentlemen discussing Drummond's disappearance. Shange interjected commenting 'What a hero that fellow was, he died trying to save the life of a child. As you know Drummond spoke Zulu and whilst Ulundi was in flames he heard the anguished cries of a mother shouting that her child was trapped in a burning hut. Drummond dismounted and rushed into the hut to save the child. Unfortunately the hut collapsed and the two were engulfed in the flames.' As Drummond and Dabulamanzi knew each other from their hunting days before the war, Drummond's demise entered into Dabulamanzi family oral history.[25]

Three weeks later Chelmsford was on his way home to England leaving Sir Garnet Wolseley, who now, as both H.M. High Commissioner to Southern Africa and Commander in Chief of H.M. Forces, had replaced both Frere and Chelmsford, to sort out the turmoil and civil war that would be the legacy of British chicanery. In recent years Prince Mangosuthu Buthelezi described the consequence of the British invasion of Zululand as 'Destruction on a grand scale followed the events of 1879 and the dignity of our kingdom has not yet been fully restored'.

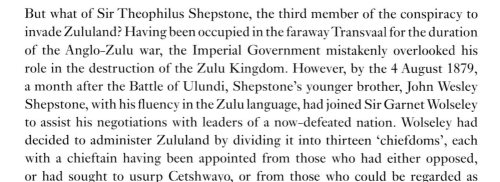

But what of Sir Theophilus Shepstone, the third member of the conspiracy to invade Zululand? Having been occupied in the faraway Transvaal for the duration of the Anglo-Zulu war, the Imperial Government mistakenly overlooked his role in the destruction of the Zulu Kingdom. However, by the 4 August 1879, a month after the Battle of Ulundi, Shepstone's younger brother, John Wesley Shepstone, with his fluency in the Zulu language, had joined Sir Garnet Wolseley to assist his negotiations with leaders of a now-defeated nation. Wolseley had decided to administer Zululand by dividing it into thirteen 'chiefdoms', each with a chieftain having been appointed from those who had either opposed, or had sought to usurp Cetshwayo, or from those who could be regarded as

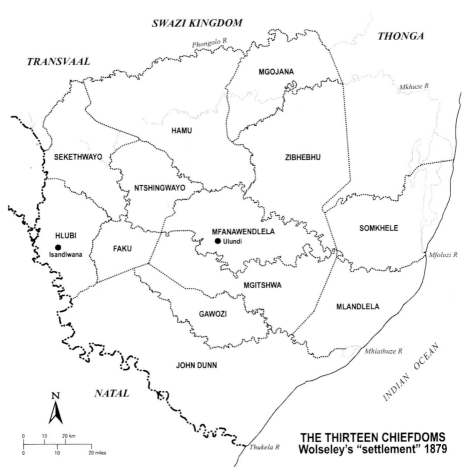

Map 7: Sir Garnett Wolseley's division of the Zulu Kingdom into thirteen chiefdoms. John Dunn receiving one of the largest and most fertile portions.

'trusty'. For instance, Prince Hamu kaMpande, a half-brother of Cetshwayo, and the Zulu general Zibhebhu kaMaphitha fell into the first category while John Dunn, for instance, who received the largest slice of the old kingdom, could be so regarded. Rather surprisingly, General Ntshingwayo kaMahole, the victor of Isandlwana, was also given a portion of the old kingdom. Intriguing as that may be, surely there was more significance to Ntshinwayo's award? What is pertinent is Ntshingwayo clearly met with both John Shepstone and Sir Garnet on or about 1 September 1879, less than a month following the Battle of oNdini, as recorded on the document illustrated opposite which reads:

Signed at Ulundi on the first day of September 1879
This is the mark of chief 'X' Tshingwayo
This is the mark of inDuna 'X' Nikizwayo
This is the mark of inDuna 'X' uNpopoma
[followed by Sir Garnet Wolseley's signature]
General Commander of Forces in South Africa and her majesty's High
Commissioner for South-eastern Africa
This document has been faithfully interpreted from word to word
by me to the chief [there follows a name which has been crossed out
and superimposed with the name Tshingwayo] who declared fully to
understand and approve of the contents thereof.
[signed] J W Shepstone'

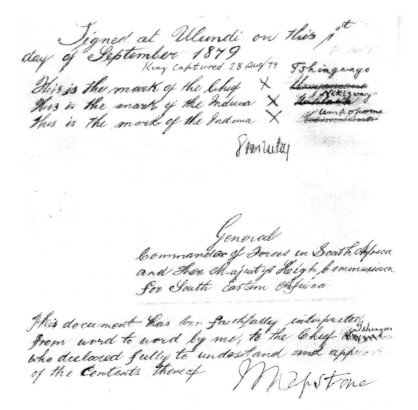

An enhanced copy of the faded front page to the document signed 1 September 1879, by
Chief Tshingwayo, Sir Garnett Wolseley, John Shepstone and others.

Unfortunately, it is not possible to reveal the contents of the document as, at the time the title page was found by the author in the Pietermaritzburg City Archives, the remaining pages were missing. If the absent pages are somewhat of a mystery, their absence is as by no means as puzzling as Wolseley, in his published diary, making no mention of Ntshingwayo whatsoever. Even though Wolseley's entry for 1 September in part reads: 'The chiefs who have been assembling here for some days past assembled this afternoon in front of my tent and I made them a long speech, Shepstone was interpreting …'. Wolseley's entry for the day was a lengthy one closing with: 'weather becoming rather warmer and the flies are becoming a plague. Cetshwayo [*sic*] was crowned this day 6 yrs. ago.'[26] Despite Ntshingwayo not having been mentioned, clearly he and Wolseley were in contact. That being the case it is difficult to believe that Wolseley, of all people, would not have been passionate to hear, direct from Ntshingwayo himself, full details of the Zulu tactics and deceptions prior to and during the Battle of Isandlwana. One can only speculate as to Wolseley's failure to question Ntshingwayo or, alternatively, if he did in fact interrogate the Zulu general, why did he decide not to mention it? Wolseley had, however, two days previously, mentioned with great glee, that his army of imperial, colonial and native troops, plus a number of the King's former chiefs, had finally captured King Cetshwayo. What of Cetshwayo's fate? He was immediately sent into exile in the Cape where it was intended he should remain. However, due to public opinion in England, he was finally granted an audience with Queen Victoria herself and permitted to return to Zululand. Once home, he was enmeshed in a web of intrigue and civil war; he was wounded in battle and later defeated by his former general, Zibhebhu kaMaphitha. Thereafter, Cetshwayo found sanctuary with the colonial government, his minder being none other than Henry Francis Fynn junior. He died at Eshowe, under suspicious circumstances, on 8 February 1881.

Chapter 17

Reconciliation

Under the title 'Former Foes Meet at Anniversary', *The Natal Mercury* of Monday, 23 January 1929 published a picture of the Isandlwana Battlefield (see below). Where the ox wagons had been parked fifty years previously the ground was covered in motor cars and trucks. But it was an occasion for old adversaries who, on 22 January 1879, did their very best to kill each other, to come together like old cronies of the same regiment, and swap yarns, boast and show their scars. It was a ceremony that would be repeated until there were no old cronies left. Nevertheless, each year at the Sunday closest to 22 January, a wreath-laying ceremony continues to be held. Then, in January 1997,

FORMER FOES MEET AT ISANDHLWANA ANNIVERSARY

In January 1929, the 50th anniversary of the battle, a ceremony was held at Isandlwana with old adversaries mingling together in friendship. Could the horsemen in the foreground be survivors of the Natal Native Horse?

Four veterans of the battle at the January 1929 ceremony. On the right, highly decorated and now a lieutenant colonel in the British Army, William Clarke who, at the time of Isandlwana, was a trooper in the Natal Mounted Police.

At the 1929 ceremony on the Isandlwana battlefield, an old warrior describes Zulu tactics to an attentive audience.

a ceremony of a most singular nature took place, not at Isandlwana Battlefield but at Mtubatuba Barracks, South African Army, Northern KwaZulu-Natal: the affiliation parade between the Royal Regiment of Wales, the descendant regiment of the old 24th, and 121 SA Infantry ('Zulu') Battalion, a regiment recruited in Zululand, amongst whom undoubtedly there would be those whose forefathers had fought at Isandlwana. The concept of affiliation had been the inspiration of Brigadier D. de G. Bromhead, a great-great-nephew of Lieutenant 'Gunny' Bromhead VC, of Rorke's Drift fame, during a visit to South Africa in 1994. However formal approval was to be required. First the South African National Defence Force sanctioned the request followed shortly by the approval of Her Majesty Queen Elizabeth.[1]

The ceremony itself was a stirring and colourful occasion with King Goodwill Zwelithini a direct descendant of King Cetshwayo, and Brigadier Brommhead as guests of honour. It was an iconic event, the only known occasion in the history of the British Army where a British regiment has affiliated with that of a former foe.

In 1997, the Royal Regiment of Wales and 121 South African Infantry ('Zulu') Battalion, affiliated. During the ceremony, King Goodwill Zwelithini and Brigadier D. de G. Bromhead applaud the band of 121 Battalion.

Notes

Chapter 1
1. PRO WO 32/7301.
2. Ibid.
3. Wolseley, G., *Sir Garnet Wolseley's South African Diaries (Natal) 1875*, edited by Adrian Preston, Cape Town, 1971, p. 135.
4. Laband, John (ed.), *Lord Chelmsford's Zululand Campaign, 1878–1879*, Stroud, 1994, p. 75.
5. James Stewart Archive, Vol. 2, Pietermaritzburg, 1976, p. 17.
6. Ibid., p. 113.
7. Moodie, D.C.F., *John Dunn, Cetywayo & The Three Generals*, Pietermaritzburg, 1886, p. 5.
8. Ibid.
9. Samuelson, R.C., *Long, Long Ago*, Durban, 1974, p. 230.
10. James Stewart Archive, Vol. 2, Pietermaritzburg, 1976, p. 17.
11. Mackeurtan, Graham, *The Cradle Days of Natal*, Pietermaritzburg, 1948, p. 141.
12. Laband, John, *Rope of Sand*, Cape Town, 1995, p. 114.

Chapter 2
1. Wright, J.E., and Manson, A., *The Hlubi Chiefdom in Zululand-Natal*, Ladysmith, 1983, p. 35.
2. Ibid., p. 51.
3. Ibid., p. 65.
4. The Blamey Papers, 'The Crowning of Cetshwayo', Oldhouse Museum, Durban.
5. Moodie, *John Dunn, Cetywayo & The Three Generals*, p. 40.
6. The Blamey Papers, 'The Crowning of Cetshwayo', Oldhouse Museum, Durban.
7. James Stewart Archive, Vol. 4, Pietermaritzburg, 1976, p. 126.
8. Ibid.
9. Ibid.
10. The Blamey Papers, 'The Crowning of Cetshwayo', Oldhouse Museum, Durban.
11. Binns, C.T., *The Last Zulu King*, London, 1963, p. 35.
12. Ibid. p. 59.
13. Natal Blue Books for August 1873.
14. Binns, *The Last Zulu King*, p. 87.

Chapter 3
1. Herd, Norman, *The Bent Pine*, Johannesburg, 1976, p. 13.
2. Ibid., p. 12.
3. Stalker, John, *The Natal Carbineers*, Pietermaritzburg, 1912, p. 64.
4. Ibid., p. 68.
5. Ibid., p. 69.

6. Ibid.
7. Ibid., p. 70.
8. Ibid., p. 71.
9. Ibid., p. 73.
10. Herd, *The Bent Pine*, p. 35.
11. Wright and Manson, *The Hlubi Chiefdom in Zululand-Natal*, p. 73.
12. Herd, *The Bent Pine*, p. 95.
13. Ibid., p. 87.

Chapter 4
1. Nürnberger, Margarette, *Maqhamusela Khanyile's Life & Testimony*, n.d., p. 36.
2. Ibid.
3. French, Gerald, *Lord Chelmsford and the Zulu War*, London, 1939, p. 43.
4. Mackeurtan, *The Cradle Days of Natal*, p. 225.
5. Moodie, *John Dunn, Cetywayo and The Three Generals*, p. 91.
6. Durban Municipal Library, reference 968.303
7. Ibid., p. 32.
8. Ibid.
9. Gon, Philip, *Send for Carrington*, Johannesburg, 1984, p. 15.
10. Tomasson, W.H., *With the Irregulars*, London, 1881, p. 129.
11. Symons, Fred, 1879, M/S diary.
12. Dawney, C., *Campaigns in Zululand 1879*, Cambridge, 1989, p. 5.
13. Fenn, C.E., 'How I Volunteered for the Cape', private M/S.
14. Letters of Captain the Hon. Fitzwilliam Elliot, 93rd Foot.
15. *The Red Book, a Compilation of 1879 Natal Press Reports*, privately printed.

Chapter 5
1. *The Red Book, a Compilation of 1879 Natal Press Reports*, privately printed, p. 106.
2. *The Natal Witness*, 30 January 1879.
3. Symons, Fred, 1879, M/S diary.
4. Krige, E., *The Social Systems of the Zulus*, London, 1936, p. 269.
5. James Stuart Archive, Vol. 3, Pietermaritzburg, 1976, p. 327.
6. Symons, Fred, M/S Diary.
7. The first casualty of the Anglo–Zulu War was Lieutenat S.C. Alexander of the NNC who died of dysenteric diarrhoea at Pietermaritzburg on Sunday, 5 January 1879. *The Red Book*, p. 5.
8. S.B. Bourquin, *The NNC and Associated Units During the Zulu War of 1879*, privately published, n.d., p. 106; Lock, R., and Quantrill, P., *Zulu Victory*, London, 2002, p. 62.
9. There is a Harford Road in Pinetown, KZN, named after the site of the Harford family farm.
10. *The Red Book, a Compilation of 1879 Natal Press Reports*, privately printed, p. 10.
11. Ibid.
12. *The Natal Witness*, 1 February 1879.
13. Letter to Sir Henry Ponsonby, 27 January 1879.

Chapter 6
1. Nathan, Manfred, *The Voortrekkers of Southern Africa*, London, 1937, p. 253.
2. Laband, *Rope of Sand*, p. 352.
3. French, Gerald, *Lord Chelmsford and the Zulu War*, London, 1939, p. 63.

4. Ibid., p. 62.
5. Drummond, *The Natal Witness*, 1 February 1879.
6. James Stuart Archive, Vol 1, Pietermaritzburg, 1976, p. 8.
7. Laband (ed.), *Lord Chelmsford's Zululand Campaign*, p. 52.
8. Ibid., p. 85.
9. Fynn, H.F.F., *The Natal Witness*, 22 January 1913.
10. Drummond, *The Natal Witness*, 1 February 1879.
11. Fynn, H.F.F., *The Natal Witness*, 22 January 1913.
12. Shamase, M.Z. , *S.A. Military History Society Journal*, Vol 1, No 4 (1969), p. 133.
13. James Stuart Archive, Vol 1, Pietermaritzburg, 1976, p. 174.
14. Ibid., p.175
15. Ibid., Vol 3, p. 136.
16. Ibid., Vol 5, p. 88.
17. PRO WO 32/7725
18. Maxwell, G., Private letter to Colonel Edward Durnford, November 1879, Campbell Collections, University of Natal, Durban.
19. Ibid.
20. Ibid.
21. Symons, Fred, 1879, M/S diary.
22. Drummond, *The Natal Witness*, 1 February 1879
23. Fynn, H.F., *The Natal Witness*, 22 January 1913.
24. PRO WO 32/7725.
25. Drummond, *The Natal Witness*, 1 February 1879.
26. Ibid.
27. PRO WO 33/34 Enclosure 1 No. 101.
28. Milne, PRO ADM 16486 S6333.
29. TNA (PRO) WO 32/7725.
30. Milne, PRO ADM 16486 S6333.
31. Laband (ed.), *Lord Chelmsford's Zululand Campaign*, p. 74.
32. Isaacs, N., *Travels and Adventures in Eastern Africa (Natal)*, 1836.

Chapter 7
1. James Stuart Archive, Vol 3, Pietermaritzburg, 1976, p. 314.
2. Ibid.
3. Ibid.
4. Child, Daphne (ed.), *The Zulu War Diary of Col. Henry Harford*, Pietermaritzburg, 1878, p. 24.
5. Milne, PRO ADM 16486 S6333.
6. PRO WO 33/34 56333.
7. Alison Letters, Brenthurst Library, Johannesburg.
8. Ibid.
9. TNA (PRO) WO 33/34, Enclosure 1 in No 72.
10. PRO WO 30/129 S6316.
11. Ibid.
12. Symons, Fred, 1879, M/S diary.
13. Maxwell, *The Natal Witness*, Xmas 1895.
14. Higginson, PRO WO 32/7726.
15. Drummond, *The Natal Witness*, 1 February 1879.

16. Symons, Fred, 1879, M/S diary.
17. Ibid.
18. Ibid.
19. PRO WO 32/7711 S6316.
20. Penn Symons, Private Journal, 24 February 1879.
21. Drummond, *The Natal Witness*, 1 February 1879.
22. Miss Mary Frere writing to Sir Henry Ponsonby, 27 January 1879.
23. Hamilton-Browne, G., *A Lost Legionary in South Africa*, London, 1912, p. 126.
24. Ibid.
25. Royal Archives, Windsor, VIC/O 33/118.
26. Ibid.
27. Clarke, S., *Zululand At War*, South Africa, 1984, p. 78.
28. Knight, Ian, *Zulu Rising: The Epic Story of Isandlwana and Rorke's Drift*, London, 2010, p. 308.
29. Maxwell, *The Natal Witness*, Xmas 1895.
30. Symons, Fred, 1879, M/S diary.
31. Penn Symons, Private Journal, 24 February 1879.
32. Ibid.
33. Mansel, G., Papers, Killie Campbell Africana Library, Durban, ref. 89/9/32/1 (a).
34. PRO WO 32/7731 S6316.
35. Ibid.
36. PRO WO 32/7711 S6316.
37. Hamilton-Browne, *A Lost Legionary in South Africa*, p. 132.

Chapter 8
1. Killie Campbell Africana Library, Ref KCM/98/69/13/5.
2. A narrative written in 1929 by Mr S.B. Jones of 23 Wood Grove, Pinetown, Natal. Mr Jones had been a trooper in the Newcastle Mounted Rifles and had witnessed Hayhoe's arrival. Hayhoe's subsequent fate has long been a mystery, his body alone amongst the Carbineers was never discovered. He was therefore recorded as 'missing', it not having previously known that he was witnessed talking to Major Dartnell. Having delivered his message, it is likely that Hayhoe was ordered back to Isandlwana, there to report that reinforcements were on their way, and in doing so lost his life.
3. Drummond, *The Natal Witness*, 1 February 1879.
4. Ibid.
5. Ibid.
6. Milne, PRO ADM, 16486 S6333.
7. Mansel, G., Killie Campbell Africana Library, Durban.
8. M/S Tpr. W.J. Clarke, Killie Campbell Africana Library, Durban.
9. David Rattray, in a private letter, 11 November 2005.
10. Drummond, *The Natal Witness*, 1 February 1879.
11. Ibid.
12. M/S Tpr W. J. Clarke, Killie Campbell Africana Library, Durban.
13. Hallam Parr, H., *A Sketch of the Kafir and Zulu Wars*, London, 1990.

Chapter 9
1. Symons, Fred, 1879, M/S diary,
2. M/S Tpr W. J. Clarke, Killie Campbell Africana Library, Durban.

3. Mansel, G., Killie Campbell Africana Library, Durban.
4. Ibid.
5. M/S Tpr W. J. Clarke, Killie Campbell Africana Library, Durban
6. Wolseley, G., *South African Journal 1879–80*, Capetown, 1973, p. 72.
7. Curling, H.T., private letter to his mother.
8. Penn Symons, Private Journal, 24 February 1879.
9. Laband (ed), *Lord Chelmsford's Zululand Campaign*, p. 76.
10. Maxwell, *The Natal Witness*, Xmas 1895.
11. Bourquin, S.B., *The NNC During the Zulu War*, Private Pub., 1979.
12. Fynn, H. F. F., *The Natal Witness*, 22 January 1913.
13. *The Natal Witness*, June 1879.
14. Drummond, *The Natal Witness*, 1 February 1879.
15. Wolseley, G., *South African Journal 1879–80*, London, 1973, p. 43.
16. Laband (ed.), *Lord Chelmsford's Zululand Campaign*, p. 115.
17. Wolseley, G., *South African Journal 1879–80*, London, 1973, p. 43.
18. Thompson, P.S., *The Natal Native Contingent in the Anglo-Zulu War of 1879*, Pietermaritzburg, 1997, p. 162.
19. Ibid.
20. Smith, K.I., *Select Documents: A Zulu War Source Book*, Doncaster, 2006.
21. Maxwell, *The Natal Witness*, Xmas 1895.
22. Norris-Newman, C.L., *In Zululand With the British Throughout the War, 1879*, London, 1880, p. 72.
23. *The Red Book, a Compilation of 1879 Natal Press Reports*, privately printed, p. 72.

Chapter 10
1. *The Red Book, a Compilation of 1879 Natal Press Reports*, privately printed, p. 39.
2. Ibid., p. 37.
3. Ibid., p. 39.
4. PRO WO 32/7706, S6316.
5. Laband (ed), *Lord Chelmsford's Zululand Campaign*, p. 71.
6. RA VIC/ADD E1/8514.
7. Frere, Mary, RA VIC/0 34/20.
8. RA VIC/ADD E1/8514.
9. Ibid.
10. Ibid.
11. PRO WO 32/7706 S6316.
12. RA VIC/ADD E1 8513.
13. Ponsonby, A., *Henry Ponsonby, His Life*, London, 1942.
14. RA VIC/O 33/49.
15. RA VIC/O 33/67.
16. *The Red Book, a Compilation of 1879 Natal Press Reports*, privately printed, p. 64.

Chapter 11
1. Russell, George, *History of Old Durban*, Durban, 1971, p. 294.
2. Laband (ed.), *Lord Chelmsford's Zululand Campaign*, p. 89
3. Maxwell, *Natal Witness*, Xmas 1895.
4. Symons, Fred, 1879, M/S Diary.
5. TNA (PRO) WO 33/44, Enclosure 5 in 96.

6. Ibid.
7. TNA (PRO) WO 33/44, Enclosure 8 in No. 96.
8. Ibid.
9. Ibid.
10. Clarke, S., *Zululand at War*, p. 102.
11. TNA (PRO) WO 33/44, Enclosure 8 in No. 36.
12. Ibid.
13. RA VIC/ADD/E1/8629

Chapter 12
1. TNA (PRO) WO 30/129.
2. RA VIC /0 33/83.
3. TNA (PRO) WO 33/343, No. 49.
4. Issued by General Order, Pietermaritzburg, 4 March 1879.
5. RA VIC/ADD E1/8578.
6. RA VIC/0 34/20.
7. RA VIC/0 33/92.
8. Clarke, S., *Zululand at War*, Johannesburg, 1984, p. 15.
9. Norris-Newman, *In Zululand with the British Throughout the War*, p. 15.
10. Penn Symons, Private Journal, 24 February 1879.
11. Drummond, *The Natal Witness*, 1 February 1879.
12. Snook, rorkesdriftvc.com, Discussion Forum, Oct. 2013.
13. Knight, *Zulu Rising*, p. 298.
14. Laband, J., and Mathews, J., *Isandlwana*, Pietermaritzburg, 1992, p. 31.

Chapter 13
1. Letter from Chelmsford, dated 19 December 1879, addressed to 'Dear Colonel Glyn'. No reference.
2. Clarke, S., *Zululand at War*, p. 122.
3. Historical Records of the 24th Regiment.
4. Mansel, G., Killie Campbell Africana Library, Durban.
5. M/S Tpr. W.J. Clarke, Killie Campbell Africana Library, Durban.
6. Bourquin, S.B., *The NNC & Associated Units*, privately printed, 1879.
7. Historical Records of the 24th Regiment.
8. Smith-Dorrien, H., M/S dated 1907, South Wales Borderers Museum, Brecon.
9. Clarke, S., *Zululand at War*, p. 89, n. 20.
10. Durnford, E.C.L., *A Soldier's Life and Work in South Africa*, London, 1882, p. 7.
11. Directive to the Colonial Secretary of October 1878.
12. Durnford, *A Soldier's Life and Work in South Africa*, p. 7.
13. Ibid.
14. Morris, Donald, *The Washing of the Spears*, London, 1966, p. 360.
15. PRO WO 32/7726.
16. Stalker, *The Natal Carbineers*, p. 99.
17. Ibid.
18. Curling, H.T., letter to his mother dated Helpmekaar 2 February 1879.
19. Brickhill Papers, Killie Campbell Africana Library, Durban.
20. *The Natal Witness*, 2 October 1879.
21. *The Graphic*, 22 March 1879, p. 286.

22. *Royal Engineer Journal*, 2 February 1880.
23. Wood, E., *From Midshipman to Field Marshal*, London, 1906.
24. PRO WO 32/7711.
25. Killie Campbell Africana Library, Encl. 1 to 24/9/227.
26. Coupland, R., *Zulu Battle Piece, Isandlwana*, London, 1948, p. 79.
27. TNA WO 33/44 Enclosure 2 in No. 80.
28. TNA (PRO) WO 30/129, Sir Charles Ellice, War Office, 6 March 1879.
29. TNA (PRO) WO 30/129.
30. TNA (PRO) WO 33/34 Enclosure 1 in No. 61.

Chapter 14
1. Stalker, *The Natal Carbineers*, p. 99.
2. Curling, H. T., private letter to his mother.
3. Smith-Dorrien, H., *Memories of Forty Eight Years Service*, London, 1925, p. 13.
4. South Wales Borderers Regimental Museum, Brecon.
5. Higginson's M/S report dated 'Rorke's Drift, Feb., 17, 1879'.
6. Durnford, *A Soldier's Life and Work in South Africa*, p. 206.
7. Smith-Dorrien, H., M/S dated 1907, South Wales Borderers Museum, Brecon.
8. Clarke, S., *Zululand at War*, p. 83.
9. Cochrane in evidence, Court of Enquiry. Helpmekaar, 27 January 1879.
10. PRO WO 33/34 Enclosure 1 in No 30.
11. Smith-Dorrien, H., M/S dated 1907, South Wales Borderers Museum, Brecon.
12. Higginson's letter addressed to The Officer Commanding the Forces in South Africa, dated 17 February 1879.
13. Ibid.
14. Ibid.
15. Vause's Diary, *The Daily News*, 22 January 1969.
16. Ibid.
17. Cochrane, PRO WO 33/34 Enclosure 1 in No 86.
18. AZW 16200 – 039 C.M. Etheridge, Solicitor, 22.3.79.
19. Davies, PRO WO 33/34 S6333.
20. Curling, H.T., letter to his mother dated 2 February 1879.
21. Historical Records of the 24th Regiment, p. 230.
22. Milne, PRO ADM 16486 S6333.
23. TNA (PRO) WO 33/34 Enclosure 1 in No 91.
24. Ibid.
25. (Hamer) NAM, 6807 – 386 – 8 – 14.
26. (Nyanda) TNA (PRO) WO 33/34 Enclosure 2 in No 91.
27. Ibid.
28. Fynn, *The Natal Witness*, 22 January 1913.
29. (Nyanda) TNA (PRO) WO 33/34 Enclosure 2 in No 91.
30. Raw, TNA (PRO) WO 33/34 Incolsure 1 in No 91
31. Higginson TNA (PRO) WO 33/34 Enclosure 3 in No 96.
32. Reeves, K., *Medal News*, August 1990, p. 13.
33. Ibid.
34. TNA (PRO) WO 33/34, Enclosure 2 in No 96.
35. Ibid.
36. Ibid.

37. PRO WO32/7387 55603.
38. TNA (PRO) WO 33/34, Enclosure 2 in N. 96.
39. Smith, Keith I., *Studies in the Anglo-Zulu War*, Doncaster, 2008, p. 67.
40. PRO WO 33/34, Enclosure 1 in No 80.
41. Ibid.
42. Stalker, *The Natal Carbineers*, p. 100.
43. TNA (PRO) WO 33/34, Enclosure 3 in No 101.
44. TNA (PRO) WO 33/34, Enclosure 2 in No 96.
45. TNA (PRO) WO 33/34, Enclosure 1 in No 80.
46. TNA (PRO) WO 33/34, Enclosure 2 in No 96.
47. Ibid.
48. TNA (PRO) WO 33/34, Enclosure 4 in No 96.
49. Archives of Zululand, *The Anglo-Zulu War*, p. 103.
50. Brickhill, J.A., 'The Isandlwana Disaster', *The Natal Magazine*, Vol II, 1879, p. 255.
51. Ibid.
52. Lord Chelmsford to Secretary of State for War, 27 January 1879.
53. Clarke, S., *Zululand At War*, p. 83.
54. Letter to *The Times*, 12 April 1879.
55. Court of Enquiry, Rorke's Drift, 24 January 1879.
56. PRO WO 32/7725.
57. Brickhill, J.A., 'The Isandlwana Disaster', *The Natal Magazine*, Vol II, 1879, p. 257.
58. Chadwick, G. A., *The Zulu Armed Forces*, Zulu Monuments Pamphlet, updated.
59. TNA (PRO) WO 33/34, Enclosure 2 in No 72.
60. Curling, H.T., letter to his mother dated 2 February 1879.
61. Ibid.
62. Ibid.
63. Gardner, A., Archives of Zululand, *The Anglo-Zulu War*, p. 103.
64. Historical Records of the 24th Regiment, p. 245.
65. Smith-Dorrien, *Memories of Forty-Eight Years Service*.
66. Ibid.
67. Brickhill, J.A., *The Natal Magazine*, Vol II, 1879, p. 255
68. Symons, J.M.P., 'A Paper Compiled at Rorke's Drift', 24 February 1879.
69. Raw, TNA (PRO) WO 33/34, Enclosure 1 in No. 91.
70. Higginson, W., Letter dated Rorke's Drift, Feb. 17, 1879.
71. Letter in *The Times*, 10 April 1879.
72. Curling, H.T., letter to his mother dated 2 February 1879
73. Symons, J.M.P., 'A Paper Compiled at Rorke's Drift', 24 February 1879.
74. KCAL M/S 1072, Symons papers.
75. Haggard, H.R., *The True Story Book*, London, 1893.
76. *The Natal Witness*, 19 January 1929.
77. Mtanzi, C., late Curator of the Isandlwana Battlefield, in a letter to the Author, 22 February 2000.
78. *The Red Book, a Compilation of 1879 Natal Press Reports*, privately printed, p. 192.
79. TNA (PRO) WO 33/34, Enclosure 2 in No 91.
80. Gardner, in evidence, Court of Enquiry, Helpmekaar, 27 January 1879.
81. Curling, H.T., letter to his mother dated 2 February 1879.
82. *The Oldham Weekly Chronicle*, 26 April 1879.
83. Reeves, K., *Medal News*, August 1990.

84. Ibid.
85. Henderson, a letter to his father, Helpmekaar, January 1879.
86. Chard, An account specially written at the request of H.M. Queen Victoria, 21 February 1880, Royal Archives, Windsor.
87. TNA (PRO) WO 33/34, Enclosure 2 in No 96.
88. Ibid.
89. PRO WO 33/34, Enclosure 1 in No 80.
90. Wood, E., *Winnowed Memories*, London, 1918, p. 239.
91. Curling, H.T., a letter to his mother dated 2 February 1879.
92. Stalker, *The Natal Carbineers*, p. 101.
93. Ibid.
94. Symons, Fred, 1879 M/S Diary.
95. Ibid.
96. Stalker, *The Natal Carbineers*, p 106.

Chapter 15
 1. Archives of Zululand, *The Anglo-Zulu War*, p. 103.
 2. Supplement to *The London Gazette*, 14 March 1879.
 3. Curling, H.T., a letter to his mother, 2 February 1879.
 4. Ibid.
 5. PRO WO 33/34, Enclosure 1 in No 80
 6. Supplement to *The London Gazette*, 15 March 1879.
 7. Written at the request of the officers of the South Wales Borderers, 1907.
 8. TNA (PRO) WO 33/34, Enclosure 3 in No 101.
 9. TNA (PRO) WO 33/34, Ennclosure 2 in No 96.
10. Ibid.
11. Ibid.
12. TNA (PRO) WO 33/34, Enclosure 1 in No 91
13. NAM 6807 – 386 – 8 – 14.
14. TNA (PRO) WO 33/34, Enclosure 3 in No. 96
15. Stalker, *The Natal Carbineers*.
16. M/S Document dictated by W.H. Stafford, January 1938.
17. Brickhill, J.A., 'The Isandlwana Disaster', *The Natal Magazine*, Vol II, 1879.
18. Ibid.
19. *Port Elizabeth and the Eastern Province Standard*, 14 February 1879.
20. Ashe, W., and Wyatt-Edgell, E.V., *The Story of the Zulu Campaign*, London, 1880.
21. PRO WO 32/7723.
22. PRO WO 30/129 S6316.

Chapter 16
 1. Arthur, M., *Symbol of Courage*, London, 2004, p. 12.
 2. Ibid.
 3. PRO WO 32/7387 55603.
 4. Ibid.
 5. Ibid.
 6. Ibid.
 7. Ibid.
 8. Ibid.

9. Ibid.
10. Smith-Dorrien, *Memories of Forty-Eight Years Service*, p. 18.
11. Stalker, *The Natal Carbineers*, p. 121.
12. Stafford, W., statement made in 1939.
13. *The Cape Argus*, May 1879.
14. *The Scotsman*, May, 1879
15. Cmdt., F.X. Schermbrucker, *The Friend*, 1 May 1879.
16. Moodie, *John Dunn, Cetywayo and The Three Generals*, p. 119.
17. French, *Lord Chelmsford and The Zulu War*, p. 172.
18. Emery, F., *The Red Soldier*, London, 1977, p. 120.
19. Knight, I., *Fearful Hard Times*, London, 1994, p. 199.
20. Laband, J.P., and Thompson, P.S., *The War in Zululand*, Pietermaritzburg, 1983, p. 41.
21. Vijn, C., *Cetshwayo's Dutchman*, South Africa, 1880; reprinted London, 1988, p. 40.
22. Molyneux, W.C.F., *Campaining in South Africa and Egypt*, London, 1896, p. 186.
23. Harness, A., autographed letters, Brenthurst Library M/S 158.
24. W.H. Wilkinson (Trumpet Major), *Journal of the Anglo-Zulu War Research Society*, Vol. 3, Issue 1, 1998.
25. Oral history by courtesy of John Young.
26. Wolseley, *The South African Journal of Sir Garnet Wolseley*, p. 104.

Chapter 17

1. Affiliation Parade 26 January 1997.

Bibliography

Unpublished Sources and Private Information

Alison, Sir Archibald, Autograph letters, 6 March 1878–26 October 1881, MS 165.

Blamey, A., Old House Museum, Durban.

Bourquin, S.B., *The NNC and Associated Units.*

Chatham, The Durnford Papers, Royal Engineers Museum, Chatham.

Curling, H.T., Private letters to his mother 1879, by courtesy A.J. Lucking.

Diary of Sgt. Major Cheffins, property of Lindsay Reyburn, Pretoria.

Fenn, C.E., How I Volunteered for the Cape.

Frere, Mary, Letters to Sir Henry Ponsonby.

Hamer, J.H., Papers.

Harness, Arthur, Autograph Letters, 4 January 1878–2 October 1879. MS 158, Brenthurst Library, Johannesburg.

Manuscripts and papers of: James Brickhill; William James Clarke; T.H. Cunningham; Henry F. Fynn; Ashley Thomas Goatham; Charles Rawden Maclean; W. Stafford; Frederick Symons; Sir Evelyn Wood; and G. Maxwell.

Penn Symons, Private Journal, February 1879.

Rattray, David, private letter, 11 November 2005.

Rorkesdriftvc.com, Discussion Forum, October 2013.

Sir Evelyn Wood Papers.

Smallwood, V.S., a paper titled 'The Role of the Royal Regiment of Artillery in the Battle of Isandlwana'.

Stamford, W.H., M/S dictated January 1932.

Symons, Fred, M/S diary.

The Royal Archives, Windsor.

Various papers reference PRO and PRO/WO.

Various papers, as enumerated in the notes, by gracious permission of Her Majesty Queen Elizabeth II.

Vause, R., The Vause Diaries and Papers – property of Robin Stayt, Durban.

W. Higginson Papers, Rorke's Drift, February 1879.

Killie Campbell Africana Library (KCAL) Durban.

Natal Archives, Pietermaritzburg.

National Army Museum, London.

Public Records Office, Kew.

Royal Engineers Museum, Chatham.

The Royal Archives Windsor.

Newspapers, Journals and Periodicals
South Africa
The Bloemfontein and Free State Gazette.
The Cape Argus.
The Farmer's Weekly News.
The Friend.
The Natal Mercury.
The Natal Witness.
The Port Elizabeth Telegraph and Eastern Province Standard.
S.A. Military History Society Journal.
The Times of Natal.

United Kingdom
The Anglo-Zulu War Historical Society Journal.
The Anglo-Zulu War Research Society Journal.
Fraser's Magazine.
The Graphic.
The Illustrated London News.
The London Gazette.
Medal News.
Military Illustrated.
Oldham Weekly Chronicle.
Soldiers of the Queen (Journal of the Victorian Military Society).
The Society for Army Historical Research Journal.
The Times (London).
The Times Weekly Edition.

Published Sources
Arthur, M., *Symbol of Courage*, London, 2004.
Ashe, Major, and Wyatt-Edgell, E.V., *The Story of the Zulu Campaign*, London, 1880.
Binns, C.T., *The Warrior People*, London, 1975.
Brooks, E.H., and Webb, C. de B., *A History of Natal*, Natal, 1965.
Buthelezi, oMntwana Mangosuthu G., *The Anglo-Zulu War – A Centennial Reappraisal, 'The Bias of Historical Analysis'*, Durban, 1979.
Child, D. (ed.), *The Zulu War Diary of Col. Henry Harford*, Pietermaritzburg, 1978.
Clarke, Sonia, *Invasion of Zululand*, Johannesburg, 1979.
Clarke, Sonia, *Zululand at War, 1879*, Johannesburg, 1984.
Clarke, Sub-Inspector W., *A Record of the Services of the Natal Mounted Police*, Pietermaritzburg, n.d.
Coghlan, Mark, *Pro Patria* [History of the Natal Carbineers 1945–95], Pietermaritzburg, n.d.
Coupland, Reginald, *Zulu Battle Piece – Isandhlwana*, London, 1948.
Dawney, Guy C., *Campaigns: Zulu 1879, Egypt 1882, Suakin 1885*, Cambridge, 1989.
Durnford, E.C.L., *A Soldier's Life and Work in South Africa*, London, 1882.
Ellis, Peter Berresford, *H. Rider Haggard, A Voice from the Infinite*, London, 1978.
Emery, Frank, *Marching Over Africa*, London, 1986.
Emery, Frank, *The Red Soldier*, London, 1977.
Filter, H., and Bourquin, S., *Paulina Dlamini*, Pietermaritzburg, 1986.

Forbes, Archibald, *Barracks, Bivouacs and Battles,* London, 1892.

French, Major The Hon. G., *Lord Chelmsford and the Zulu War,* London, 1939.

Furneaux, Rupert, *The Zulu War: Isandlwana and Rorke's Drift,* London, 1963.

Fynn, Henry Francis, *My Recollections of a Famous Campaign and a Great Disaster,* M/S KCAL, Durban, 1913.

Fynney, F.B., *The Zulu Army,* M/S Pietermaritzburg, 1878

Gon, P., *Send For Carrington,* Johannesburg, 1984.

Gon, P., *The Road to Isandlwana,* Johannesburg, 1979.

Haggard, H. R., *The True Story Book,* London, 1893.

Hallam Parr, Henry, *A Sketch of the Kaffir and Zulu Wars,* London, 1990.

Hamilton-Browne, Col. G., *A Lost Legionary in South Africa,* London, 1912.

Hattersley, Alan F., *Carbineer; The History of the Royal Natal Carbineers,* Aldershot, 1950.

Herd, N., *The Bent Pine,* Johannesburg, 1976.

Holt, H.P., *The Mounted Police of Natal,* London, 1913.

Isaacs, N., *Travels and Adventures in Eastern Africa (Natal),* 1836.

Knight, Ian, *Zulu Rising, The Epic Story of Isandlwana and Rorke's Drift,* London, 2010.

Krige, Eileen Jensen, *The Social System of the Zulus,* Pietermaritzburg, 1957.

Laband, J.P. (ed.), *Lord Chelmsford's Zululand Campaign, 1878–1879,* Stroud, 1994.

Laband, J.P., *Rope of Sand,* Johannesburg, 1995.

Laband, J.P., and Knight, Ian, (eds), *Archives of Zululand: The Anglo-Zulu War 1879,* London, 2000.

Laband, John, and Mathews, Jeff, *Isandlwana,* Pietermaritzburg, 1992.

Laband, J.P., and Thompson, P.S., *Field Guide to the War in Zululand,* Pietermaritzburg, 1979.

Laband, J.P., and Thompson, P.S., *Kingdom and Colony at War,* Pietermaritzburg, 1990.

Laband, J.P., and Thompson, P.S., with Henderson, Shiela, *The Buffalo Border Guard, 1879. The Anglo-Zulu War in Southern Natal,* Durban, 1951.

Lock, Ron, *Blood on the Painted Mountain,* London, 1995.

Lock, Ron, and Quantrill, Peter, *The Red Book. Natal newspaper reports on the Anglo-Zulu War, 1879,* Compilation, Pinetown, KwaZulu-Natal, 2000.

Mackeurtan, G., *The Cradle Days of Natal,* Pietermaritzburg, 1948.

Mackinnon, J.P., and Shadbolt, Sydney, *The South African Campaign,1879,* London, 1880; reprinted London, 1995.

Maxwell, J., *Reminiscences of the Zulu War,* Cape Town, 1979.

McKay, James, *Reminiscences of the Last Kaffir War,* Cape Town, 1970.

Milton, John, *The Edge of War,* Cape Town, 1983.

Mitford, Bertram, *Through the Zulu Country,* London, 1883; reprinted London, 1988.

Molyneux, W.C.F., *Campaigning in South Africa and Egypt,* London, 1896.

Moodie, D.C.F., *John Dunn, Cetywayo and the Three Generals,* South Africa, 1886.

Moodie, D.C.F., *The History of the Battles and Adventures of the British, the Boers and the Zulus, etc. in Southern Africa from the Time of the Pharaoh Necho to 1880,* Cape Town, 1888.

Morris, Donald R., *The Washing of the Spears,* London, 1966.

Natham, M., *The Voortrekkers of Southern Africa,* London, 1937.

Newark, George and Christopher, *Kipling's Soldiers,* Romford, 1993.

Norris-Newman, Charles L., *In Zululand with the British Throughout the War of 1879,* London, 1889; reprinted London, 1988.

Notes on Transport, Pamphlet published by the 2nd Battalion, Oxford Light Infantry (revised 1897).

Ponsonby, A., *Henry Ponsonby, His Life*, London, 1942.

Preston, Adrian (ed.), *Sir Garnet Wolseley's South African Journal, 1879–80*, Cape Town, 1973.

Regulations Field Forces South Africa 1878, example consulted courtesy of Professor John Laband, University of Natal, Pietermaritzburg.

Roberts, Brian, *The Zulu Kings*, London, 1974.

Russell, George, *History of Old Durban*, Durban, 1971.

Samuelson, L.H., *Zululand its Traditions, Legends, Customs and Folklore*, Durban, 1974.

Samuelson, R.C.A., *Long, Long Ago*, Durban, 1929.

Schiel, Adolf, *23 Jahre Sturm und Sonneshein in Süd Afrika* ('Twenty-three Years Storm and Sunshine in South Africa'), Leipzig, 1902.

Smith, Keith I., *Select Documents: A Zulu War Sourcebook*, Doncaster, 2006.

Smith, Keith I., *Studies in the Anglo-Zulu War*, Doncaster, 2008.

Smith-Dorrien, Horace, *Memories of Forty-Eight Years' Service*, London, 1925.

Stalker, J., *The Natal Carbineers: History of the Regiment from its Foundation 15 January 1855 to 30 June 1911*, Pietermaritzburg, 1912.

Stewart, J., *Archive, Vol.2.*, Pietermaritzburg, 1976.

Stuart, James, and Malcolm, D. (eds), *The Diary of Henry Francis Fynn*, Pietermaritzburg, 1986.

Taylor, Stella, *Shaka's Children*, London, 1994.

Thompson, P.S., *The Natal Native Contingent in the Anglo-Zulu War, 1879*, Pietermaritzburg, 1997.

Tomasson, W.H., *With the Irregulars in the Transvaal and Zululand*, London, 1881.

Tylden, G., *The Armed Forces of South Africa 1659–1954*, Johannesburg, 1954.

van Warmelo, N.J., (ed.), *History of Matiwane and the amaNgwane Tribe*, Pretoria, 1938.

Vijn, Cornelius, *Cetshwayo's Dutchman*, London, 1880; reprinted London, 1988.

von Kehrhahan, J., *Das Filter-Larsen Denkmal*, South Africa, 1938.

War Office, *Narrative of the Field Operations Connected with the Zulu War of 1879* (compiled by J.S. Rothwell), London, 1881; reprinted London, 1907 and 1989.

War Office, *Precis of Information Concerning Zululand*, London, 1895.

Webb, C. de B., and Wright, J.B., *A Zulu King Speaks*, Pietermaritzburg, 1978.

Wolseley, G., *South African Journal 1879 – 80*, Cape Town, 1973.

Wood, Evelyn, *From Midshipman to Field Marshal*, London, 1906.

Wood, Evelyn, *Winnowed Memories*, London, 1918.

Wright, John B., *Bushmen Raiders of the Drakensberg 1840–1870*, Pietermaritzburg, 1971.

Wright, John, and Manson, Andrew, *The Hlubi Chiefdom in Zululand-Natal*, Pietermaritzburg, 1983.

Young, John, *They Fell Like Stones; Battles and Casualties of the Zulu War, 1879*, London, 1991.

Index

Page numbers in *italics* refer to illustrations